BEYOND THE SCOREBOARD

Youth employment opportunities and skills development in the sports sector

To Joan,

with gratitude for your intervention in the Conference this morning, refreshing, inspirational and passionate.

with my wishes —

[signature]

I would like to take this opportunity to underscore the importance of the topics discussed in this book, as they are key issues in the global economy today: youth employment and skills development. They represent the new frontier for both development and peace building. What is needed in the global economy is strong professionalism, life skills and dedication. The sports sector, the subject of this book, is essential for a balanced approach to life and relationships. Sport provides a neutral ground to discuss issues that are often controversial, such as the local and global economy, HIV/AIDS prevention, physical literacy and education, and social inclusion of youth. For the above reasons, the contributions that make up this book illustrate the challenges related to the sports sector, as well as opportunities for new services, training and jobs for youth.

This research is part of a much broader framework supported by the ILO/Universitas programme, which brings together academic institutions, private and public stakeholders and the tripartite social partners, along with local and global organizations, to develop methodologies for decent work to address youth employment and social inclusion. I am very proud that this programme is supported by the Development Cooperation, Italian Ministry of Foreign Affairs.

Minister Giuseppe Deodato
Director-General Development Cooperation
Italian Ministry of Foreign Affairs

BEYOND THE SCOREBOARD

Youth employment opportunities and skills development in the sports sector

Edited by Giovanni di Cola

INTERNATIONAL LABOUR OFFICE • GENEVA

di Cola, G. (ed.)
Beyond the scoreboard: Youth employment opportunities and skills development in the sports sector
Geneva, International Labour Office, 2006

Sport, youth, youth employment, employment opportunity, skill, social integration, developed countries, developing countries. 08.17.2

ISBN 978-92-2-117968-9

ILO Cataloguing in Publication Data

Typeset by Magheross Graphics, France & Ireland *www.magheross.com*
Printed in Switzerland   PCL

FOREWORD

by Adolf Ogi, Under-Secretary-General and Special Advisor to the United Nations Secretary-General on Sport for Development and Peace

I congratulate the International Labour Organization (ILO) on compiling this remarkable volume intended to broadcast the positive message of sport to future generations. It underlines the importance of giving young people the opportunity to promote social and economic development through sport to help create a better world.

Education plays a vital role in a young person's life. Sport is "the best school of life", teaching basic values and life skills that are important for the holistic and well-balanced development of younger generations. Honesty, fair play, self-confidence, mutual respect, adherence to rules and how to cope with victories as well as defeats are all examples of the values connected to the immense resource that is sport.

Since my appointment as Special Adviser to UN Secretary-General Kofi Annan in 2001, I am mandated to consult with the UN agencies, programmes and funds engaged in development, peace-making and peace-building, in order to identify programmes and tasks that could benefit from the involvement of sport organizations.

Resolution 60/9, adopted by the General Assembly on 3 November 2005, recalls the importance of sport as a means to promote education, health, development and peace.* It also invites governments, as well as the UN system, to seek new and innovative ways to use sport for communication and social mobilization, and to develop strategic partnerships with the wide range of stakeholders involved in "sport at all levels".

The International Year of Sport and Physical Education (IYSPE 2005) has provided an opportunity for key sports players to meet with the world of

---

* UN General Assembly resolution A/RES/60/9, in force 17 Jan. 2006.

development. These players have responded to the international community's call with concrete policy and project initiatives. The ILO has carried out an outstanding review, using the 358 existing sport and development projects of the UN System, the European Union and NGOs as a reference to identify the sport community's values and the core skills.

It is important at this stage to benefit from the lessons learned so far. This volume contributes highly to general awareness by discussing the positive effects that sport has on our communities and the numerous challenges that sport itself will face in the future. The outstanding quality of contributions demonstrates the serious commitment of the international, governmental and academic community in encouraging sport as a means to promote education, health, development and peace.

PREFACE

by Djibril Diallo, Director, United Nations New York Office of the Special Advisor to the Secretary-General on Sport for Development and Peace

The authors of this book, differing in their regional backgrounds and experiences, share the rationale that sport can play an influential role in positively shaping the lives of youth in both developed and developing countries. In Africa, Latin America, Europe and elsewhere, thorough analysis by experts indicates that civil society and governments must engage and foster the development of youth in the sports sector to create quality jobs for them, to improve their skills and ultimately achieve sustainable development through sport.

The authors of this book have illustrated that development of sporting activities under the necessary conditions of transparency is found to be dependent on national public policies. However, sport and particularly physical education are in need of additional budgetary support if the sector is to develop youth nationwide. This is far from the case in most of the selected countries.

Global and regional partnerships are necessary to promote sport and its related industries. In Europe, the completion of a global collective agreement at the European Union level, specific to the sports sector, would help facilitate the creation of quality jobs in sport and include the stakeholders as part of a unique strategic approach. Countries in Latin America such as Peru and El Salvador, which share common cultural elements, can use sport to build upon their similarities and history while promoting development. Sports events can create growth in the local economies and related industries, and attract tourists and foreign investments.

Likewise, in Africa, collaborative approaches are necessary to create a viable sports sector. If the East African Community created a wider market by strengthening ties between Kenya, Uganda and the United Republic of Tanzania, greater financial resources would be available to develop sport infrastructures. Given East Africa's geographical location and favourable climate, and established attractive wildlife reserves and tourist resorts, the area is well suited to host major international sporting events and serve as the region's athletics centre. The East African culture and the record of sport performances, particularly in track and field, would further attract international competitions into the region, and would open new opportunities for service-oriented athletic programmes and bids for global and regional events.

Civil society and governments globally are encouraged to collaborate with public authorities and private institutions to develop sport, sport tourism and social events.

Scholars, universities and academic leaders should also play an influential role in identifying opportunities in physical education and sport science, facilitating international discourse on the core elements required to train professionals and physical education teachers to ensure quality physical education, and identifying specific new services and related career opportunities in the areas of sport science. Universities should engage in knowledge sharing via various distance-learning programmes, and eventually as a single data management system.

Through sport, women acquire leadership skills, and the book stresses the importance for leaders from international sport organizations to promote the progression of women in sport, as well as providing employment and job opportunities. One way of achieving higher standards for women in sport is by supporting research action and ad hoc training that will assist the Olympic Movement and encourage women's leadership skills and empowerment.

The United Nations (UN) has long acknowledged the importance of sport in society and has established strong ties to the world of sport. Its agencies, funds and programmes have undertaken a wide variety of sports-related activities to help improve the lives of poor or marginalized people, particularly women and youth.

The UN, the ILO and the World Bank have forged alliances to promote social integration and economic opportunities for youth with the establishment of the Youth Employment Network. The world of sport must put forth greater energies and establish more alliances in order to continue developing sport specific for youth.

In November 2003, this work was strengthened when the UN General Assembly adopted Resolution 58/5 recognizing the power of sport as a means to promote education, health, development and peace. The resolution also proclaimed 2005 as the International Year of Sport and Physical Education (IYSPE 2005). At the launch of the International Year, UN Secretary-General Kofi Annan underlined the importance of sport.

IYSPE 2005 and young people's strong interest in sport provide an entry point for drawing on sport to help youth promote health, education and development in order to accelerate the attainment of the Millennium Development Goals (MDGs). In connection with activities related to the IYSPE 2005, the UN is encouraging partnerships between sport institutions and UN agencies, funds and programmes to develop projects and policies concerning sport for development.

The UN, through a number of youth-oriented activities, including the Global Youth Leadership Summits, plays a strong role in the social development of young people, establishing dialogue between communities to reach out to youth to increase their awareness of key challenges, and encourage them to become engaged in development strategies and initiatives.

United Nations efforts to assist countries to achieve the MDGs include encouraging various actors working in partnership for sustainable development and peace. In particular, the eighth MDG calls for concerted action to cultivate "a global partnership for development" and to create opportunities for youth employment and skills development. This is an essential step towards realizing the objectives of the UN, and it can only be achieved if civil society, with support from governments and international agencies, is fully engaged. We are happy to see that this partnership on sport is moving forward, and the contribution of this book is a way towards a better recognition of the role of each and every one of the players.

ACKNOWLEDGEMENTS

I should like to thank those who inspired this book, in particular youth sport professionals and amateurs. Without determination, willingness to learn, adaptability and, most of all, creativity, there would probably be no decent working conditions for the majority of workers or new opportunities in the global economy for youth. We know that these opportunities exist, but they need to be brought to light. Good attitudes, a positive spirit and openness are required. Often specific skills and competences through youth sport are there to show the way. This book is dedicated to those young people who have, it is hoped for a short while only, lost the above attitudes. I hope that it will inspire them in the same way that a game brings inspiration to those who participate enthusiastically in it.

A big thank you goes to all those who have greatly contributed to the book by exchanging ideas with me. These include not only the authors, whose work deserves to be mentioned, but also friends and colleagues encountered throughout the journey, in particular Jesse Drawas, Lisa Grimm, Ron Hochbaum, Rock Shenk and Jeff Trigilio, as well as some prominent "sports figures" and friends such as Phil Craven, Tommi Ganda Sithole, Bruce Kidd, Katia Mascagni and Kiran Mehra Kerpelman. I would also like to thank Rosemary Beattie, Meredith Coburn and May Hofman for the editing and production, and Lauren Elsaesser and Martine Jacquinod for the promotion, of this book.

CONTENTS

Boxes

Figures

Tables

ABOUT THE CONTRIBUTORS

Roger Blanpain – Professor Blanpain taught Comparative Labour Law and Industrial Relations at the University of Leuven in Belgium (1967–98). He has also taught at the University of Limburg (Netherlands). During his career he has served as the president of the Fédération Internationale des Footballers Professionnels (FIFPro – International Federation of Soccer Players), the International Industrial Relations Association and the International Society for Labour Law and Industrial Relations. He serves as the editor in chief of the *International encyclopaedia for labour law and industrial relations*. He holds a Master's degree in Political Science from Columbia University and a PhD in Law from the University of Leuven.

Cheri Blauwet – Ms Blauwet is a medical student at Stanford University and a Paralympic Gold Medallist. She was the winner of the Women's Wheelchair division in the 2004 and 2005 Boston Marathons, and was nominated for the 2005 Laureus World Sport Award for Best Athlete with a Disability. In 2004, she was awarded the Paul Hearne Leadership Award by the American Association of People with Disabilities, given to three individuals annually who display outstanding leadership potential in promoting disability rights and equality.

Mike Boit – Mr Boit joined Kenyatta University as a senior lecturer in 1987. In 1990 he was appointed Kenya's Commissioner for Sport. He would later rejoin Kenyatta to teach Human Anatomy in 1997. In 2002 he was promoted to chairman of the Department of Exercise and Sport Science, becoming an associate professor. Apart from teaching, he is currently coordinating the International Association of Athletics Federations (IAAF) Athletic Academy. His sporting accomplishments are impressive: at the 1972 Olympic Games in Munich he won a bronze medal. He received two Master's degrees from Stanford University and a Doctorate in Education from the University of Oregon.

Jean Camy – Professor Camy was the first chairperson of the European Network of Sports Sciences in Higher Education (1989–93), and the first director of the Master Européen de Management des Organisations Sportives (1993–99). He founded the European College of Sport Science and the European Observatoire of Sport Employment, of which he is chairperson. He coordinated and co-authored the report *Sport and employment in Europe* for the European Commission in 1999, and conducted research on "Social partners in the sport sector in the EU countries" in 2002. He holds a PhD in Sociology from Lumière Université de Lyon.

Jean-Loup Chappelet – Professor Chappelet has been a professor of Public Management at the Swiss Graduate School of Public Administration (IDHEAP – Institut des Hautes Etudes en Administration Publique) of the University of Lausanne since 1993. He has served as the IDHEAP director since 2003. He specializes in sport management and sport policy, with particular emphasis on the organization of the Olympic Games and other sporting events as regional and national public policies. He is currently director of the Master Exécutif en Management des Organisations Sportives programme, supported by the European Olympic Committees, Olympic Solidarity and the European Union.

Michele Colucci – Dr Colucci works at the Legal Service of the European Commission. He serves as a member of the FIFA Dispute Resolution Chamber, and as fiduciary of the Italian trade union football organization. He is a researcher at the University of Salerno (Italy) and has published in the field of European and comparative law. He is director of the *Revista di Diritto ed Economia dello Sport.*

Phil Craven – Sir Phil Craven spent a large portion of his career working for the British Coal Corporation. From 1970 to 1993, he served Great Britain on their Paralympic swimming and wheelchair basketball teams. He also served multiple terms as chairperson of Great Britain's Wheelchair Basketball Association, and as president of the International Wheelchair Basketball Federation for over a decade. In 2001, he was elected President of the International Paralympic Committee. In 2005, Her Majesty Queen Elizabeth bestowed on him a Knighthood; he was also awarded a Member of the Order of the British Empire in 1991. He graduated with honours from Manchester University.

Giovanni di Cola – Dr di Cola joined the ILO in 1988 after field experience with UNESCO in Senegal and with UNICEF in Niger. He has served on field assignments in Latin America and Africa. He currently works at ILO headquarters in Geneva as programme coordinator of the Universitas programme. Since 2002, he has represented the ILO on the UN Task Force and the UN Communication Group on Sport and Development. He is a visiting professor at the University of Teramo (Italy) in its doctorate programme on Social and Economic Critics of Sport. He is also a member of the Scientific Committee of the *Rivista di Diritto ed Economia dello Sport*. He holds a Doctorat en Economie Internationale from Université Paris X.

Djibril Diallo (Senegal) is the director of the United Nations New York Office of the Special Advisor of the Secretary-General on Sport for Development and Peace, established in October 2004. As spokesperson of the president of the 59th General Assembly, H. E. Mr Jean Ping, Minister for Foreign Affairs, Cooperation and Francophonie of the Republic of Gabon, he oversees all press events and media relations for the president of the General Assembly. He was previously director of the Communications Office/Office of the Administrator, responsible for sharpening the United Nations Development Programme (UNDP) corporate identity and image through media and advocacy outreach, and as a senior official of the United Nations Children's Fund (UNICEF), acting as both Special Advisor to the Executive Director and Deputy Director of Public Affairs. He holds a PhD in Linguistics and Communication from the University of London.

Gudrun Doll-Tepper – Dr Doll-Tepper is president of the International Council of Sport Science and Physical Education, and a professor at the Free University of Berlin. She is a member of the German National Olympic Committee. She served as chair of the Sport Science Committee of the International Paralympic Committee from 1993 until 2001, and is the scientific director of the Information Agency for Adapted Physical Activity in Berlin. She was the main force behind numerous international symposia such as the World Summit on Physical Education in 1999. Among her numerous awards is the Order of the Federal Republic of Germany.

Amy Farkas – Ms Farkas has been development manager for the International Paralympic Committee (IPC) since 2003. Previously she worked in the field as a programme manager for the Sports For Life programme with the Vietnam Veterans of America Foundation in Kosovo, and before that as an information specialist at the United States National Center on Physical Activity and Disability (NCPAD). She holds a Master's degree in disability studies.

Gregg Hartley – Mr Hartley is vice-president of Marketing and Operations at Sporting Goods Manufacturers Association International (SGMA International). He has also served as vice-president of Marketing and Development at SGMA and as executive director at the Athletic Footwear Association. He has been a member or served on the board of a number of organizations, including the United States Olympic Committee, the National Operating Committee for Standards for Athletic Equipment, the Arthur Ashe Athletic Association and Virginia Commonwealth University. He received a BSc and completed his postgraduate studies at Appalachian State University, South Carolina.

Ian Henry – Dr Henry is professor of Leisure Policy and Management, and director of the Institute of Sport and Leisure Policy in the School of Sport and Exercise Science at Loughborough University, United Kingdom. From 1976 to 1980 he worked in facility management and sports administration in local government before becoming a lecturer at Ilkley College in 1980 and Leeds Polytechnic in 1987. His research is focused on issues relating to leisure policies, politics and governance at the transnational, national, urban and regional levels. He holds a Master's degree and a PhD from Loughborough University.

Dan Kellams is an independent communications consultant with more than 30 years' experience in corporate and agency management, dealing with issues in crisis management, corporate communications and marketing support. He has also directed national publicity activities for a series of outdoor adventure and sports marketing programmes. He has received a Bronze Anvil Award from the Public Relations Society of America for Reebok's global newsletter and a Big Apple Award from PRSA-NY for an internal communications programme for Citicorp. He holds a Master's degree from Columbia University's Graduate School of Journalism.

Don Porter – Mr Porter is president of the International Softball Federation (ISF) and has held posts as executive director of the Amateur Softball Association (ASA) and secretary-general of the ISF. He has served as chairperson and member of a number of committees for the United States Olympic Committee (USOC), including their Board of Directors. He has also served four consecutive terms (currently) on the Executive Council of the General Association of International Sports Federations (GAISF) and was re-elected to the post of secretary-general in 2002. He was elected to the ISF Hall of Fame in 1983 and to the ASA Hall of Fame in 1988.

Laurent Rivier – Dr Laurent Rivier was involved in research concerning organic trace analysis in biological matrices. In 1984, he was appointed head of the Laboratory of Analytical Toxicology at the Institute of Legal Medicine of the University of Lausanne and, in 1990, he created the Swiss Laboratory for Doping Analysis. He teaches at both the University of Lausanne and the University of Tromsø in Norway. He received his PhD in Chemistry from the University of Lausanne.

Betty Siegel – Dr Siegel is an internationally known educator, scholar and advocate for women's leadership and diversity. She has served as the president of Kennesaw State University (KSU) for the past 25 years, moving the university from a small four-year college to the third largest university in Georgia. Through her efforts, the Institute for Leadership, Ethics and Character was established at KSU, and the Betty L. Siegel Chair of Leadership, Ethics and Character was endowed within the institute. She is co-founder and co-director of the International Alliance for Invitational Education.

Richard Sowell – Professor Sowell is dean at Wellstar College of Health and Human Services. He has served as editor in chief of the *Journal of the Association of Nurses in AIDS Care* (JANAC) for the past decade. He has published extensively on the psychosocial issues associated with HIV/AIDS, focusing specifically on women in the southern United States.

Mike Spino – Mr Spino is director of the Office of International Sport Education at Kennesaw State University. He organized the 1984 Pre-Olympic Track and Field camp for the 1984 Olympic Games in Los Angeles. A former director of the Esalen Sports Center, he is the author of six books on the mental and physical aspects of sport. His cross-country and track teams at Georgia Tech and Life Universities broke numerous records including 12 national championships at Life, where he was nominated national coach of the year on three occasions.

Eleni Theodoraki – Dr Theodoraki developed her interest in the management of sports organizations during her studies at Loughborough University, where she completed her PhD on organizational analysis of the national governing bodies of sport in Great Britain. Her first academic appointment in 1994 was as lecturer in Sports Management at De Montfort University in Leicester. In October 1996, she returned to Loughborough as lecturer in Recreation Management.

Geoff Thompson – Five times world karate champion, Mr Thompson was appointed to the Great Britain Sports Council in June 1990 following the close of an outstanding career. His numerous titles include 1982 World Heavyweight Champion and 1985 World Games Heavyweight Gold Medallist. In 1993, he founded the Youth Charter for Sport, Culture and the Arts (YCSCA). He has also advised and contributed to the Manchester, Nagano and South African summer and winter Olympic bids, and acted as consultant for the 2002 Commonwealth Games bid.

Anita White – Ms White is an independent consultant working in the field of national and international sport policy and sports development, and a visiting professor at Loughborough University. She is currently president and chair of the Board of Great Britain Olympic Hockey, chair of the United Kingdom Coordinating Group on Women and Sport, and a member of the International Working Group on Women and Sport (IWG).

Dho Young-shim – Ambassador Dho Young-shim served the National Assembly of the Republic of Korea in various internationally oriented roles, including chief of staff for the Foreign Affairs Committee. From 1988 to 1992, she served as a member and vice-chairperson of the Foreign Affairs Committee of Korea's National Assembly; she then became president of the Institute of Korean–American Affairs in Seoul. She was appointed Korea's Ambassador of Cultural Cooperation. She is the chairperson of the Korea Culture and Tourism Policy Institute and represents Korea on the Board of Governors of the UNWTO ST-EP Foundation.

ACRONYMS AND ABBREVIATIONS

AAHPERD	American Alliance for Health, Physical Education, Recreation and Dance
ACSM	American College of Sports Medicine
AEHESIS	Aligning a European Higher Education Structure in Sport Science
AIOWF	Association of International Olympic Winter Sports Federations
ANOC	Association of National Olympic Committees
ARISF	Association of Recognized IOC International Sports Federations
ART	antiretroviral therapy
ASOIF	Association of Summer Olympic International Federation
ATC	Australian Tourist Commission
B2B	business to business
BASI	British Association of Snowsports Instructors
BJSM	*British Journal of Sports Medicine*
BOA	British Olympic Association
BPA	Swiss Office for Accident Prevention
CAF	Confederation of Africa Championships
CCPR	Central Council of Physical Recreation (UK)
CDDS	Center for Drug Develop Science
CEO	chief executive officer
COES	National Olympic Committee of El Salvador
COMESA	Common Market for Eastern and Southern Africa
CONGO	Congress of Non-Governmental Organizations
COSMoS	Social Council of the Sport Movement

CREPS	Centre Régional d'Education Physique et Sport (French Regional Centre of Physical Education and Sport)
CSLA	Community Sports Leaders Awards
DCMS	Department of Culture, Media and Sports (UK)
DEUAPA	European University Diploma in Adapted Physical Activity
EAC	East African Community
EASM	European Association of Sport Managers
EFPL	European Professional Football Leagues
EMDAPA	European Master's Degree in Adapted Physical Activity
ENFA	European Network Fitness Association
ENSSEE	European Network of Sport Science, Education and Employment
EOC	European Olympic Committees
EOSE	European Observatoire of Sport Employment
EPO	erythropoietin
EU	European Union
FIEP	Fédération Internationale d'Education Physique
FIFA	Fédération Internationale de Football Association/ International Football Association Federation
FIFPro	Fédération Internationale des Footballers Professionnels
FIMS	Fédération International de Médécine Sportive
FS3	Fondation Sport, Science et Société/Foundation Sport, Science and Society
GAISF	General Association of International Sports Federations
GNP	gross national product
IAAF	International Association of Athletics Federations
IAKS	International Association for Sports and Leisure Facilities
IAPESGW	International Association of Physical Education and Sport for Girls and Women
IBLF	International Business Leaders Forum
ICCA	International Congress and Convention Association
ICHPER	International Council for Health, Physical Education and Recreation
ICPES	International Charter of Physical Education and Sport
ICSP	International Committee of Sport Pedagogy
ICSPE	International Council of Sport and Physical Education
ICSSPE	International Council of Sport Science and Physical Education
IIPT	International Institute for Peace through Tourism
ILDE	Local Development and Employment Initiatives

INSEP	Institut National du Sport et de l'Education Physique (France)
IOC	International Olympic Committee
IPC	International Paralympic Committee
IRLT	Institute for Research on Learning Technologies (UK)
ISRM	Institute of Sport and Recreation Managers
ISCO	International Standard Classification of Occupations
ISLP	Institute of Sport and Leisure Policy (Loughborough University)
IT	information technology
IYSPE	International Year of Sport and Physical Education
JANAC	*Journal of the Association of Nurses in AIDS Care*
JSLA	Junior Sports Leaders Award
KAAA	Kenya Amateur Athletic Association
KDI	Korea Development Institute
LDC	least-developed countries
MDGs	Millennium Development Goals
MEMOS	Executive Master's in Sports Organisation Management
MINEPS	International Conference of Ministers and Senior Officials responsible for Physical Education and Sport
NACE	Statistical Classification of Economic Activities in the European Community
NASPE	National Association for Sport and Physical Education
NGO	non-governmental organization
NOC	National Olympic Committee
NPC	National Paralympic Committee
OECD	Organisation for Economic Co-operation and Development
OFSPO	Office fédéral du Sport (Switzerland)
PAY	Physically Active Youth (Canada)
P.E.4 Life	Physical Education for Life
PRSP	Poverty Reduction Strategy Papers
R&D	research and development
RI	Rehabilitation International: Rights and Inclusion
SADC	Southern African Development Community
SDC	Swiss Agency for Development and Cooperation
SGMA	Sporting Goods Manufacturers' Association International Market Intelligence
SKU	stock keeping unit
SOA	Swiss National Olympic Committee
SpinEd	Role of Physical Education and Sport in Education

ST-EP	Sustainable Tourism for Elimination of Poverty
SUVA	Swiss National Accident Insurance Organization
TEC	European Community Treaty
THENAPA	Thematic Network on Educational and Social Integration of Persons with a Disability through Adapted Physical Activity
UEFA	European Football Union
UNCG	United Nations Communications Group
UNCT	United Nations Country Team
UNCTAD	United Nations Conference on Trade and Development
UNDAF	United Nations Development Assistance Framework
UNDP	United Nations Development Programme
UNEP	United Nations Environment Programme
UNESCO	United Nations Educational, Scientific and Cultural Organization
UNICEF	United Nations Children's Fund
VET	vocational education and training
WADA	World Anti-Doping Agency
WFSGI	World Federation of Sporting Goods Industry
WHO	World Health Organization
WiFi	Wireless Fidelity
WOA	World Olympians' Association
WSSD	World Summit on Sustainable Development
WTO	World Trade Organization
WTTC	World Travel and Tourism Council
YCS	Youth Charter for Sport
YCSCA	Youth Charter for Sport, Culture and the Arts
YEN	Youth Employment Network (ILO)
YSP	Youth Sport Programme (ILO)

INTRODUCTION

Giovanni di Cola

The relationship between the International Labour Organization (ILO) and the International Olympic Committee (IOC) is long and illustrious. It all started in 1922, in the aftermath of the Treaty of Versailles, which concluded the First World War, when the IOC President, Baron Pierre de Coubertin, and the first ILO Director-General, Albert Thomas, agreed to collaborate on a number of far-reaching and visionary links for that time.

In 1924, the 6th Session of the International Labour Conference, with the support of the Baron, entrusted the ILO with the issue of "workers' spare time" to promote "district or local (sport) committees, composed of representatives of the public authorities, of employers' and workers' organizations, and of cooperative associations for coordinating and harmonizing the activities of the various institutions providing means of recreation".[1] The leaders of the respective organizations also identified additional areas for joint collaboration. These included workers' education at the university level and access to sport-related services and physical activities, all of which would promote decent working and living conditions. Workers should be able to access permanent and non-permanent infrastructures for sport, they felt. Finally, educational curricula, even at the university level, should include issues regarding physical education and sport for workers to enhance the physical and social well-being of both youth and workers.

The IOC and the ILO continue to use sport to promote the social well-being of all members of society. Recently, they embarked on sports projects that created decent job opportunities for youth and income-generating activities for women in Albania, El Salvador and Mozambique as part of the ILO Youth Sport Programme (YSP) and its Common Framework. A number of different partners, such as the International and National Olympic

1

Committees, the International and National Sport Federations and the World Federation of Sporting Goods Industry (WFSGI) are working together on important issues related to youth employment, gender equality and women's empowerment, and the elimination of child labour. In 2004 the IOC adopted the ILO code of practice, *HIV/AIDS and the world of work* (published in 2002) as a major policy tool for the Olympic Movement.

The ILO Universitas programme, in collaboration with universities in Canada, Italy, Switzerland and the United States, is developing a curriculum on youth leadership and skills development through sport. It includes a needs assessment conducted in developing countries.

The Universitas programme shared the lessons learned from partnership creation to foster economic development at the local level with the International Business Leaders Forum (IBLF). The IBLF published a brochure with the aim of sharing best practices in the field of sport and business partnership. The ILO contributed again with its perspective on sport and local economic development: "By not knowing what local needs are, business miss the opportunity for providing services and creating jobs."[2]

As part of the United Nations (UN) system-wide effort, the ILO has provided full support to the UN Inter-Agency Task Force on Sport for Development and Peace Report. In March 2003, the Task Force handed UN Secretary-General Kofi Annan the report, produced under the leadership of General Adolf Ogi, former President of Switzerland and Under-Secretary-General of the UN. The ILO perspective on sustainable development in sport is recognized as a powerful tool for socio-economic development at both the global and local levels. It gives youth the skills necessary for social insertion and access to decent jobs. Sport has proved to be an innovative solution to address issues such as youth unemployment, child labour and HIV/AIDS prevention.

Over the past few years the UN General Assembly has adopted three resolutions stressing sport as a means to promote education, health, development and peace. The first resolution[3] was approved in November 2003; its text, recalling all the important steps undertaken by the UN and the specialized agencies, invited all Governments and sport-related actors to mainstream sport in their development programmes to fulfil the Millennium Development Goals (MDGs) and, at the same time, launched the International Year of Sport and Physical Education (IYSPE). The UN General Assembly subsequently adopted a new resolution[4] encouraging Governments and the UN specialized agencies to develop strategic partnerships with the stakeholders involved in sport, including sports organizations, sports associations and the private sector. In November 2005 the General Assembly adopted the resolution marking the 2005 IYSPE.[5] The resolution specifically requested the UN Secretary-General to create an action plan with the scope of expanding and strengthening partnerships with governments, sport-related organizations and the private sector. It also requested the boosting of advocacy and social mobilization through well-targeted communication activities.

In order to improve coordination among UN agencies on Sport for Development and Peace, the United Nations Communications Group (UNCG) elaborated a Business Plan in September 2005. The plan offers a framework for a more systematic and coherent use of sport as a means to promote education, health, development and peace. Its medium-term objective is to use the assets of sport at various levels, starting with sports values, and to enhance opportunities for socio-economic change and a shift of attitude, particularly for youth.[6]

The ILO's concrete contribution to the Business Plan is the implementation of key activities based on the YSP, as noted above.[7] The ILO also carries out these projects and activities in collaboration with the national ministries of labour, youth and sport, the NOCs and the UN Country Teams.

About the book

This book compiles various contributions from authors belonging to all the sport-related partners involved in this venture. It is divided into three parts.

Part I, "Challenges in the sports sector", explains the critical challenges that sport faces, such as physical education, gender and women's empowerment in sport, and social insertion of people with a disability through sport, as illustrated by the International Paralympic Committee (IPC). This section also presents ethical values and a safe environment without doping in sports as a way to confront some of the difficulties inherent in the sector.

Part II, "Opportunities at the global and regional levels", gathers experiences on both local and global sports-sector-related situations and needs. It includes both African and Latin American local economic development initiatives inspired by sport. This part reports on European tripartite social dialogue and sports sector employment opportunities, together with a sporting goods market assessment over the next decade. An overall picture of the Sport Federation organizations is also included, showing how the sector acts as a vehicle between local and global markets.

Part III, "The contribution of sport to youth development", shows how sport can promote youth social development. First, it highlights key areas where policies regarding sport development can benefit youth. Other articles indicate clear opportunities (tourism and sport projects aimed at youth crime and violence reduction) where society can use sport for social insertion. Finally, the ILO Youth Sport Programme methodology is explained, and its results analysed to illustrate how sport can develop core employability skills.

Annexes provide case studies of the General Association of International Sports Federations (GAISF), women and leadership and the Olympic Movement, and youth insertion through sport in Mozambique.

Sport-specific skills should be included in the core skills employability framework. This concrete step would officially recognize the importance of sport values. Such values are of overriding significance not only in sports, but also for the benefit of youth in a global decent work environment.

Notes

[1] The Utilisation of Spare Time Recommendation, 1924 (No. 21); withdrawn.

[2] Intervention by Dr di Cola, ILO Senior Development Official, at the International Business Leaders' Forum: "Shared goals. Sport and Business for Partnerships for Development", July 2005.

[3] UN General Assembly Resolution A/RES/58/5, 17 Nov. 2003.

[4] UN General Assembly Resolution A/RES/59/10, 8 Sep. 2004.

[5] UN General Assembly Resolution A/RES/60/9, 3 Nov. 2005.

[6] Business Plan Elements, UN New York Office of Sport for Development and Peace, 2005.

[7] The UN Country Team (UNCT) office in Maputo, Mozambique, is carrying out a workshop on Sport and Development with both sport and development partners to reduce vulnerability and poverty (November 2005).

PART I

CHALLENGES IN THE SPORTS SECTOR

KEY QUESTIONS FOR POLICY DECISIONS IN SPORT

1

Jean-Loup Chappelet and Eleni Theodoraki

Introduction

Before discussing issues in sport development, we need to acknowledge the multifaceted nature of the sports industry. With an industry of numerous public, voluntary and commercial providers involved in recreation, sport education and competitive sport, it is important to avoid making generalizations when describing developments. Nevertheless, common answers arise when we contemplate what is good and bad within the sector.

This chapter proposes a strategy for sport management that leads to sustainable development on local, national and global levels. According to the International Charter for Physical Education and Sport adopted by UNESCO in 1978, sport is a fundamental right for all. We must ask ourselves, however, how the current (Western) sports model can be exported elsewhere and, above all, whether it favours sustainable development.

This is, in fact, questionable. The media report all possible negative or harmful behaviours within sport, such as anorexic gymnasts, doped athletes, violence in the stadium, corrupt sports officials, or the gigantism of sports facilities and events. The President of the International Olympic Committee (IOC) often attributes these harmful aspects to sport's damaged credibility (Horisberger, 2002). Sport has unfortunately contained these forces for a long time, and they are now a reflection of today's society. They are also becoming more widespread, which is a problem because they detract from the more obvious benefits of sport.

Is sport always healthy, educational and socially valid, as those who promote it have been affirming for over a century? The central question for this chapter thus becomes the following: What sort of sport do we want to practise, teach, manage, organize, promote or simply watch, with a view towards sustainable and ethical development? And how should we manage it in order for sport to remain a tool for positive development and not a factor that simply exacerbates the quality of life?

The state of sport today is examined according to the four main reasons for promoting sport in developed and developing countries: to maintain good health; to contribute towards education and the social agenda; for economic performance; and for sustainable development. The Government of Switzerland advances these main reasons in its sports policy concept (OFSPO, 2000a), which moreover explicitly recognizes that the State should "oppose the negative aspects of sport" and, with the sport organizations, fight against its excesses.

For the British, sport matters a great deal and the Government of the United Kingdom is committed to the value of sport both in itself and in the wider life of the community. The Department of Culture, Media and Sport's "Social Inclusion Action Plan" provides ample evidence of the role sport plays in combating social exclusion and tackling the neighborhood renewal agenda. The document also argues that sport is employed to remove barriers and maximize opportunity, to recognize and challenge inequality, and to create an environment in which everyone who wishes to participate in sport can do so without disadvantage or discrimination (DCMS, 2001).

Health: What evidence?

Good health is usually the first reason given when encouraging sport practice and when justifying public authority support. A healthy population is a basic condition of sustainable development. It has now also been scientifically proven that daily physical activity, even gentle forms of exercise, will maintain fitness and prevent a whole series of health problems (e.g. cardiovascular diseases, diabetes, cancer of the colon, prostate or breast, stress, osteoporosis, etc.). It is vital to encourage people to exercise regularly, since a sedentary lifestyle and its inherent problems are a threat to many of us. According to Swiss Federal Statistics, about 45 per cent of the Swiss population does not practise sport or perform any other kind of physical exercise (OFSPO, 2000b, p. 36).

There is ample research evidence that links physical activity to health outcomes. The chronic diseases of the twenty-first century are more difficult to cure in light of the obesity epidemic, children's inactivity and the ageing population (Hardman and Stensel, 2003, p. 4). Although differences in methodology make it difficult to compare the findings of national surveys of physical activity levels, two features are common: there is a rapid decline in activity with increasing age, and levels of activity are typically higher in men than in women. The national fitness survey for England determined that nearly one-third of men and two-thirds of women would find it difficult to sustain a walking pace of about 4.8 km per hour up a 5 per cent slope for more than a few minutes (ibid., p. 15). In developing countries, a decline in physical activity sadly appears to follow in the wake of economic growth, meaning that the prevalence of inactivity in the world may rise as the economies of such countries develop.

Generally speaking, sport contributes to the public's health. However, parallel to this positive aspect is evidence that some exaggerated and/or careless practices of sport are developing. A very high number of sprains, fractures and other injuries are occurring among the many "Sunday athletes" (i.e. those who exercise infrequently). The Swiss Office for Accident Prevention (BPA) publishes these statistics and evaluates the related economic and social costs every year. For example, in 1999 there were 34,592 skiing accidents in Switzerland, of varying degrees of gravity, costing approximately 180 million Swiss francs. The BPA, collaborating with the Swiss National Accident Insurance Organization (SUVA), launches regular publicity campaigns encouraging these "Sunday athletes" to take precautions. In their publications, certain doctors, for example Cascua (2002), Koralzstein (1986) and Solomon (1985), do not hesitate to stress the dangers of extreme sports.

Even in non-extreme sports elite athletes are frequently injured or ill, and this phenomenon is growing. Studies published in the *British Journal of Sports Medicine* (2000) reveal that there are now twice as many rugby injuries reported since it became a professional sport five years ago (Bottini et al., 2000; Gabbett, 2000). In 2002 FIFA (the International Football Federation Association) launched a study on the "fatigue threshold" of professional players, which could lead to the development of a licence limiting the number of matches in which a footballer can play per season (Davet and Potet, 2002). Scientific studies in Scandinavia and the United States are beginning to reveal major health problems for those seriously involved in endurance sports. At a world pneumonology conference held in Florence in September 2000, doctors denounced pulmonary damage caused to marathon runners, swimmers and cross-country skiers. According to researchers at Innsbruck Hospital, those who regularly practise mountain biking run the risk of major testicular cancer. In order to help doctors, in 1981 the World Medical Association adopted the Principles of Health Care for Sports Medicine, and has subsequently amended them several times in order to take into account the dangerous developments in sport.

Exercise-related injuries are quite common. Most are to the muscles and skeleton, caused by either overuse or trauma. The majority of injuries are to the lower limb and two out of three occur during team sports. Vigorous exertion is also one of the prime triggers of heart attacks. On average, people are between two and six times more likely to have a heart attack during or shortly after exercise than at other times. Furthermore, this transient increase in risk is much greater among sedentary people than among those accustomed to vigorous exercise, and it is outweighed by the decrease in risk long term (Hardman and Stensel, 2003, p. 239). Menstrual dysfunction is also common among women who engage in large amounts of vigorous endurance exercise, and even when menstrual periods are regular there may be abnormalities that will reduce fertility. Bone mineral density is lower in athletes with amenorrhoea than in those with normal menstrual periods, and there is concern that this bone loss may be largely irreversible. Lastly, our immune systems may be compromised after prolonged exertion, providing a "window of opportunity" for infections to gain a foothold.

Non-communicable diseases are a major and increasing public health burden in developing countries, and sedentary living puts people at greater risk in contracting several of these diseases. Increasing physical activity levels would have an important impact on the incidence of these diseases. It can be argued that, like drugs, physical activity has some adverse effect but these diseases are mainly avoided if the intensity of activity is at least moderate. Similarly, some health hazards may be prevented through specialist protective equipment (Hardman and Stensel, 2003).

Evidence shows that those who practise a sport very intensively can develop a form of dependence on it, and reveal withdrawal symptoms if they stop (Bauche, 2001). Statistics from the Swiss Institute for the Prevention of Alcohol and Drug Problems reveal links between the practice of certain sports (such as football, snowboarding, volleyball and badminton) among adolescents and the excessive consumption of alcohol, tobacco or drugs. In an attempt to combat these links, in 2001 the Swiss Federal Office for Public Health launched the "Ola" project to inform young athletes of these problems. It has also become evident that an increasing number of sportsmen and women are taking all kinds of "dietary supplements" and pharmaceutical products in order to participate in competitions at various levels, or simply to achieve a personal goal (Rivier and Romain, 2002). Several participants in the "20 km de Lausanne" (a half-marathon open to the public) falsely stated that they were asthmatics in order to be allowed to use performance-enhancing medication for this condition. More and more occasional athletes are falling into the trap of dangerous substance use (Waddington, 2000).

One extreme outcome of this substance abuse is doping, which today represents a public health problem since it affects an ever-increasing number of athletes, and most notably the younger generation. The fact that doping has become commonplace is revealed by several studies, such as the one carried out on 5,500 Swiss schoolchildren in 2000. It established that 38 per cent of young athletes admitted to consuming substances such as caffeine, creatine, alcohol, analgesics or amphetamines (Hirzel, 2000). Many bodybuilding centres have become veritable sources of supply for forbidden substances. More than half of the EPO (erythropoietin) sold in Switzerland is apparently used to improve sports performance (Terrani and Oberli, 2000). The "Calcio widows" controversy (premature deaths of Italian professional footballers), which started in 2001, reveals the long-term effects of EPO and other doping substances.

The World Anti-Doping Agency (WADA) was created in 1999 in order to unite public authorities and the Olympic Movement in the fight against this phenomenon, which is potentially lethal not only for athletes but also for the image of competitive sport (Chappelet, 2002). At a municipal level, the city of Lausanne in Switzerland wants to adopt a "Clean Sport Charter", which will have to be implemented by local clubs in order for them to receive grants from the city. Another initiative by the local pentathlon club led to the creation of a comic strip entitled *Doping or No Doping?*, showing the dangers of abusing drugs in sport. This comic strip was translated into nine languages (Borter et al., 2000).

Education or violence?

Education and training are vital to the sports industry, while sport is becoming an increasingly important component of the education sector (British Council, 2003). Participation in sport is beneficial to youth development; therefore physical education has been included in the curriculum to help improve students' abilities. Indeed, part of the function of the British National Curriculum is to realize the aims of the Education Reform Act 1998 to "promote the spiritual, moral, cultural, mental, and physical development of pupils at school and of society, and to prepare pupils for the opportunities, responsibilities and experiences of adult life" (United Kingdom Parliament, 1988). In other words, sport is perceived as aiding pupils' preparation for citizenship and the workplace.

Physical activity and sport promote not only fitness, but the cultural and moral education of those who practise them as well (Arnold, 1997). Healthy sports competition is an excellent school of life: the combination of effort, loyalty and fair play represents just some of the moral qualities that have led physical education to gain such esteem in most schools throughout the world. In addition to the educational benefits come the advantages for society, such as team spirit, fraternity, socialization and integration. Numerous studies confirm these raisons d'être for sport in schools, and serve as an example for elite sport. See, for example, the synthesis of the role of sport in society published by the Council of Europe (Vuori et al., 1995).

Sport teaches discipline, respect and the virtue of effort, helping participants to avoid getting into trouble and to be more productive. Physical education links the physical and the emotional to the intellectual, and is a vital component in the overall development of young people. The competitive aspect of sport helps young people to express their emotions in a controlled way, to work in groups and to build self-confidence. At its most basic level, physical education introduces "physical literacy" – the ability to control movement, to jump, to throw, to hit a ball and so on. A number of programmes and projects use the appeal of sport to attract young people and promote other aspects of education. For example, young children's sports equipment in the United Kingdom is colour- and number-coded, and teachers are trained to use the equipment to promote literacy and numeracy (British Council, 2003).

Of course there is also the negative side of young sportsmen and women sacrificing their natural growth for sporting excellence by taking prohibited drugs and leading unbalanced lives of constant struggle with little personal happiness or tranquillity. Like everything else, sport needs to be experienced in moderation along with other aspects of life, such as being with family and friends, and finding ways to express yourself whether it be artistically, culturally and so on. Our education systems are so obsessed with academic and applied performance that resource limitations leave sport education marginalized in the curriculum, fighting for legitimacy and recognition.

Unfortunately, violence in sport is developing and endangering its educational benefits. Books by Dominique Bodin (2001) and Jeffrey Goldstein (1985) detail various forms of violence seen in different sports. We are aware of the problems of football hooliganism, which has caused many deaths both within the stadium and beyond it (Heysel, Sheffield, etc.). The phenomenon also exists in North American football, baseball and ice hockey, as Jon Leizman reveals in his book: *Let's kill 'em: Understanding and controlling violence in sports* (1999). The development of violence and racism between fans and players is another burning issue. The case of the footballer Eric Cantona is well known, but is far from being an isolated incident. In 2002, the UEFA (the European Football Union) launched a ten-point guideline aimed at fighting racism and violence in the stadium. However, violence on the pitch is becoming an almost daily event, notably in football. In amateur leagues, French referees are applying a new rule, the "white card", which means that the player responsible for an incident is sent off the pitch for ten minutes. Player violence has also affected other sports, such as tennis, with the incidents during the Chile–Argentina Davis Cup match in April 2000, and ice hockey, when a Boston Bruins player struck another player with his stick, resulting in concussion for the victim.

Professional sport does not have a monopoly on related violence. Attacks (including those of a sexual nature) on the occasion of everyday sports activities have become so frequent that they are the subject of numerous articles or discussions (Brackenridge, 2001). The French department of Seine-Saint-Denis in the Paris region cancelled all amateur football matches for several weeks in 2001 as a result of serious incidents of this nature. Violence in sport is affecting the perceptions of young people more and more through the behaviour of their family members. In the United States, fights between referees and parents who are hoping to see their offspring become sports stars have become commonplace. In his book, *Why Johnny hates sports* (2002), Fred Engh reveals how this can make children disenchanted with sport. In Europe, many in the education sector have protested against intensive training for children at an early age, claiming that it endangers their physical and psychological development. Cases in which the young athlete's entourage and parents push the child to excel in sport occur far too frequently. We therefore see that examples of aggressive competition and intensive involvement in sport too early in life can destroy the educational benefits that are commonly expected from sport, notably for the majority who do not reach the "top".

In 2002 the Swiss National Olympic Committee (SOA) published a code of ethics with seven points aimed at fighting violent forms of behaviour, doping and dependence on narcotics (SOA, 2002). The Council of Europe annexed a Code of Sports Ethics to the European Sport Charter adopted in 1992, which gives a definition of fair play ("the winning way") and outlines the respective responsibilities of the sport organizations, governments and athletes.

Regardless of how widespread the benefits of sport participation are, managers and policy makers need to promote sport within an ethical framework, so that the negative effects are limited. If the sports system is obsessed with excellence in global competition, then, inevitably, there will be a number of losers who may look at fast and immoral ways of improving. On the other hand, if efforts are praised, then the educated person learns a different lesson, one of perseverance and unfailing effort to improve, not to be better than the other but better than oneself.

Performance or corruption?

Over the past 30 years, sport has become an important sector of the economy, and in Europe it generates approximately 2 per cent of consumer expenditure (Andreff et al., 1994). Sport participation and entertainment have given rise to an entire industry of sporting goods manufacturers and sports service providers. The media and advertising are devoting more and more attention to sport. A large proportion of this "sport consumption" is indirect: most tennis shoes purchased are not used when playing tennis, and many of those who watch rugby on television take no part in any kind of physical activity. However, the development of this new economic sector provides an indirect justification for public authorities to promote sports activities. This "performance cult" (to use the expression of French sociologist Alain Ehrenberg) appears beneficial to companies and their employees. Sport-induced performance capacity is useful in today's working environment, which is becoming increasingly competitive.

To the chagrin of the sporting world, corruption is threatening sports executives and athletes alike. In 1999 around 20 members of the International Olympic Committee (IOC) were expelled or issued warnings for accepting various benefits from the Salt Lake City candidature for the Olympic Games. Over the past 15 years, other major competitions have also been implicated in corruption because the economic stakes have been enormous and the competition increasingly fierce. When sporting events involve contracts bringing in millions in revenue, those who award these contracts are subject to the same temptations as those in the business world. While this reasoning does not serve as an excuse, it does begin to explain the dilemma facing competitive sports. Corruption is a form of doping for sports executives and, like doping in athletes, it is a reflection on the state of society.

The astronomical sums that circulate in the business of team sport incite managers of clubs or federation executives to hide huge deficits or to cover up underhand dealings. Andreff (1999; 2001a) revealed the extremes related to financing this type of sport. In 2002 the honesty of the presidents of several Swiss football clubs and the president of the Swiss Ice Hockey League was questioned regarding the management of their sports organizations. Faced with similar problems, the 25 European Olympic Committees proposed, in 2001, rules for the good governance of sport organizations (EOC, 2001) and, in 2002, the IOC adopted conflict-of-interest guidelines for its members.

Perhaps even more troubling is the fact that corruption is reaching the playing fields, with athletes and referees involved in distorting match results. One infamous example was the fixed match between Valenciennes and Olympique de Marseille, which caused the (temporary) downfall of French businessman Bernard Tapie. Another case was the Auxerre–Grasshoper match, which led to the UEFA's lifelong suspension of Swiss referee Kurt Röthlisberger. In Greece, the reaction has been to adopt a law aimed at redressing underhand business practices and recurring cases of match fixing in football, and in sport in general. However, despite efforts like these the corruption pandemic is spreading. At the beginning of 1999, several Italian football clubs admitted to having given sumptuous Christmas gifts to referees. In 2000, eight players from Italy's premier football division were accused of sports fraud under the same law that convicted the cyclist Marco Pantani for doping.

False passports are now a common method enabling footballers from overseas to participate in major European championships. Some of these players are extremely young, and at times taken away from their parents and homeland. In January 2003, UNESCO's Final Declaration of the Sports Ministers' Conference (MINEPS IV) recognized the problems arising from "muscle drain" (paralleling the "brain drain" from less-developed countries to richer ones). To fight the "muscle drain", Andreff (2001b) proposes that fines be levied against corruption in sport, and that a tax be paid on the transfer of players.

It is important to note that corruption is certainly not limited to the game of football. Journalists have revealed examples of corruption in boxing, motor racing, cricket, cycling, gymnastics, judo and figure skating (even at the Olympic Games!). During the 1999 Golden League, the world saw a long-distance runner yield his victory to the athlete placed second, after admitting that they discussed sharing the jackpot if the latter agreed to let him place first. Taking matters to the extreme, certain athletes and officials are prepared to eliminate the glorious incertitude of sport in order to obtain a better profit on their investments or their wagers. In doing so, however, they run the risk of destroying the very attraction of sport as a form of entertainment. Jean-Marie Brohm, renowned for attacking sport as being a tool for alienating the masses, speaks of "rampant criminalization" within sport as an institution. While such a claim seems a little extreme, we must be cognizant of the fact that the risk exists. With that in mind, the IOC created an Ethics Commission in 1999 to study and judge all cases of dispute concerning the Olympic Movement. Furthermore, sports ethics centres have been created in certain countries, including Australia, Canada, Great Britain, Switzerland and the United States.

Sustainable development or gigantism?

All sporting pursuits take place in a given environment that is not immune to athlete intervention. Even a runner leaves an ecological footprint causing soil erosion. More threatening, however, is the impact of facility construction, air pollution and inevitable waste generation. Apart from sport harming the environment, environmental change poses a threat to sport, with climate change and loss of natural habitat attraction. The reality is that the way the sporting community acts in the boardroom or on the playing field is entirely consistent with the way society at large acts, which often counteracts the ideals of sport (Chernushenko et al., 2002, pp. 9 and 33).

Over the past 15 years, the organizers of major sports events have realized the importance of taking the environment into consideration. The Olympic Winter Games in Albertville (France) in 1992 and in Lillehammer (Norway) in 1994 marked a turning point in sporting event organization. Today, the idea of organizing large or small sports events without taking measures to protect the environment, notably regarding their logistics (transport, waste, energy, etc.), is inconceivable. Several publications on this subject include the pioneering book by Chernushenko (1994) or the story of the Swiss Gymnastics Festival, which unites thousands of participants in Switzerland every six years (FSG, 1997). The Swiss National Olympic Committee has recently introduced a prize to be awarded for the most ecological sports event organized in Switzerland.[1]

The idea of sustainable development gained ground in sport community circles after the Earth Summit held in Rio de Janeiro in 1992. In 1997, the candidature of Sion (Switzerland) for the 2006 Winter Games suggested for the first time that the Games could be the catalyst for sustainable development, notably concerning social aspects and tourism (AJOH, 1998). These ideas were taken up by the city of Turin (the host of the 2006 Winter Olympics), which is currently setting up an environmental management system to this effect (Furrer, 2002). In 1999, the IOC also adopted its own Agenda 21 to serve as a reference tool for the sporting world in the protection of the environment and the promotion of sustainable development (IOC, 1999). Agendas adapted to the specific Olympic sports are currently in preparation under the aegis of the IOC's Sport and Environment Commission (Tarradellas, 2002).

Despite these commitments being made to promote sustainable development, major sports events such as the Olympic Games and other World or European Championships are becoming even more gigantic. This makes their organization risky or too expensive, even for the largest of countries (e.g. Atlanta, 1996, and Nagano, 1998). That being said, it would be impossible for developing countries to organize similar events, with rare exceptions (e.g. the World Volleyball Championships in Argentina, 2002). The Olympic Games have never been held in Africa or South America. The football World Cup will be held in Africa in 2010 following a decision taken by FIFA, but it is questionable what kind of development it will bring to the "lucky" country. In 2001, the IOC president acknowledged the problem of Olympic gigantism by nominating a commission to study the size and cost of the Games, and to propose solutions for limiting their complexity. The commission's final report was delivered in July 2003, and proposes more than 100 ideas to progressively reduce the gigantism of the Olympic Games.

The National and International Federations have gradually imposed norms for building sports facilities. These norms are often too luxurious and unsuitable, making it costly to build and run these facilities. Their spectator capacity is frequently too large, leading to the construction of "white elephants" that are rarely filled once the major event for which they serve as a venue is over. One flagrant example of the "white elephant" scenario is the 20 stadiums built or renovated for the 2002 FIFA World Cup in the Republic of Korea and Japan. Furthermore, despite the success of the 2000 Sydney Games, the post-Games use of the Olympic Park created for the occasion in

Homebush Bay is proving to be problematic. Although the stadium was built on top of an industrial wasteland, which has now been rehabilitated, today it is a concrete desert that is rarely used or visited by the local population.

Sophisticated television broadcasting (notably on wide screens and with high definition) should assist in avoiding the gigantism dilemma and help promote sustainable development. Initiatives for the construction of appropriate facilities, such as the project being put forward by the Olympafrica Foundation,[2] should be encouraged. The principles developed for sustainable sport facilities and events within the framework of the Sustainable Active Living Framework proposed by UNESCO and the United Nations Environment Programme (UNEP) should be made better known and applied.

In a proposal by Chernushenko and UNEP (Chernushenko et al., 2002, p. 227), sustainability in sport must be seen as a triathlon. The tri-athlete company, facility or event manager will be working to improve environmental, social and economic practices as a package. In doing so, the manager will arguably also find that steps taken to improve environmental performance, when adopted as part of an overall sustainability strategy, will have the additional effect of improving social and economic performance as well.

Education and training needs

Evidence of the increasing professionalization of sports management exists through the number of qualified graduates in the related disciplines, the creation of professional associations and the work of scholars in the epistemic community of sport. The need for continuous learning by the above agents is all the more important, as:

- sport business grows;

- the position of sport and physical education is unstable in congested curricula; and

- negative effects of sport are on the increase.

Inherent in sport is learning, and improving upon new skills, not only for athletes but also for coaches, officials, professionals and voluntary administrators. Improvements in skill and performance can only be achieved through education and training, whether on the field or in the classroom. Modern sport is a large and complex industry, within which elite athletes form only the pinnacle. In a well-functioning sports system, this pinnacle rests on the solid foundation of physical education in school and sport for all at a community level. Around 60 per cent of adults in the United Kingdom take part in some form of sport or organized physical recreation. A large number of people are needed to make this system work, including professionals (750,000 people work in sports recreation and allied industries) and volunteers (an estimated 2 million) (British Council, 2003).

Given its size, the sports and recreation industry is a major employer in its own right. Careers are open in physical education, coaching, sports physiotherapy and massage, sports science, sports centre management, sports administration and management, sponsorship and other related areas. In the United Kingdom alone, more than 50 institutions offer undergraduate courses in sport and 40 institutions offer postgraduate sports education. Educational institutions must provide managers with the needed business and analytical skills. Moreover, sport could not function without the unpaid army of volunteers who run clubs, fund-raise, chair meetings and organize competitions. Since all those functions are skilled work, the training, recognition and retention of volunteers are major challenges facing modern sport.

Education and training for athletes have traditionally focused primarily on honing skills that will improve performance. However, a range of other issues are now also important to the modern coach and athlete, including safety, ethics (particularly sexual and drug abuse) and what is called "lifestyle management". Such education will provide athletes with the skills that will make them more rounded people and, ultimately, more effective athletes during their sporting careers (British Council, 2003).

The United Kingdom has a number of resources in many areas of sports education and training. The subsections below paint a picture of the types of expertise available.

Sport in the curriculum

The Department for Education and Employment and the Youth Sports Trust (a non-governmental organization) are promoting innovative solutions in the delivery of sport and physical education in schools, in the form of new materials, new teaching techniques and in-service training for teachers. Nevertheless, the current financial crisis in British schools has meant that sport education also suffers.

Vocational and pre-vocational education for sport

Higher and further education in the United Kingdom offers a wide range of courses and in-service training for all aspects of the sports industry. Behind the United States, the United Kingdom has the second-greatest offering of courses in this area – over 400. Many of these courses already attract foreign students and/or offer opportunities for distance learning. Despite all these education opportunities, reforms in higher education funding have led to under-funding of research, the introduction of tuition fees and increasing reliance on international fee-paying students.

Athlete personal development

The UK Sports Institute is developing over 30 modules designed to provide elite athletes with the skills to complement their athletic education: time management; dealing with injury; financial planning; dealing with the media, etc. Life management training for professional athletes is pertinent following a British Olympic Association report (1996) that reveals the high extent of debt that elite athletes and their families face.

Volunteers

Running Sport and the Volunteer Involvement Programme are two programmes designed to recognize, train and motivate the volunteers who run sport. The role of volunteers in British sport has never been underestimated, but certain management modernization programmes have undermined the legitimacy of their voices in strategic issues. As decision-making power moves away from the hands of the volunteers to paid executives, volunteers are slowly marginalized in the higher echelons of sport management (Theodoraki, 1999).

A bridge to the classroom

The Department for Education and Employment is working with professional football clubs across England to establish after-school study centres sponsored by the clubs (British Council, 2003).

Overall the level of training of those involved in sport is improving and the growing professionalism in the field will surely lead to further changes in the way sport is played, organized, funded and strategically managed. Just as curriculum developers need to be sensitive about what aspect of sport they promote at school, so too do agents in the sport industry need to be taught how to develop a professional conscience that binds them to serving society and not just economic interests.

The possibility of improvement through greater professionalization of the field is encouraging, but there are still many so-called sport managers and sport policy makers who have not been educated in the subject and come from other professional backgrounds. Sports ministers in the United Kingdom have a reputation of being too weak to lead other departments, which is indicative of the type of people that are sometimes attracted to public and voluntary sector sport management positions. The role of the international and national professional bodies such as the European Association of Sport Managers (EASM) and the Institute of Sport and Recreation Managers (ISRM) come into play here as legitimate protectors of the profession. If medical doctors take the Hippocratic oath to protect the patient at all costs before they are allowed to practise medicine, sport managers should have their own oath that will professionally bind them to acceptable behaviour. However, debating what is acceptable can be a very protracted enterprise that must involve philosophers, educationalists and professional representatives.

Effective sport development

Although the future of sport is guaranteed as access and opportunities for participation increase, we must constantly re-evaluate its effect on our lives and moral development. Educators preparing individuals for careers in sport management, students studying in this area and those already holding sport management positions are responsible for ensuring that sport and those associated with sport maintain moral character. According to DeSensi and Rosenberg (1996), ethical reform within sport will occur when self-reflective dialogue among those involved takes place. During such dialogue, values, beliefs and goals must be examined in conjunction with the programme values and the ways in which each of these compares with larger society. When the effectiveness of a system is considered, attention needs to be given to the criteria of effectiveness employed. The literature suggests that effectiveness is a multidimensional concept (Chelladurai and Haggerty, 1991) that is difficult to measure operationally; and also that various stakeholders hold different views of the attributes that make a system or a policy effective. Houlihan (1999) also discusses crowded policy spaces where it is challenging to disentangle the intended and unintended outcomes of policy programmes, and the motives of the key agents and agencies involved.

If holistic, healthy and sustainable sport development is required, the challenge to future providers is to make the transition from a preoccupation with targets to a critically reflective analysis of processes. This, however, would be nearly impossible to evaluate using the current target system. In the British context, broader institutional management has been increasingly subject to external influences, stressing concepts of financial efficiency and management within the sporting enterprise. The terms "new public management" or "managerialism" are usually taken to refer to some combination of processes and values that have developed in the last decade. The term, in essence, refers to the incorporation and application of private sector management systems and techniques in public services. Some of its features include: introduction of strategic management; specific structural change (such as the development of new middle-management positions); use of financial efficiency as a measure of organizational effectiveness; the incorporation of market values in public policy areas; the demise of collectivist approaches (e.g. provision on the basis of expert opinion instead of user consultation); seeing the public as clients; and, finally, department budgets giving way to contracts with notionally cheaper and "better" private providers (Farnham and Horton, 1993; Schedler, 1995; Clarke, Gewirtz et al., 2000).

In response to the question, "How does one evaluate current sport development systems?", the current approach includes the use of targets. The learning of athletes is judged by international performance and post-competition career. For sport managers, evaluation is based predominantly on financial efficiency and how well they embrace the modernization agenda. For volunteers, assessment is centred on conformity to managers' whims and compliance with professionals' opinions. The British Government's Department for Culture, Media and Sport is also primarily focused on searching for quantifiable, tangible outputs to justify its funding and guide its policies. Its research policy document calls for prioritizing the analysis of future trends, understanding the sponsored sectors, enforcing evidence-based policy and developing a prototype data framework and monitoring/evaluation (DCMS, 2003, p. 34). In this context, qualitative research findings are perceived by the Department as secondary to quantifiable evidence that is legitimate to base policy upon. Paradoxically, it is traditionally the qualitative research that most often reveals abuse in the sports system, be it harassment, corruption or self-harm.

In order to improve the sports system, we must begin a dialogue about values. When sport, in its current form, is examined and challenged from various perspectives, it is necessary for the sports manager to look for the positive and negative aspects of this environment: How are individuals (participants and public) affected? Is the realm of sport consistent with the values, issues and problems of a multicultural and diverse society? What value does sport bring to society as a whole? How is moral excellence achieved and maintained through sport? Herein lies the ethical responsibility of sport managers in the future.

Ethics in sport management and the SAFE principles

Optimists argue that the sports industry has the potential to mature and evolve in such a way that it promotes economic prosperity, human fitness, environmental conservation and community development, along with many other traditional values. What is needed according to Chernushenko et al. (2002, p. 34) is a common ethic that embodies shared principles. Sport remains an eminently valid tool for policies of health, education and socio-economic development, but remains a tool that is rather new and somewhat unpolished, with capricious effects: to paraphrase the Greek fabulist Aesop, sport can be the best and worst of things. Over the twentieth century, sport has become a paramount social factor, having the tendency to reflect the ills of society as a whole. Therefore, it is essential to reflect on the harmful effects of sports activity and on ways in which we can minimize them in an attempt to preserve sport's beneficial effects and to earn greater endorsement among public officials. The Olympic motto, *Citius, Altius, Fortius* (Faster, Higher, Stronger), can be dangerous in that it appears to imply a sport without limits (Chappelet, 1994). It is no longer sufficient to quote the famous *Mens Sana in Corpore Sano* (a healthy mind in a healthy body), which is why we must endeavour to make sport safe for all those who practise it and ensure that it contributes towards sustainable development in those countries where it receives support (in the form of funding from intergovernmental or non-governmental organizations).

The sport movement must proceed, taking into account the three major priorities of the Olympic Movement's Agenda 21 (improvement of socio-economic conditions; preservation and sustainable management of resources; and reinforcement of the role of women, young people and indigenous populations) (IOC, 1999). Sports organizations must be managed in accordance with the principles of the Triple Bottom Line (financially stable, socially progressive and environmentally conscious), drawn up under the aegis of UNEP (Chernushenko et al., 2002, p. 10). This implies using Olympic Solidarity programmes like MEMOS (Executive Master's in Sports Organisation Management) to train managers. Finally, sport teachers and coaches should use educational tools for young athletes such as those proposed by the FS3 Foundation in Lausanne (FS3, 2001). Moreover, self-regulating and incitement mechanisms for athletes, sponsors and the media must be established in order to combat the lethal dangers in sport, thereby permitting sport to remain safe for those who practise it and for society in general, and to serve harmonious human development everywhere. To this effect, the regulatory intervention of public authorities is indispensable, and should be in close partnership with the governing bodies of sport.

With this being said, we must begin to defend a certain notion of sport. This notion is embodied in the slogan "SAFE Sport", i.e. sport that is Sustainable, Addiction-free, Fair, and Ethical:

* *Sustainable* – to avoid sport leading to the construction of inappropriate facilities or organizing gigantic events, and conversely for sport to facilitate balanced development;

- *Addiction-free* – to avoid sport leading to the abnormal use of all kinds of substances that are harmful to the individual, and instead for sport to contribute towards better health;

- *Fair* – to avoid sport degenerating into physical or moral violence, and to ensure that sport remains an incomparable educational tool;

- *Ethical* – to avoid sport becoming corrupted or criminal, and for it to remain a factor that contributes to a sound and effective economy.

This slogan was proposed and accepted by the World Sport and Development Conference held in Maggligen, Switzerland, in February 2003. A number of concrete recommendations were also included in the final declaration (SDC, 2003).

Conclusion

This chapter has weighed the pro and cons of the use of sport as a means for development, discussing the effects of sport participation at the various levels, and for the relevant agents involved. In the light of documented, unwanted effects and identified future threats, the authors consider the need for ethically grounded, sustainable sport management as embodied in the spirit and the letters of the SAFE Sport slogan. With SAFE Sport, it will be possible to meet the needs of today's sportsmen, sportswomen and fans without further harming sport or compromising the ability of future generations to enjoy sport at its best.

It is clear that current sport systems are bound by the political and economic realism facing the government(s) or private interests that control them and, in such a context, investment in sport is seen as a means to certain ends (health, social development and control, national pride, wealth accumulation, etc). However, despite our good intentions, involvement in sport will not always yield positive outcomes. Sports managers must act as ethically responsible professionals, remembering to debate what values are being promoted (Pelegrinis, 1997). Ultimately this debate must lead to the choice of guiding principles, and while being aware of the demands that accrue from these principles, sports professionals should act according to these principles alone.

Notes

[1] Prix ECOSPORT: Le prix écologique des manifestations sportives (Ecological prize for sporting events): see www.prox-ecosport.ch, accessed 24 Feb. 2006.

[2] See Association of National Olympic Committees in Africa (www.anoca/info/olympicafrica.php, accessed 24 Feb. 2006).

Bibliography

Andreff, W. 1999. "Les finances du sport et l'éthique sportive", in *Revue d'économie financière* (Paris), No. 55.

—. 2001a. "Jusqu'à l'extrême: l'escalade dans le financement du sport", in Baddeley, M. (ed.): *Sports extrêmes, sportifs de l'extrême, la quête des limites.* Geneva, International Academy of Sports Science and Technology (AiSTS) and Georg, pp. 175–181.

—. 2001b. "The correlation between economic underdevelopment and sport", in *European Sport Management Quarterly*, Vol. 1, No. 4, Dec.

—, et al. 1994. *Les enjeux économiques du sport en Europe*. Paris, Dalloz.

Arnold, P. 1997. *Sport, ethics and education*. London, Cassell.

Association pour les Jeux Olympiques d'hiver (AJOH). 1998. *Sion 2006 Switzerland: Rainbow paper on sustainable development*. Sion.

Barcelona Declaration. 1998. *Seventh World Sport for All Congress "Sport for All and the Global Educational Challenges"*. Barcelona.

Bauche, P. 2001. *Conséquences psychiques et psychopathologiques de l'arrêt de la pratique sportive chez l'athlète de haut niveau*, unpublished doctoral thesis. Paris, 13-Villetaneuse.

Bello, S. 2003. *Strategic development for sport in Albania*, unpublished MEMOS project. June.

Bizzini, L. 1999. "Balance and imbalance in children's sport", in *Olympic Review* (Lausanne), Vol. XXVI, No. 26, Apr.–May, pp. 25–28.

Bodin, D. 2001 (ed.). *Sports et violences*. Paris, Chiron.

Borter, F; Ayats, R; Durbec, A. 2000. *Doping or no doping?* Lausanne, Panathlon.

Bottini, E., et al. 2000. "Incidence and nature of the most common injuries sustained in Argentina (1991–1997)", in *British Journal of Sports Medicine*, Vol. 34, pp. 94–97.

Brackenridge, C. 2001. *Spoilsports: Understanding and preventing sexual exploitation in sport.* London, Routledge.

Brennan, J.; Shah, T. 1994. "Higher education policy in the United Kingdom", in L. Goedegebuure et al.: *Higher education policy: An international comparative perspective.* Oxford, Pergamon Press.

British Council. 2003. "Sport, education and training". London (see: http://www.britcoun.org/work/sport/ed.htm, accessed May 2003).

British Olympic Association. 1996. *Athletes' Commission Report 1996*. London, The British Olympic Association.

Cascua, S. 2002. *Le sport est-il bon pour la santé ?* Paris, Odile Jacob.

Chappelet, J. 1994. "Olympisme, nature et culture", in IOC: *Texts and summaries of interventions at the Olympic Centennial Congress*. Lausanne, pp. 39–40.

—. 2002. "L'Agence mondiale antidopage: un nouveau régulateur des relations sportives internationales", in *Relations Internationales* (Paris), Vol. X, No. 131, Autumn.

—. 2003. *Managing a safe and sustainable sport*, Sport and Development International Conference, Macolin, 16–18 Feb. 2003.

Chelladurai, P.; Haggerty, T. 1991. "Measures of organisational effectiveness of Canadian National Sport Organisations", in *Canadian Journal of Sport Science* (Ontario), Vol. 16, No. 2.

Chernushenko, D. 1994. *Greening our Games: Running sports events and facilities that won't cost the earth.* Ottawa, Centurion.

—; van der Kamp, A.; Stubbs, D. 2002. *Sustainable sport management: Running an environmentally, socially and economically responsable organization.* Nairobi, UNEP.

Chifflet, P.; Gouda, S. 1996. "Olympisme et identité nationale en Afrique noire francophone", in *Revue STAPS* (France), Vol. 17, No. 14, Nov., pp. 93–105.

Clarke, C. 2003. Speech to the Sports Colleges Conference, Secretary of State for Education and Skills Rt Hon Charles Clarke MP. United Kingdom.

Clarke, J.; Gewirtz, S.; et al. 2000. *New managerialism new welfare?* London, Sage.

Davet, G.; Potet, F. 2002. "La FIFA craint que le foot-business tue la santé des joueurs", in *Le Monde* (Paris), 12 Oct.

Department for Education and Employment (DFEE), United Kingom. 1995. *The English education system: An overview of structure and policy.* London.

Department of Culture, Media and Sport (DCMS). 2001. *High Level Business Plan 2000–2001.* London (see: http://www.culture.gov.uk/NR/rdonlyres/6D01FB42-715A-4E90-AC5B-3BA236BF32CA/0/dcmsbusplan200001.pdf, accessed 4 Apr. 2006).

—. 2003. *Framework for the future.* London, Feb.

DeSensi, J. T.; Rosenberg, D. 1996. *Ethics in sport management.* Morgantown, WV, Fitness Information Technology.

Ehrenberg, A. 1991. *Le culte de la performance.* Paris, Calmann-Lévy.

Engh, F. 2002. *Why Johnny hates sports.* New York, Square One Publishers.

European Olympic Committee (EOC). 2001. "The rules of the Games", Conference on the Governance of Sport, Brussels, 26–27 Feb.

Farnham, D.; Horton, S. 1993. *Managing the new public services.* London, Macmillan.

Farrar, Straus and Giroux (FSG). 1997. *Manifestations sportives et environnement: L'exemple de la Fête fédérale de gymnastique Berne 96, Concept, mesures, bilan et recommendations.* Berne, FSG, AOS and IRLT.

Foundation Sport, Science and Society (FS3). 2003. *Safe sport.* Sion, Gessler SA.

Fondation Sport, Science et Société (FS3). 2001. *Sport, science and society*, brochure published by the FS3 on the occasion of the Third World Sport Forum (Lausanne), Sep.

Furrer, P. 2002. "Sustainable Olympic Games: A dream or a reality? ", in *Bollettino della Società Geografica Italiana* (Italy), Series XII, Vol. VII, 4.

Gabbett, T. J. 2000. "Incidence, site, and nature of injuries in amateur rugby league over three consecutive seasons", in *British Journal of Sports Medicine*, Vol. 34, pp. 98–103.

Goldstein, J. 1985. *Sports violence*. New York, Springer.

Griffith, R. 2000. *National Curriculum: National disaster. Education and citizenship*. London, Routledge.

Hardman, A. E.; Stensel, D. J. 2003. *Physical activity and health: The evidence explained.* London, Routledge.

Hirzel, F. 2000. "Un tiers des jeunes sportifs en danger", in *24 Heures* (Lausanne), 29 Mar., p. 36.

Horisberger, C. 2002. "Dopage, corruption et violence nuisent à la crédibilité du sport", Interview with Jacques Rogge, *Swiss-Sport* (Berne), Sep., pp. 6–7.

Houlihan, B. 1999. *Sporting excellence, schools and sports development: The politics of crowded policy spaces*, paper presented to the CRSS-EPER Conference on PE and Excellence, University of Leicester, Sep.

—; White, A. 2002. *The politics of sports development: Development of sport or development through sport?* London, Routledge.

International Olympic Committee (IOC). 1999. *Agenda 21 of the Olympic Movement: Sport for sustainable development.* Seoul, Sport and Environment Commission.

Koralzstein, J.-P. 1986. *La santé à l'épreuve du sport.* Grenoble, PUG.

Leizman, J. 1999. *Let's kill 'em: Understanding and controlling violence in sports.* New York, University Press of America.

Office fédéral du Sport (OFSPO). 2000a. *Concept du Conseil fédéral pour une politique du sport en Suisse.* Macolin, 30 Nov.

—. 2000b. *Enquête suisse sur la santé: Santé et comportements vis-à-vis de la santé en Suisse 1997.* Neuchâtel.

Pelegrinis, T. 1997. *Ethical philosophy*. Athina, Ellinika Gramata (in Greek).

Rivier, L.; Romain, D. 2002. "Resolution for the Fourth World Sport Forum" (Lausanne), Sep.

Schedler, K.1995. *Ansätze einer wirkungsorientierten Verwaltungsführung.* Berne, Haupt.

Solomon, H. 1985. *Le sport à tout prix, le mythe de l'exercice physique.* Paris, Payot.

Swiss Agency for Development and Cooperation (SDC). 2003. "Final Declaration of the World Sport & Development Conference", Magglingen, Switzerland, 17–18 Feb. 2003.

Swiss National Olympic Committee (SOA). 2002. "Charte éthique: Ensemble en faveur d'un sport sain, respectueux et correct!", in *Swiss-Sport* (Berne), Sep., p. 4.

Tarradellas, J. 2002. "The Olympic Games and sustainability", in *Proceedings of the Symposium on the Legacy of the Olympic Games* (Lausanne), Nov.

Terrani, Y.; Oberli, P. 2000. "Le sport absorbe plus de 50% de l'EPO vendue en Suisse: parole d'expert", in *Le Temps* (Geneva), 10 June, p. 21.

Theodoraki, E. 1999. "Structural change in Britain and its implications for sport", in K. Heinemann: *Sport clubs in various European countries.* Schorndorf and Hofmann.

UK Parliament. 1988. *Education Reform Act 1988*. London, HMSO.

UNESCO. 2002. *Sustainable Active Living (SAL): Integrating Sustainable Development with Quality Physical Education and Sport*, Recommendations for the Johannesburg Summit., Aug.

Vuori, I., et al. 1995. *The significance of sport for society – Health, socialisation, economy.* Strasbourg, Council of Europe Press.

Waddington, I. 2000. *Sport, health and drugs: A critical sociological perspective.* London, Spon Press.

PHYSICAL EDUCATION AND SPORT SCIENCE: CHALLENGES AND OPPORTUNITIES

2

Gudrun Doll-Tepper

Introduction

For many decades, physical education has been on the agenda of formal education systems at both national and international levels. More recently, physical education has also been discussed as part of lifelong learning, and is no longer limited to school institutions. This chapter examines developments and initiatives from a global perspective, and presents challenges and opportunities based on the most recent studies and findings. The various sport science disciplines that have evolved until now have made specific contributions to physical education. The tremendous changes with regard to specialization areas in sport science present new challenges as well. In particular, one may note the broad spectrum of scientific knowledge and its accessibility to experts and the general public, as well as new professional training opportunities at national and international level. The chapter also gives some selected examples of new joint programmes with several universities and institutions of higher learning. Finally, it presents challenges focusing on issues related to training, employment and social dialogue.

Physical education (1978–2000)

As early as 1978, the General Conference of the United Nations Educational, Scientific and Cultural Organization (UNESCO) adopted the International Charter of Physical Education and Sport, urging governments, non-governmental organizations, educators, families and individuals to implement physical education and sport appropriately, inside and outside schools and in all countries around the world. The Charter (UNESCO, 1978; 1993) highlighted that:

- The practice of physical education and sport is a fundamental right for all.

- Physical education and sport form an essential element of lifelong education in the overall education system.

- Physical education and sport programmes must meet individual and social needs.

- Teaching, coaching and administration of physical education and sport should be performed by qualified personnel.

- Adequate facilities and equipment are essential to physical education and sport.

- Research and evaluation are indispensable components of the development of physical education and sport.

- Protection of the ethical and moral values of physical education and sport must be a constant concern for all.

- Information and documentation help to promote physical education and sport.

- The mass media should exert a positive influence on physical education and sport.

- National institutions play a major role in physical education and sport.

- International cooperation is a prerequisite for the universal and well-balanced promotion of physical education and sport.

Experts and professionals from around the world have made major contributions to strengthening physical education. Despite the proven benefits of physical education, notably in school settings, governments have passed down decisions to reduce time allocation for physical education, or in some cases even to replace it with other subjects. This news was alarming and led to joint efforts at the international level to raise awareness and call for action.

In 1998, the International Council of Sport Science and Physical Education (ICSSPE) approached the International Olympic Committee (IOC) with a view to financial support for a worldwide survey on the state and status of physical education. Ken Hardman and Joe Marshall, in collaboration with many experts, undertook the task of collecting data on the current situation of physical education around the world (Hardman and Marshall, 2000). This survey was the first of its kind and clearly showed the severity of the physical education situation at that time. The findings (ibid., p. 66) included:

- decreasing time allocation;

- budgetary controls with inadequate financial, material and personnel resources;

- low subject status and esteem, occupying a tenuous place in the school curriculum and not accepted on par with seemingly superior academic subjects concerned with developing a child's intellect;

- marginalization and under-valuation by authorities.

In order to change this negative course, it became clear that joining forces at international and national levels in order to increase awareness and encourage action within relevant governments was critical. It was therefore necessary to share the results of the worldwide survey with representatives of governmental and non-governmental organizations active in the areas of physical education and sport. The first World Summit on Physical Education (1999), held in Berlin, served as a forum for the international dissemination of findings and the creation of an international call to action for government ministers. Different topics and scientific perspectives were included in the programme (Doll-Tepper and Scoretz, 2001).[1]

The World Summit on Physical Education and the Berlin Agenda for Action for Government Ministers (1999) had a remarkable impact, particularly upon the Third International Conference of Ministers and Senior Officials Responsible for Physical Education and Sport (MINEPS III), where it was accepted in Punta del Este, Uruguay (December 1999). The Declaration of Punta del Este states (para. 4):

> The reduction of physical education programmes, they [the Ministers] note, has contributed to the phenomenal rise in juvenile delinquency and violence, and rising medical and social costs. Studies undertaken at international levels indicate that $1 invested in physical activity leads to a saving of $3.20 in medical costs. In this context, they endorse the Berlin Agenda for Action adopted by the World Summit on Physical Education in 1999 and encourage Member States to ensure that sport and physical education are incorporated in school programmes or, as a minimum, that their legal requirements with respect to physical education programmes in school curricula are being met.

There is an ongoing effort to distribute the documents of the World Summit on Physical Education worldwide, and of chief importance is the translation into many different languages (e.g. English, German, Chinese, Japanese, Polish). Researchers in Europe (e.g. Council of Europe, European Physical Education Association) undertook studies in the following years, to provide updated material about the situation of physical education.

Physical education (2000 and beyond)

In the years following the World Summit on Physical Education and MINEPS III, efforts continued to provide scientific evidence for the benefits of physical education and its indispensable role in the educational process. In 2001, a new initiative, with financial backing from the IOC, began as a follow-up to the worldwide survey. This project, called the Role of Physical Education and Sport in Education (SpinEd), was carried out under the leadership of Richard Bailey, in collaboration with the International Committee of Sport Pedagogy (ICSP), a committee within the ICSSPE. SpinEd is an international research project that aims to gather and present evidence regarding the qualitative benefits of physical education and sport for schools. This project provides a unique framework for the evaluation of the role of physical education and school sport. Data are available showing the benefits in various domains, including physical, lifestyle, affective, social and cognitive development (Bailey and Dismore, 2004, p. 12). The authors conclude that:

> The benefits of a quality physical education and school sport experience are significant, and many of these benefits are not reproducible through other areas of the curriculum, or through other sporting or physical activity settings … quality school-based education and school sport should be available to every child in every school system, as an educational entitlement.

The SpinEd report was one of the chief documents presented at UNESCO's Fourth International Conference of Ministers and Senior Officials Responsible for Physical Education and Sport (MINEPS IV), providing well-documented evidence of the importance of physical education to representatives from around the world. During MINEPS IV, important recommendations were formulated, such as the International Convention Against Doping in Sport, Physical Education and Sport as a key component of quality Education for All and Women and Sport (Bailey and Dismore, 2004). In the document of recommendations called the Declaration of Athens, "A Healthy Society Built on Athletic Spirit", the Ministers reaffirm their belief that "sport and physical education play a key role in society by contributing to national cohesion, overcoming prejudice and exercising a positive influence on public opinion through the sharing of the ethical and universal values they convey".

Physical education – New approaches and concepts

Research offering scientific evidence and the use of new methodological approaches are highly important in the fight against the global crisis of physical education. It is also essential to present new conceptual frameworks for physical education. For example, Margaret Whitehead's concept of "Physical Literacy", presented in various journals of physical education (Whitehead, 2001) and more recently at the 2004 Pre-Olympic Congress in Thessaloniki, Greece, has received worldwide attention and caused enormous debate. In her presentations, Whitehead refers to a 1991 Sports Council leaflet which states: "Physical education creates literacy in movement, which is as vital to every person as literacy in verbal expression itself" (UK Sports Council, 1991). The concept of "Physical Literacy" offers an interesting theoretical framework; however, as Whitehead concedes, many questions still remain unanswered, such as: Is it a universal concept? Where do the physically challenged and persons with a disability fit in? Does an understanding of personal health promotion have a place in this concept? (Whitehead, 2001; 2004) Many experts are currently debating these international issues on a philosophical level and it is hoped that these discussions will lead to the identification of physical education's potential in conjunction with physical literacy.

Important approaches to physical education in recent years have addressed the issues of quality and inclusion, also referred to as "quality physical education" and "inclusive physical education". The Berlin Agenda for Action for Government Ministers (November 1999) highlighted the importance of "Quality Physical Education" claiming that it:

• is the most effective and inclusive means of providing all children, whatever their ability/disability, sex, age, cultural, race/ethnicity, religious or social background, with the skills, attitudes, values, knowledge and understanding for life-long participation in physical activity and sport;

• helps to ensure integrated and rounded development of mind, body and spirit;

• is the only school subject whose primary focus is on the body, physical activity, physical development and health;

• helps children to develop the patterns of and interest in physical activity, which are essential for healthy development and which lay the foundations for adult healthy lifestyles;

• helps children to develop respect for the body – both their own and others';

• develops understanding of the role of physical activity in promoting health;

• contributes to children's confidence and self-esteem;

- enhances social development by preparing children to cope with competition, winning and losing, and cooperation and collaboration;

- provides the skills and knowledge for future work in sport, physical activity, recreation and leisure, a growing area of employment.

Recently, the terms "inclusive education" and "inclusive physical education" have become more mainstream. Since the 1990s, the term "integration" has been replaced by "inclusion" in many official documents (e.g. the Salamanca Declaration, 1994), which is especially relevant to developments and changes in educational institutions. Inclusion means that all schools and school systems need to be changed structurally in such a way that they provide education for all children, including those with a disability. "An inclusive school is a place where everyone belongs, is accepted, supports and is supported by his or her peers and other members of the school community in the course of having his or her educational needs met" (Stainback and Stainback, 1990, p. 3).

Controversial debates have accompanied these recent developments in the education system, with one side advocating the existence of special schools, the other supporting inclusive education in regular schools. A global comparative study indicates tremendous differences between countries, with some of them maintaining a traditional school system with special schools, and others starting trends towards decentralization of special education offered by schools and the closure of special schools in countries such as Australia, Canada, Denmark, Germany, Italy, Norway and the United States. The main objective of these closures is the development of a "school for all" (Hans and Ginnold, 2000).

As Reid (2003, pp. 139–140) points out: "There are some important educational implications in the concept, which have been articulated by those writing extensively about inclusion. First, all students are included, not just those with mild disabilities, as was the case with mainstreaming ... Second, the regular classroom is the starting point for instruction, not a reward for good performance elsewhere."

Despite various efforts, implementation has occurred at different rates in European Union Member States. Cross-cultural and cross-national communication and cooperation have helped to speed up this process, leading to structural changes in school systems and new approaches in teacher training and preparation. The law in Berlin, Germany, for example, requires a mandatory course on inclusive education for all students undertaking teacher training at university.

In this context, it is important to highlight the role of international agencies, such as UNESCO, the ILO, the World Health Organization (WHO) and the United Nations Childrens Fund (UNICEF). "It is a UNESCO commission which urges the international community to continue to work on achieving the goals set to make education a right and reality for children before 2015" (Eklindh, 2003, p. 25). In his chapter entitled "Education for all means all", Eklindh quotes estimates from international agencies such as UNICEF:

- More than 90 per cent of all children with disabilities in developing countries do not attend school.

- 500,000 children every year lose some part of their vision due to vitamin A deficiency.

- 41 million babies are born each year at risk of mental impairment due to insufficient iodine in their mothers' diet.

In order to reach the goal of education for all, it is necessary to:

- promote the right of every child and youth with a disability to express his/her view pertaining to his/her education and life skills;

- identify and disseminate effective practices and stimulate research in areas such as quality teacher education, school organization (including adequate and accessible facilities), curriculum and pedagogy and assistive devices and appropriate materials.

(Ibid., p. 27)

A recent paper by Sander (2004) summarizes the past, current and future developments regarding concepts of an inclusive education and distinguishes five levels:

1. Exclusion: children with a disability were/are excluded from education/ school in general.

2. Separation: children with a disability attend special institutions (special schools).

3. Integration: children with a disability can attend regular schools with special education assistance.

4. Inclusion: all children with a disability attend regular schools like their "able-bodied" counterparts. Heterogeneity and differences are appreciated.

5. Variety as "normality": inclusion is practised in every educational setting; the term inclusion can be omitted.

Despite the fact that they have been developed for general education, current concepts of physical education need to take these five levels of inclusion into account. Inclusive education is not a marginal theme, but rather a challenge for the professional, who should provide appropriate responses to the broad spectrum of children's learning needs.

Since the 1990s, adapted physical activity/education professionals have debated issues regarding the "inclusion movement" (DePauw and Doll-Tepper, 2000). It is important to acknowledge that this debate is primarily a discourse which initially took place in the United States. However, in November 1999 at the World Summit on Physical Education in Berlin, it became clear that similar debates also existed in other countries. It is obvious that concepts of inclusion exist and some understand it as one universal placement for all. Others define inclusion not as a place or placement, but rather as an attitude or process (ibid., p. 139):

> … to re-examine the assumptions about general physical education: (a) general physical education programmes are of high quality with individualized instruction; (b) class sizes are similar to general education class rooms, and most typically, developing children are well behaved and motivated; (c) physical educators are willing to take on the challenge of working with children with a disability; and (d) physical educators do and will continue to receive training from adapted physical educators.

It is clear that these assumptions need to be examined with regard to the trend towards progressive inclusion and acceptance. "Inclusion must be seen as a philosophy, a process, and as an attitude" (ibid., p. 140). In order to contribute to changes in society in general and to education, particularly physical education, dialogue needs to be intensified between the professionals in different disciplines and areas of expertise.

Comparative studies undertaken by Hardman and Marshall (2000) and by Hardman (2004) show remarkable differences in this process:

> Opportunities for disabled pupils in physical education seem to be increasing but there are regional variations: in central and eastern Europe the level of integration is considerably lower than in the rest of Europe. Problems in realising integration embrace: the lack of official policy to address and to raise broader awareness of integration issues; shortage of material; resources; a shortage of trained specialist personnel; physical barriers to access; class management inadequacies; programme content and class size. (Hardman, 2004, pp. 5–6)

Hardman (ibid., p. 13) also reports that "countries such as England, Sweden, Canada, Australia, Finland and Israel have in place specific programmes to support the inclusion of children with disabilities into physical education. Undoubtedly, these programmes are making progress and are beginning to cater for a much more diverse group of children than ever before".

In his report, Hardman identifies several challenging issues, such as the perceived additional burden for physical education teachers, the lack of driving forces within and from the Education Departments for inclusive physical education, and the ongoing debate concerning the role of specialist providers of adapted physical education teachers. He concludes by saying that "world-wide, there appears to be a lack of recognition, mostly from education itself, of the important role that children with disabilities play in our playgrounds" (ibid.).

Sport science – A historical perspective

In their publication, *The history of exercise and sport science* (1997), Massengale and Swanson give an overview of the beginnings of sport science and its development, which can be characterized by increased specialization during the twentieth century. They listed nine areas of specialization.[2]

During the 1960s and 1970s, sport began to receive worldwide attention, particularly in the context of high-performance sport shown at the Olympic Games and other international sporting events. These developments were closely linked to a rising number of competitive sport events at regional, national and local levels.

With that in mind, a new approach to sport began: the IOC's Sport for All movement (see Palm, 1991; Hartmann-Tews, 1996; DaCosta and Miragaya, 2002). In many countries around the world, experts highlighted the need for all people to practise physical activity and sport, focusing less on competitive elements than on recreational benefits with regard to both physical and psychosocial improvements. Despite a growing interest in sport, physical education received less attention, making it necessary to create new links between physical education and sport. This led to the creation of international organizations, such as the International Council of Sport and Physical Education (ICSPE) in 1958. "Overall, ICSPE was providing a forum for extensive research and information exchange – between sport scientists who were serving both sport and physical education" (Bailey, 1996, p. 79). Other organizations such as UNESCO, the Fédération International d'Education Physique (FIEP), the International Council for Health, Physical Education and Recreation (ICHPER), the International Association for Sports and Leisure Facilities (IAKS) and the International Association of Physical Education and Sport for Girls and Women (IAPESGW) were also involved in these efforts at the international level. The internationalization of sport required more scientific and pedagogical discussion (Bailey, 1996), which consequently led to a name change of ICSPE to the International Council of Sport Science and Physical Education (ICSSPE) in 1983.

"The period from 1983 until 1990 was characterized by the further differentiation and consolidation of disciplinary fields of sport science" (Bailey, 1996, p. 255). Changes not only occurred in organizations of physical education, sport and sport science, but also with regard to the introduction of new specialized degrees in universities and institutions of higher learning. They were no longer limited to the training of future physical education teachers. The increased variety of sport science disciplines is reflected in the third edition of ICSSPE's *Directory of sport science* (2004).[3]

The following section will highlight how the expansion of studies in sport science has influenced the development of education and training in physical education.

New professional training opportunities – A European perspective

During the late 1980s, efforts were made in European countries to increase exchange opportunities for students and staff, based on the ERASMUS programme. One of the most successful European programmes, the European Master's Degree in Adapted Physical Activity (EMDAPA), coordinated by the Catholic University in Leuven (Belgium), started in 1991. At the beginning nine universities were offering this programme, with an increasing number of others joining during subsequent years. Today, over 30 universities are participating in this European Master's programme.

In 1997, another European programme in this specialization area was initiated: the European University Diploma in Adapted Physical Activity (DEUAPA). DEUAPA, originally coordinated by Italian colleagues in Milan, spread to the University of Bordeaux and later to the University of Paris (Paris X), attracting many European students and offering them a specialized education and certificate. It is important to note the growing importance and recognition of "Adapted Physical Activity" (Doll-Tepper, 2003, p. 47), which is based on three significant developments:

1. A change of the role of persons with a disability in society.

2. Rapid global developments in physical education and sport.

3. Increasing importance of scientific knowledge in all areas of society, including sport.

Similar joint study programmes focusing on physical education and sport science disciplines were discussed by members of the European Network of Sport Sciences in Higher Education (Mester, 1994). In 2004, The European

Network of Sport Science, Education and Employment (ENSSEE)[4] listed numerous programmes in physical education and sport science.[5]

The Aligning a European Higher Education Structure in Sport Science (AEHESIS) project, coordinated by the German Sport University in Cologne (and on behalf of ENSSEE – European Network of Sport Science, Education and Employment), evaluates the degree to which higher-education institutions align themselves with the Bologna agreement's principles, in four areas: physical education; coaching; health and fitness; and sport management. The Bologna agreement is also seeking to develop harmonized programmes across the EU Member States. Clearly, there are implications here for the future of sports science programmes. In years two and three of the AEHESIS project, each of the four areas is looking at employment opportunities and skills/competences required in their respective areas. The EU Commission has asked for the formulation of a common curriculum, and therefore each area group will focus on this aspect during the next 18 months (years two and three).

Joint programmes enabled the mobility of students and staff within Europe. A highly attractive programme, the Executive Master's in Sports Organisation Management (MEMOS) was founded in Europe in 1995 as a joint venture by a number of National Olympic Committees, the European Network of Sport Sciences in Higher Education and several universities, and was financially supported by the IOC and the Socrates programme: "The aim of MEMOS was to provide a higher level of training to European sport managers. MEMOS, soon after, began to attract sport managers from other continents, and in the summer of 2002, the MEMOS Steering Committee voted to adapt the programme to an international participation" (Miro, 2003).

Consequently, in 2003, MEMOS VI was conducted in three continents (Europe, Asia, Africa) and was opened to all National Olympic Committees. The programme includes topics such as strategic management and sport governance, marketing management and sport markets, human resource and intercultural management of sport, as well as performance management of sport organizations. Students who successfully complete the programme are awarded a postgraduate degree from the University Claude Bernard of Lyon (France).

In 2004, in honour of the European Year of Education through Sport, the European Commission supported four studies investigating the following issues (EU Office, *Monthly Report*, Jan. 2005):

- The situation in Europe with regard to the education of young sportsmen and sportswomen and their ability to return to school or the workforce once their sporting careers were finished. The study was carried out by PMP Consultancy in collaboration with the Institute of Sport and Leisure Policy (ISLP) at Loughborough University (United Kingdom).

- The situation in Europe regarding the training for careers in the sporting industry, with specific reference to the creation of jobs in this field (Vocasport). The European Observatoire of Sports Employment (EOSE) and the Vocasport Group conducted this project.

- The contribution of sport as an instrument of non-formal education directed at a multicultural dialogue between young people, and the role it plays in facilitating the integration of young people with different socio-cultural backgrounds. The study was carried out by PMP Consultancy in collaboration with the ISLP at Loughborough University.

- Young people's lifestyles and sedentary behaviours, and the role of sport in the context of education and as a means of restoring the balance. The project was carried out by the University of Paderborn and the University of Duisburg-Essen (Germany).

Another recent development is the introduction of an Erasmus Mundus Master's programme in Adapted Physical Activity, which was due to start in 2005. The European Commission approved a proposal from a consortium of four European universities including Leuven (Belgium), Limerick (Ireland), Olomouc (Czech Republic) and Oslo (Norway) to begin this programme. The objectives are to improve the quality of higher education in Europe and promote intercultural understanding through cooperation between students and staff from countries inside and outside Europe. The specific attraction to students lies in a multidisciplinary and interdisciplinary education that provides them with solid professional training as a basis for their future professional career. An overview of Vocational Training in Adapted Physical Activity by De Potter, Van Coppenolle, Van Peteghem, Djobova and Wijns (2003/2004) analysed the current situation in different European countries and offered recommendations for action at the national level. This document, as well as a publication entitled *Inclusion and integration through adapted physical activity* (Van Coppenolle, De Potter, Van Peteghem, Djobova and Wijns, 2004), was released as part of the initiatives within the Thematic Network on Educational and Social Integration of Persons with a Disability through Adapted Physical Activity (THENAPA), supported by the European Commission.

These joint efforts at the European level are a clear indication of the need to improve vocational opportunities in specialized areas of sport science. Developments in society, which are related to inclusive approaches, are no longer limited to children and youth with a disability, but have also led to the establishment in 2004 of a Thematic Network on Ageing and Adapted Physical Activity, also coordinated by the Catholic University Leuven (Belgium).

Worldwide developments in professional training in sport science and physical education

The previous section provided a detailed report on developments in European countries. It explained increased efforts to provide quality training for professionals in physical education and the various disciplines of sport science, as well as the implementation of new programmes that are open to students from all parts of the world. Parker (2000) gave an overview of professional training in exercise and sport science from an Australian perspective. He points out that a growing number of universities in Australia are offering courses in exercise and sport science, stemming from an increased demand from students and the growth of career opportunities. He states that "in exercise science, the future of the profession will be strongly influenced by changes in the health care system. Managed care will be important, but it will need to be more effective, oriented towards prevention, and customised" (Parker, 2000, p. 15). Amusa and Toriola (2000) focus on professional issues in exercise, sport science and physical education in Africa. Like Parker they report:

> In many African institutions, there has been a gradual shift of emphasis from traditional physical education that focuses on the development of physique and training sport persons, to health promotion and sport science. Realising the role of physical activity in disease prevention, there has been a growing interest in the influence of exercise in preventing lifestyle-related diseases, such as diabetes, hypertension and obesity. (Ibid., p. 25)

That being said, discussion of the establishment of centres of excellence in physical education and sport science has commenced. The American College of Sports Medicine (ACSM) and the Fédération Internationale de Médécine Sportive (FIMS) have introduced important initiatives for career development and certification.

Thompson and Stewart (2000) provide an overview of the certification programmes of ACSM that draws a distinction between the health/fitness themes and the clinical themes offering specific education and training for professionals inside and outside the United States. FIMS provides certificates and specific training in sport medicine and exercise science for professionals from all over the world. The National Association for Sport and Physical Education (NASPE) and the American Alliance for Health, Physical Education, Recreation and Dance (AAHPERD) have developed basic standards for professional preparation in exercise science. The AAHPERD website lists these competencies for seven areas.[6]

Chin, Hensley, Cote and Chen (2004) report that in Asian countries there is a growing interest in physical education and sport science degrees, referring also to a growing demand for highly qualified professionals. The growing interest for improved professional training is reflected in numerous courses, seminars, symposia and congresses at national, regional and international levels. Events such as the Pre-Olympic Congress in 2004 in Thessaloniki, Greece have been excellent opportunities for professionals to exchange the most recent scientific knowledge. Evidence-based information is required – to a growing extent – for decision-making processes at government levels, with regard to both the introduction of new professional training and new employment opportunities.

Conclusion

Physical education and sport science, as areas of scientific expertise and professional training, have changed rapidly over the past four decades. Societies around the world are demanding evidence-based knowledge and highly qualified professionals, while governments are requesting data on which political decisions can be based. Examples of such a development can be given in the context of MINEPS (Ministers and Senior Officials Responsible for Physical Education and Sport). In 1999 UNESCO's MINEPS III produced important recommendations and declarations, many of them based on scientific data from experts in the field of sport science and physical education. Of particular importance are the documents produced by these professionals at the World Summit on Physical Education in Berlin (1999). The Berlin Agenda for Action for Government Ministers and the scientific documents attached to it provided important input for the deliberations and recommendations of the ministers. This process continued during the following years and led to improved communication and collaboration, in particular on the occasion of the MINEPS Round Table in Paris (2003) and MINEPS IV in Athens (2004).

Important professional input was also given to the WHO in preparation for its Global Strategy on Diet, Physical Activity and Health, which was approved by the WHO General Assembly in 2004. The ICSSPE was commissioned by the WHO to prepare a series of technical papers as resources, in particular for young people, in the context of the World Move for Health Day (ICSSPE Bulletin, No. 43, 2005).[7]

The advisory role of professional organizations in physical education and sport science to these important international developments at governmental level continues to grow. At the same time, there is a growing labour market for professionals in physical education and sport science; however, career opportunities must be viewed in the light of new demands in society. Service provision is no longer limited to meet the demands of some selected segments of the population, as it was in the past (for children in schools, and to a larger extent for the elderly population, and those with chronic disease and other health-related conditions). Parker (2000, p. 15) considered these developments and challenges when he said:

> The viability and progress of our profession will be very much dependent on our abilities to deliver and communicate outcomes such as cost effectiveness, patient/client satisfaction, and the quality of the data collected to measure these outcomes. It will also depend on our ability to establish key partnerships with other related professionals, and to clearly define the distinctive service that we provide.

In addition to identifying and providing specific new services in the areas of sport science, it is important to ensure that well-trained physical education teachers teach quality physical education. Their training and further education should be based on the most recent scientific findings, as well as practical experience. Despite certain issues and approaches that are particularly relevant for each country, there is also a need for an international discourse on core elements in the training of professionals, including physical education teachers.

Among the many challenges that the sports profession is currently facing is an ever-increasing number of programmes that use information technologies and distance learning programmes, creating additional challenges regarding quality control. It is recommended that information on these various programmes be assembled onto a database (similar to the European Observatoire of Sports Employment), which could be of great value for all interested parties, including those involved in research, training, and various sectors of employment.

Notes

[1] *World-wide survey on the state and status of school physical education* (Hardman and Marshall, United Kingdom); The Case for Physical Education (Talbot, United Kingdom); Good Practice in Physical Education (Solomons, South Africa); Physical Education and its Physical Domains (Malina, United States); Psychological Outcomes and Social Benefits of Sport Involvement and Physical Activity – Implications for Physical Education (Brettschneider, Germany); Physical Education, Health and Wellbeing (Matsudo, Brazil); The Economic Case for Physical Education (Kidd, Canada); and Nutritional Needs for Physical Activity in Young People (Williams, United Kingdom).

[2] Sport Pedagogy; Adapted Physical Activity and Education; Sport Sociology; Sport History; Philosophy of Sport; Motor Behaviour; Sport and Exercise Psychology; Biomechanics; Exercise Physiology.

[3] Adapted Physical Activity; Biomechanics; Coaching Science; Comparative PE and Sport; Kinanthropometry; Neuromotor Psychology, Motor Learning and Control; Philosophy of Sport; Political Science of Sport; Sociology of Sport; Sport and Exercise Physiology; Sport and Exercise Psychology; Sport Facilities; Sport History; Sport Information; Sports Law; Sport Management; Sports Medicine; Sport Pedagogy; Sports Vision.

[4] See www.enssee.org, accessed 4 Feb. 2005.

[5] TN Project: European Observatoire of Sports Employment (EOSE) Dissemination of Results; ODL Project: Information Technologies in European Sport and Sport Science (ITES); Thematic Network in Adapted Physical Activity – THENAPA (Master's Programme; Sport Management and EASM – European Association of Sport Managers (Master's Programme); Health and Fitness (Master's Programme); Physical Activity for Elderly People (Master's Programme); Physical Education (Master's Programme); Physical Education in a European Perspective; Biology of Physical Activity (Master's Programme); Exercise and Sport Psychology; Sport History; Training and Coaching; Exercise and Fitness – ENFA (level 2–4); Children and Physical Activity.

[6] Foundational Core; Exercise Prescription for Normal and Special Populations; Health Promotion; Administrative Tasks; Human Relations; Professional Development; and Practical Experience (see: http://www.aahperd.org, 8 Feb. 2005).

[7] These papers include: *An update on the status of physical education in schools world-wide* (Ken Hardman); *Girls' participation in physical activities and sport: Benefits, patterns, influences and ways forward* (Richard Bailey, Ian Wellard and Harriet Dismore); *Physical activity and its impact on health behaviour among youth* (Diane Jones-Palm and Jürgen Palm); *Young people with disability in physical education, physical activity and sport, in and out of schools* (Claudine Sherrill).

Bibliography

American Alliance for Health, Physical Education, Recreation and Dance (see: www.aahperd.org, accessed 8 Feb. 2005).

Amusa, L.; Toriola, A. 2000. "Professional issues in exercise, sport science and physical education in Africa", in *ICSSPE Bulletin*, No. 20, p. 25.

Bailey, R.; Dismore, H. 2004. *SpinEd – The role of physical education and sport in education*, Project report to the Fourth International Conference of Ministers and Senior Officials Responsible for Physical Education and Sport (MINEPS IV), Athens.

Bailey, S. 1996. *Science in the service of physical education and sport*. Chichester, Wiley.

Chin, M.-K.; Hensley, L. D.; Cote, P. M.; Chen, S.-H. (eds.). 2004. *Global perspectives in the integration of physical activity, sports, dance and exercise science in physical education: From theory to practice*. Hong Kong, China.

DaCosta, L.; Miragaya, A. (eds.). 2002. *Worldwide experiences and trends in sport for all*. Aachen/Oxford, Meyer and Meyer Sport.

DePauw, K.; Doll-Tepper, G. 2000. "Toward progressive inclusion and acceptance: Myth or reality? The inclusion debate and bandwagon discourse", in *Adapted Physical Activity Quarterly*, Vol. 17, No. 2, pp. 135–143.

De Potter, J.-C.; Van Coppenolle, H.; Van Peteghem, A.; Djobova, S.; Wijns, K. (eds.). 2003/2004. *Vocational training in adapted physical activity*. Leuven.

Doll-Tepper, G. 2003. "Adapted physical activity and sport", in *Lifelong Learning in Europe*, Vol. 4, p. 47.

—; Scoretz, D. (eds.). 2001. *World Summit on Physical Education Proceedings*. Schorndorf, Hoffman-Verlag.

Eklindh, K. 2003. "Education for all means all", in *Lifelong Learning in Europe*, Vol. 4, pp. 24–27.

EU Büro des deutschen Sports. 2005. *Monthly Report*, Jan. Brussels.

European Network of Sport Science, Education and Employment (see: www.enssee.org, accessed 4 Feb. 2005).

Hans, M.; Ginnold, A. (eds.). 2000. *Integration von Menschen mit Behinderung – Entwicklung in Europa*. Berlin, Neuwied, Kriftel.

Hardman, K. 2004. *An update on the status of physical education in schools worldwide*, technical report for the World Health Organization, unpublished document on behalf of International Council of Sport Science and Physical Education (ICSSPE).

—; Marshall, J. 2000. *World-wide survey of the state and status of school physical education, final report*. Manchester.

Hartmann-Tews, I. 1996. *Sport für Alle!* Schorndorf, Hofmann-Verlag.

International Council of Sport Science and Physical Education (ICSSPE). 2004. *Directory of sport science*, CD-Rom, third edition. Paris.

ICSSPE Bulletin (Berlin), No. 43. 2005.

Massengale, J.; Swanson, R. 1997. *The history of exercise and sport science*. Champaign, Human Kinetics.

Mester, J. (ed.). 1994. *Sport sciences in Europe 1993 – Current and future perspectives*. Aachen, Meyer and Meyer Verlag.

Miro, P. 2003. "Foreword", in MEMOS VI, Feb.– Nov. Lausanne.

Palm, J. 1991. *Sport for all – approaches from utopia to reality*. Schorndorf, Verlag Carl Hofman.

Parker, T. 2000. "Professional developments in exercise and sport science: An Australian perspective", in *ICSSPE Bulletin*, No. 30, pp. 12–13.

Reid, G. 2003. "Moving towards inclusion", in R. Steadward, G. Wheeler and E. J. Watkinson (eds.): *Adapted Physical Activity*. Edmonton, University of Alberta, pp. 11–25.

Sander, A. 2004. "Konzepte einer Inklusiven Pädagogik", in *Zeitschrift für Heilpädagogik*, No. 5, pp. 240–244.

Stainback, S.; Stainback, W. 1990. "Inclusive schooling", in W. Stainback and S. Stainback (eds.): *Support networks for inclusive schooling*. Baltimore, Paul H. Brookes, pp. 3–24.

Thompson, W.; Stewart, C. 2000. "American College of Sports Medicine: Career development and certification", in *ICSSPE Bulletin*, No. 30, pp. 16–17.

UK Sports Council. 1991. "The case for sport", publicity leaflet.

UNESCO (ed.). 1978 and 1993 (revised). *International Charter for Physical Education and Sport*. Paris.

—. (ed.). 1999. *Third International Conference of Ministers and Senior Officials Responsible for Physical Education and Sport – MINEPS III, Declaration of Punta del Este*. Punta del Este.

Van Coppenolle, H.; De Potter, J.-C.; Van Peteghem, A.; Djobova, S.; Wijns, K. (eds.). 2004. *Inclusion and integration through adapted physical activity*. Leuven, Thematic Network Educational and Social Integration of Persons with a Disability through Adapted Physical Activity (THENAPA).

Whitehead, M. 2001. "The concept of physical literacy", in *British Journal of Teaching Physical Education*, Vol. 32, No. 1, Spring, pp. 6–8.

—. 2004. "Physical literacy – a debate", in V. Klissouras, S. Kellis and I. Mouratidis, (eds.): *2004 Pre-Olympic Congress – proceedings*. Thessaloniki, pp. 117–118.

THE PARALYMPICS: RIGHT TO PARTICIPATE, RIGHT TO WIN[1]

3

Sir Philip Craven, Cheri Blauwet and Amy Farkas

Since the turn of the twenty-first century, the United Nations and other large peace-keeping organizations have promoted an agenda of "Sport for Development", that is, using sport as a cost-effective tool to stimulate international development and promote human rights within developing nations. In addition, it has been proved that sports and recreation have a positive health impact on athletes by increasing physical activity and mitigating the effects of many chronic health problems. The Paralympic Movement is attempting to harness the potential of these positive impacts and support both grass-roots and elite sporting opportunities for individuals with a disability[2] worldwide.

Promoting health as a human right

The Paralympic Games are a powerful demonstration of the vitality and achievements of disabled persons world-wide... .

Kofi Annan, United Nations Secretary-General (letter dated 7 September 2004)

The International Paralympic Committee (IPC) is the international governing body of sports for athletes with a disability. It supervises and coordinates the organization of the Paralympic Summer and Winter Games and other world and regional competitions at the elite sport level, of which the most important are world and regional championships for the 13 IPC sports (for which the IPC functions as the International Federation). The IPC also develops sporting opportunities around the world for athletes of all levels, from grass-roots to elite. In March 2003 it approved a new vision statement: "To enable Paralympic athletes to achieve sporting excellence and inspire and excite the world." In short, the IPC aims to create worldwide opportunities for athlete empowerment through self-determination (*Vision and Mission, Athens, 2004*). In addition to this expected mission, the IPC has recently increased its focus on development and continues to advocate for human rights globally.

In September 2004, the IPC adopted a position statement on human rights that serves to reinforce its core belief that every individual should enjoy access to and opportunities for leisure, recreation and sporting activities. This right should be granted and guarded by the legal and administrative systems of responsible governments and communities. The IPC believes both sport and human rights are for all (box 3.1).

On 17 September 2004, in Athens, 3,837 athletes from 136 nations were present to participate in the Opening Ceremony of the XII Paralympic Games. On the same day, the IPC, in collaboration with RI (which stands for Rehabilitation International, as well as Rights and Inclusion) hosted the first International Paralympic Symposium on Human Rights. The event aimed to promote the draft United Nations (UN) Convention on the Rights and Dignities of People with Disabilities, advocating the human rights of both Paralympic athletes and citizens with a disability at large. These include but are not limited to: the right to play; the right to sport and recreation; and the right to full participation in society. It is vital that persons with a disability and organizations working with such persons are educated in the process and get

---

Box 3.1   IPC position statement on human rights

The IPC believes all individuals should enjoy equal access and opportunities for leisure, recreation and sporting activities, and such rights be granted and guarded by the legal and administrative systems by the responsible governments and communities.

The IPC firmly believes in the unlimited athletic potential of persons with a disability, and thereby embraces the sporting achievements of Paralympic athletes. Equal opportunities for sporting development, participation, training, and recognition of achievement should be provided for all persons in all schools, sport clubs and venues, sports organizations and communities.

The IPC believes in sport as a vehicle to promote peace, which will result in preservation of lives and quality of life.

The IPC shall promote the above philosophy and actualize its policy through the Paralympic Games and all other sporting activities, and through its membership and work with nations, regions, sports and groups representing persons with a disability.

involved in their own communities to support the work of the UN towards a Human Rights Convention.

While improvements have been made in some countries, the fact remains that without an International Human Rights Convention, the rights of these members of society cannot be effectively guaranteed. As the largest minority group in the world, these individuals have not received the same assurances or rights that other minorities have achieved. A UN Convention will have a global effect and will strengthen the ability to advocate for human rights both locally and nationally.[3] In addition to the IPC, many other international organizations have taken on the cause of promoting the right to health. For over 50 years, the focus on physical activity and sport as a means of achieving health for individuals with a disability has grown in the global discourse surrounding health and human rights:

- Beginning in 1948, the UN Universal Declaration of Human Rights asserted that all human beings are born free and equal in dignity and that all persons have the right to "a standard of living adequate for the health and well-being of himself and of his family" (Article 25). In the same year, the World Health Organization (WHO) declared in its Constitution that "the enjoyment of the highest attainable standard of health is one of the fundamental rights of every human being" (WHO, 1948).

- Thirty years later, in 1978, the United Nations Educational, Scientific and Cultural Organization (UNESCO) stated in its International Charter of Physical Education and Sport that every person is entitled to participate in sport, including especially women, young people, the elderly and those with a disability.

- In 1993, the UN Standard Rules on the Equalization of Opportunities for Persons with Disabilities (Rule 11: Recreation and Sports) were developed to encourage sports organizations to create opportunities for individuals with a disability to participate at a level equal in quantity and quality to the population of persons without a disability (United Nations, 1993).

- The UN has now established an ad hoc committee that is currently drafting the International Convention on the Protection and Promotion of the Rights and Dignity of Persons with Disabilities. Article 21 of this draft Convention states that "[a]ll persons with disabilities have the right to the enjoyment of the highest attainable standard of health without discrimination on the basis of disability". In addition, Article 24 outlines the right to "participation in sport, recreation, and leisure", and specifically notes that all individuals with disabilities should have equal access to sporting opportunities and facilities (ibid.).

By integrating the two international ideals of the right to health and sport for development, the Paralympic Movement can gracefully and efficiently move this agenda forward.

> The Paralympics are one of the world's most prominent events where people with disabilities show their tremendous talent and energy. We take this opportunity to admire the skill and determination of these athletes, but at the same time we must reflect upon the fact that globally, too many people with disabilities do not enjoy even the most basic human right.
>
> *Dr Etienne Krug, Director of the WHO Department of Injuries and Violence*
> *Prevention, International Paralympic Symposium on Disability Rights*

Promoting health through Paralympic sport: Participation in sport improves physical and mental health outcomes

The benefits of participating in organized sport versus simply being "active" have been shown to have unique impacts beyond that of physical conditioning. Organized sport fosters positive socializing influences such as interactions with teachers and coaches, and the requirements of team membership may establish constructive incentives for both youth and adults. In addition, the necessary time commitment of organized sport may divert people, especially youth, from negative influences (Jones-Palm and Palm, 2004).

For individuals with a disability, the physical and societal barriers to participating in physical activity and sport are often difficult to overcome. One recent survey showed that 56 per cent of persons with a disability reported participating in no daily exercise, versus 36 per cent of persons without a disability (Rimmer at al., 2004). Discrimination and lack of access in several key areas have been shown to discourage individuals with a disability from participating in physical activity and sport. A number of studies show that, within developed countries, some of these include:

- the inaccessibility of sport facilities and equipment (i.e. front entrances of buildings, shower and bathroom areas, adaptive exercise equipment) (Rimmer et al., 2004; Tregaskis, 2003);

- the cost of participating in sport activities (Rimmer et al., 2004);

- a lack of adequate and knowledgeable coaching (Sherrill and Williams, 1996);

- negative attitudes and behaviour of persons without a disability who may work in sport facilities or instruct physical education (Rimmer et al., 2004; Leiberman et al., 2002; Grimes and French, 1987).

For individuals living in developing nations, these barriers to participation in physical activity and sport may become even more inhibitory. Although similar areas are identified as being problematic, the societal stigma and less progressive nature with which potential athletes are treated create an even harder road to success. In many cases coaches are non-existent, and the cost of quality equipment such as prosthetics or sports wheelchairs is excessive (Crawford, 2004).

> We don't have a sufficient amount of facilities, keep in mind that what we are using is for the able-bodied. There is no single facility [that can be used] by the disabled people all the time. We have to come to the able-bodied and request from athletes to give us a few hours so that we can train in their facilities.
>
> *Marcus, table tennis coach, Kenya*

By providing sport opportunities, Paralympic sport has infinite potential to promote a positive image and improve health throughout all regions of the world. In a recreational environment, athletes can find strength and companionship in sport, thus increasing the chances of compliance with a wellness plan that includes physical activity as a form of preventive medicine. In a competitive arena, athletes can benefit physically from achieving superb fitness, and mentally from gaining the identity of "athlete". When care is taken in promoting the Paralympic Movement, and providing both developmental and elite opportunities, health benefits can be attainable for all:

- Athletes can lower their risk of obesity and all secondary health concerns associated with obesity. These include, but are not limited to, diabetes, stroke, cancer, osteoarthritis and respiratory distress (Kumar et al., 1997, p. 261). Currently, many studies have shown increased rates of obesity in individuals with a disability. For example, children with spinal cord injury have been shown to have an increased risk of obesity due to the decreasing resting metabolic rates and muscle mass that often result from living a sedentary lifestyle (Liusuwan et al., 2004).

- Athletes can be more aware of their health and therefore more likely to participate in health maintenance and preventive health practices. This includes paying attention to personal hygiene and nutrition, and making positive behavioural health decisions such as avoiding smoking and excessive alcohol consumption (Rimmer, 1999).

- Athletes, specifically those who acquire injury later in life, can regain the greatest amount of functional mobility that is possible for their type of impairment. Muscle strength, dexterity and coordination will be maintained at a pre-injury level or will improve concurrently with athletic training. Research has shown that a sedentary lifestyle and low fitness level make movement with a wheelchair much more difficult (Pate et al., 1995). Mobility becomes easier with physical fitness. Another study showed that for an experimental group of subjects with spinal cord injury, an aerobic and strength training programme undertaken for nine months improved not only maximal power output and strength, but also showed positive improvements in stress, pain and depression (Hicks et al., 2003).

- Athletes can gain confidence, self-esteem and identity through participation in sport. This will result in a more positive self-image and lead to a decreased risk of depression and other mental health illnesses. Studies have shown that physical inactivity is a leading factor in the deteriorating physical and psychological health of individuals with a physical disability (Coyle and Santiago, 1995). In addition, it has been shown that for individuals with an acquired mobility impairment, members of an "active" experimental group evaluated their physical appearance and health more highly than in comparison to a "non-active" group with similar impairments, and were also more concerned with their fitness (Yuen and Hanson, 2002).

Wheelchair racing has improved me physically in my upper body strength and mentally. It has really enriched my life because I now have the confidence to address large groups of people. Just recently I have been invited into a local school to do a morning assembly and spoke to 200 kids about how I train myself and about my personal achievements. I could never have done that before. It has also improved my self esteem … .

Anne, Olympia Wheelchair Racing, Kenya

The economic and social rationale for Paralympic programmes: Improving health and investing in human capital

If we see sport as a tool for economic development, it is undeniable that healthy individuals will be able to use their improved health status, along with the life lessons learned through sport, to contribute to the economic and social growth of their nation. As the community of persons with a disability is the largest minority group in the world, it is easy to see the enormous potential that these persons have to contribute to their nations while reciprocally gaining the respect and dignity to which they are entitled. Approximately 10–15 per cent of all human beings have a disability, representing 600 million persons worldwide (Sibilski, 2000). In the European Union, a region considered to be industrialized and quite progressive in terms of social policy, still only 26 per cent of individuals with a self-perceived "severe disability" earn an income, compared to 64 per cent of the able-bodied population. Of these individuals, 48 per cent report living on state benefits (European Commission, 2001). Globally, it is estimated that the annual loss of gross domestic product (GDP) due to having persons with a disability out of work is between US$1.37 and US$1.94 trillion (Metts, 2000).

Sports can give these citizens the physical and mental skills they need to seek and maintain employment, which increases productivity and causes a ripple effect of decreasing social welfare costs. In addition, a healthier population reduces the nationwide burden on a public health-care system. In the United States, it was found that for every US$1 spent on physical activity, US$3.20 is saved in medical costs (Pratt et al., 2000).

No country can afford to turn its back on ten percent of its population.

ILO/UNESCO/UNICEF/WHO Proclamation of 3 December 1997

In addition, Paralympic sport has the unique ability to quickly and effectively affect the social and environmental framework that surrounds all individuals with a disability. Inasmuch as physical activity and sport can improve the physical and mental health of the athlete, the surrounding social fabric must also respond and be willing to embrace the changes that are made possible through athlete empowerment. Indeed, *disability is a perceived state.* It is defined by the physical environment and social perceptions that surround an individual. How can the Paralympic Movement be the lever for change on all these levels?

• Social perceptions: Paralympic sport gives the public exciting images that instantaneously dismiss the word "disability". Outdated adjectives such as "impaired" and "handicapped" are replaced with "strong" and "capable". This direct impact is achieved through direct spectatorship of the Paralympic Games themselves, as well as world and regional events. The Paralympic Movement has the power to secure media opportunities and engage thousands in simultaneous viewership. Through this, "disability" is very quickly turned into ability in the eyes of entire societies. A perceived "disability" disappears as the social perceptions surrounding an individual become accepting, embracing and motivating. In a survey of only 17 countries, an accumulated audience of 1.8 billion watched the Athens 2004 Paralympic Games.

- Environmental change: Paralympic sport can change the physical environment. The legacy of the Paralympic Games themselves promotes accessible infrastructures through both direct action (accessible transport, communications, housing, etc.) and legislative change. In areas outside the direct reach of the Games, National and Regional Paralympic Committees create direct impact by ensuring the creation of accessible training locations for their athletes, and advocating for accessibility in educational and employment opportunities.

- Individual athlete empowerment: These broad-based impacts must occur in order to create opportunities and empowerment for the ultimate beneficiary of the Paralympic Movement: the athlete. For the individual, the opportunity to identify with this movement is a simple and quick way to gain an identity and take pride in being healthy, active and socially engaged. Getting involved in sport starts a positive cascade of events.

Initial participation in sport leads to an individual attaining better health. He or she is obtaining the physical life skills needed to keep up with a fast-paced society. In addition, through finding and overcoming the challenges met when learning a sport, the athlete also learns mental life skills such as confidence and perseverance. These lessons may at first seem abstract, although they will quickly translate into other areas of life. An athlete with a spinal cord injury may learn to transfer in and out of cars and go up and down curbs, or an athlete with a visual impairment can learn to navigate the streets that lead into town.

As these skills are acquired, the athlete begins to see the potential for success in all areas of life. He or she is able to attend school and seek education. The athlete has gained the skills needed to become physically mobile and transfer out of the home and into the school environment. The mental attributes of confidence and determination have also been built through sport and allow the individual to take this first step. In many nations, athletes will see the example that has been set by other successful individuals, and the success of their peers will become motivating rather than intimidating.

Figure 3.1 is a pictorial representation of this concept. The three larger rings represent the three primary areas of impact as outlined above: social perceptions, environmental infrastructure and individual athlete. When these three areas are simultaneously affected, as can be achieved through the Paralympic Movement, then the results presented in the overlapping region can be achieved.

Figure 3.1   The interaction between social perceptions, environmental change and the individual athlete

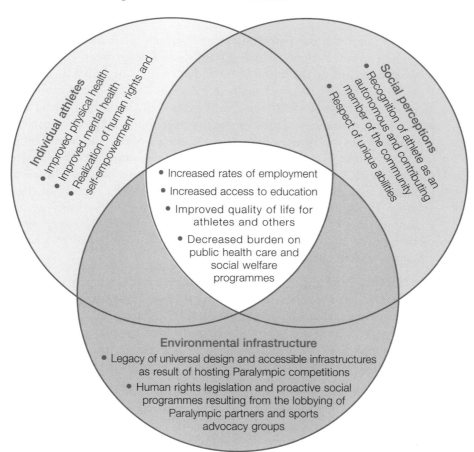

Source: © International Paralympic Committee.

Participating in sports not only benefited me in terms of my physical health, but it helped me develop life skills that enabled me to embark on the path to becoming a successful attorney, author and public speaker.

Linda Mastandrea, Wheelchair Racer, United States

Sports for us are very important [because] you see it has helped me to perform my daily activities very easily. I used to be very nervous to do anything, but since I'm playing [tennis], I am doing everything without nervousness. It has helped me for mobility in spite of no mobility infrastructure in Nepal.

Deepak K.C., Wheelchair Tennis, Nepal

Although these concepts may seem abstract, in many nations the potential for sports programmes to lead to sustainable development is being discovered:

- Beginning in 1992, the Government of Poland implemented a "Quota-Levy-Incentive" system, which establishes employment quotas for companies regarding the hiring of individuals with a disability. Businesses that do not adhere to government regulations are fined and money is directed into the Polish State Fund for People with Disabilities. This Fund is then used to finance and direct proactive programmes that serve citizens with a disability and promote a progressive model of development. Under this programme, 106 athletes and 44 support staff were funded to attend the Athens 2004 Paralympic Games, and an extensive media broadcast was produced that allowed all Polish citizens to follow the success of their athletes. In addition, the number of employees with a disability within Poland increased from 80,721 in 1992 to 174,000 in 1998. The unemployment rate for citizens with a disability is consistently equal to that of citizens without a disability (Sibilski, 2000).

- The National Paralympic Committee in Pakistan partnered with the World Bank and other national corporations in its country to create an annual art and music exposé that will serve to raise funds for Paralympic programmes. The event raises awareness about the opportunities for Paralympic athletes in Pakistan, while also bringing business and public interests together professionally to create sustainable support for the programme.

- In the Islamic Republic of Iran in 2004, nearly 8,000 persons, 4,000 of whom were girls and women, were introduced to Paralympic sport through the planning and implementation of "Paralympic Day". A nationwide festival, this annual event brought potential athletes from around the country to Tehran, where they were able to try several Paralympic sports and learn about physical fitness, nutrition and preventive health practices. The Government, several municipalities and private donors covered the expenses.

- In the United States, The Hartford Insurance Company has become a major donor to the US Paralympic Team and has incorporated an athlete incentive programme into its sponsorship. Within this programme, athletes can make appearances for The Hartford and receive income in turn for promoting the company's "Ability Philosophy". Because The Hartford is a leading supplier of insurance to large employers across the United States, this programme creates incentives for injured or chronically ill employees to return to work and become inspired by Paralympic athletes.

Although the Paralympic Movement has made great strides to spread this message into developing areas of the world, more programmes are needed to give persons with a "perceived" disability the opportunities to determine their own course in life. Sport teaches values and gives all people the opportunity to discern the best within themselves. When one sees photos of Paralympic athletes competing for gold, it is easy to see the drive and passion in their eyes. Without a doubt, this passion will translate into advocacy for future educational and career endeavours. Sport, as you can see, promotes success in all areas of life.

Notes

[1] Contributions to this chapter have been made by Rehabilitation International: Rights and Inclusion (RI) and the Center for Sport in Society at Northeastern University, Chicago, IL.

[2] It should be noted that, throughout this chapter, the phrase "with a disability" is used to describe individuals, athletes, groups of a national citizenry, and others who have unique physical attributes which traditionally place them within the minority group served by the Paralympic Movement. Realizing that this term often implies that one is at a physical or social deficit, neither the author nor the IPC wish for this implication to be associated with the term. We ask the audience to realize that the international norm of today is to use the phrase "with a disability" in a free and non-condescending manner.

[3] For more information on this topic, the IPC and the RI have published a Human Rights Toolkit in six languages available on the IPC website (see: http://www.paralympic.org, accessed 24 Mar. 2006).

Bibliography

Coyle, C. P.; Santiago, M. C. 1995. "Aerobic exercise training and depressive symptomatology in adults with physical disabilities", in *Archives of Physical Medicine and Rehabilitation*, Vol. 76, pp. 647–652.

Crawford, J. 2004. "Constraints of elite athletes with disabilities in Kenya", dissertation submitted for the degree of Master of Science in Leisure Studies in the Graduate College of University of Illinois at Urbana-Champaign.

DePauw, K; Gavron, S. 1995. *Disability and sport*. Champaign, IL, Human Kinetics.

European Commission. 2001. *Disability and social participation in Europe*. Luxembourg, Office for Official Publications of the European Community.

Grimes, P. S.; French, L. 1987. "Barriers to disabled women's participation in sports", in *Journal of Physical Education, Recreation and Dance*, Vol. 58, pp. 24–27.

Hicks, A. L., et al. 2003. "Long-term exercise training in persons with spinal cord injury: Effects on strength, arm ergometry performance and psychological well-being", in *Spinal Cord*, Vol. 41, pp. 34–43.

International Paralympic Committee. 2003. "Development department strategic plan". Bonn,

—. 2004. "Paralympic programme guiding principles". Bonn.

Jones-Palm, D.; Palm, J. 2004. "Physical activity and its impact on health behaviour among youth", in *Bulletin of the International Council of Sport Science and Physical Education*. Paris.

Kumar, V.; Cotran, R.; Robbins, S. 1997. *Basic pathology*. Philadelphia, W.B. Saunders Co.

Landmine Survivors Network. 2004. *Legal analysis of the modifications proposed at the Third UN Ad Hoc Committee Meeting,* Aug. (see: http://www.un.org/esa/socdev/enable/rights/lsncontribaug04.doc, accessed 10 Nov. 2004).

Leiberman, L., et al. 2002. "Perceived barriers to including students with visual impairments in general physical education", in *Adapted Physical Education Quarterly,* Vol. 19, pp. 364–377.

Liusuwan, A.; Widman, L.; Abresch, R. T.; McDonald, C. M. 2004. "Altered body composition affects resting energy expenditure: Interpretation of body mass index in children with spinal cord injury", in *Journal of Spinal Cord Medicine,* Vol. 27, pp. 24–28.

Metts, R. 2000. *Disability issues, trends and recommendations for the World Bank.* Washington, DC, World Bank.

Pate, R. R., et al. 1995. "Physical activity and public health: A recommendation from the Center for Disease Control and Prevention and the American College of Sports Medicine", in *Journal of the American Medical Association* (Berlin), Vol. 273, pp. 402–407.

Pratt, M; Macera, C.; Wang, G. 2000. "Higher direct medical costs associated with physical inactivity", in *The Physician and Sportsmedicine* (New York, NY), Vol. 28, pp. 63–70.

Rimmer, J., et al. 1996. "Research on physical activity and disability: An emerging national priority", in *Medical Science and Sports Exercise,* Vol. 28, pp. 1366–1372.

Rimmer, J. H. 1999. "Health promotion for people with disabilities: The emerging paradigm shift from disability prevention to prevention of secondary conditions", in *Physical Therapy Magazine* (Alexandria, VA), Vol. 79, pp. 495–502.

—; Braddock, D. 1997. *Physical activity, disability, and cardiovascular health. A National Consensus.* Champaign, IL, Human Kinetics, pp. 236–244.

—.; Riley, B.; Wang, E.; Rauworth, A.; Jurkowski, J. 2004. "Physical activity participation among persons with disabilities: Barriers and facilitators", in *American Journal of Preventative Medicine* (Washington, DC), Vol. 26, pp. 419–425.

Sherrill, C; Williams, T. 1996. "Disability and sport: Psychosocial perspectives on inclusion, integration, and participation", in *Sports Science Review,* Vol. 5, pp. 42–64.

Sibilski, L. 2000. *Social aspects of disability: Social movements, social organization, and legislative action.* Katowice, Wydawnictwo Naukowe.

Tregaskis, C. 2003. "Towards inclusive practice: An insider perspective on leisure provision for disabled people", in *Managing Leisure* (Oxford, Routledge), Vol. 8, pp. 28–40.

United Nations.1948. "Universal Declaration of Human Rights" (see: http://www.un.org/Overview/rights.html, accessed 9 Nov. 2004).

—. 1976. "International Covenant on Economic, Social and Cultural Rights", Article 12 (see: http://www.unhchr.ch/html/menu3/b/a_cescr.htm, accessed 9 Nov. 2004).

—. 1993. "Standard Rules on the Equalization of Opportunities for Persons with Disabilities" (see: http://www.un.org/esa/socdev/enable/dissre00.htm, accessed 11 Dec. 2004).

Vision and Mission: Athens, 2004 (see: http//:www.athens2004.com/en/VisionAndMission/indexpage, accessed 16 Mar. 2006).

World Health Organization (WHO). 1948. "Constitution of the World Health Organization" (see: http://www.who.int/about/en/, accessed 9 Nov. 2004).

Yuen, H. K., Hanson, C. 2002. "Body image and exercise in people with and without acquired mobility disability", in *Disability and Rehabilitation* (Taylor and Francis), Vol. 24, pp. 289–296.

WHAT DOES SPORT HAVE TO DO WITH HIV/AIDS?

4

Richard L. Sowell

Loss of optimism: The fight against HIV/AIDS

It has been approximately a year since the International HIV/AIDS Conference was held in Thailand in 2004. The Bangkok meeting was both positive and troubling for me. On a positive note, the conference was well organized and informative, and visitors could not have been shown greater hospitality. I had an unexpected opportunity to spend time with Dr Venna Jirapaet, an international editorial board member of the *Journal of the Association of Nurses in AIDS Care* (JANAC),[1] who is a nursing professor at Chulalongkorn University in Bangkok. Dr Jirapaet gave me a tour of her city, and of the largest university hospital in Bangkok. This visit reaffirmed my fond feeling for Thailand and its people.

Yet despite the wonderful experience of visiting Thailand, the conference left me with an overwhelming loss of optimism concerning the fight against HIV/AIDS. I have been going to international AIDS conferences for more than a decade, and each conference has been a positive experience in that new treatments have been announced, prevention programmes have been shared, and strength has been gained from engaging the world community in the fight. However, a sobering reality hit me in Bangkok. Despite all the wonderful work of individuals and groups, we arrive at each new AIDS conference with reports of an ever-increasing pandemic and the realization of a growing number of individuals who have been infected with HIV. Despite all the treatment advances, despite all the global awareness, despite all the political jockeying, we are not winning this fight.

With everything we have done so far, the fact remains that the HIV/AIDS pandemic continues to grow daily. By the end of 2004, there were approximately 40 million individuals diagnosed with HIV/AIDS worldwide. Women

57

and children are more and more being disproportionately affected by HIV/AIDS. These groups are not only being infected at record rates, but often women are left without support, and children are orphaned, as husbands, parents and whole families die of AIDS. For me, the Bangkok Conference underscored this reality. Further, it stressed that we are not merely fighting an infectious disease, but rather a vast array of issues that promote the spread of HIV/AIDS. It will not be enough to make antiretroviral therapy (ART) available in resource-poor countries. It will not be enough to pontificate on the responsibility of individuals to be more moral. It will not be enough to focus on other world priorities and hope all this will just go away. I suddenly gained a new awareness that it is not just an AIDS pandemic – we are in a much larger fight to respond to complex forces that converge to support the spread of HIV/AIDS around the world. With more than 95 per cent of the new cases of HIV infection (approximately 14,000 a day) in low- and middle-income countries, it is those with the least resources for education and health care that are being forced to respond to this pandemic. Poverty, stigma, discrimination, gender inequity, cultural conflict and exploitation are all factors that are significant components of the spread of HIV infection.

You do not have to be an AIDS expert to be aware of these forces and their negative outcome for the global community, which are as familiar as the nightly news. Collective reports of war, disease and inaction in feeding and sheltering the most vulnerable among us provide a clear picture that our world is in trouble. If not adequately addressed, these forces will continue to promote a world that is ripe to spawn new diseases and decrease our humanity. To underscore this situation, concerns about a new pandemic of "bird flu" spreading from poor, rural areas of Asia are being sounded internationally as I write this chapter.

To more fully understand the complexity of the situation, consider that in sub-Saharan Africa, 75 per cent of new HIV infections are among young girls and women aged 15 to 24 who are not free to abstain from sex or to get treatment when infected. Yet, clearly survival sex is not limited to the developing world. Exploitation and inequity based on gender and/or ethnicity or cultural identity is a universal condition. In many countries, there is a generation of AIDS orphans (estimated as 25 million by 2010) who are growing up without parents or support. A number of resource-challenged countries are losing a generation to HIV/AIDS – the generation that was most prepared to help advance economic improvement in these countries. The result is a worsening economic outlook. There are more than 70 regional conflicts under way in the world today. Rape has become a tool of war. Stigma and discrimination, long identified as enemies of successful responses to HIV/AIDS, continue to be commonplace not only as a response to

HIV/AIDS, but also directed against the poor, women, gays and lesbians, ethnic and religious minorities, and anyone who is viewed as "other". These universal forces are not new but provide a fertile ground in which epidemics such as HIV/AIDS grow. They need to be recognized not as isolated occurrences, but as intertwining forces that act to undermine the overall human condition and prevent any successful responses to HIV/AIDS.

The point is that those working in HIV/AIDS care and prevention, those working to support economic development in resource-limited and wealthy countries, those addressing peace and reconciliation in the world, and those working towards justice and gender equity need to understand that all these efforts are different aspects of the same, larger fight. The countries of the world seemed to have acknowledged this fact in their adoption of the Millennium Development Goals (MDGs), established by the United Nations in 2000. Human justice, health and economic stability in the world will not happen in isolation – a new commonness of purpose and action is needed.

Changing self-defeating traditions

What is needed is a new strategy to change ideas, to change self-defeating traditions, to change attitudes and to change negative role-modelling behaviour. As with every generation, the young hold the potential for a better future. But considering the forces in the world that have led us to ongoing conflict, physical and economic exploitation of the weak and poor, and hatred of those seen as different, we need new strategies to support the next generation in attaining a higher ethical reality. We need to develop new models that foster the ability to resolve conflict by negotiation within accepted rules of law, a respect for our fellow human beings, and the ability to win and lose with honour. These are key factors in our fight against HIV/AIDS. The more comprehensive fight against HIV/AIDS is a fight for basic social change.

By a series of beneficial accidents, I have become involved in a small way with a new initiative undertaken by the ILO in conjunction with the United Nations (UN) and the International Olympic Committee (IOC). This initiative, known as the Universitas programme, builds on the report of the UN Inter-Agency Task Force on Sport for Development and Peace and has at its core the goal of using the many positive aspects of sport and recreation to facilitate social change and skills development (of youth in particular). The objective of the programme is to bring together local leaders, government officials, community advocates, social service providers and representatives of international organizations to develop ways to meet the MDGs in individual countries and communities, using sport as the mechanism for collaboration. The goal is not to teach individuals to play sports but rather to use the positive environment that can be produced around sport, especially in the young, to address significant social issues. As indicated by Adolf Ogi, Special Advisor to the UN Secretary-General, "Sport is the best school of life".

When you think about it, sport does hold potential as a strategy for education, attitude formation, collaboration and friendly competition within a framework of rules. Coaches can play a vital developmental role in modelling positive attitudes, values and character. In this context, the reference to "coach" is broader than the traditional definition of athletic coach, as used in developed countries. In many regions, the coach is a respected adult who works with youth in the community, both to support youth and facilitate recreation. This goes beyond preparing elite athletes or the high-pressure approach that focuses on winning at all costs.

Figure 4.1 provides an initial conceptualization of the coach as a facilitator and promoter of a comprehensive community approach to youth development. In this model, the coach, who is often in the best position to assess the needs of individuals and groups of youth, serves as a linch-pin or conduit to link youth to available community services. Through the development of a community network with the coach as a referral agent, youth can more easily access needed services, education and skills development. Likewise, the coach can effectively act as a role model for positive attitudes and character traits such as inclusion, non-discrimination and openness to exploration of new approaches through education.

The significant effect of the coach's influence in integrating positive attitudes and practices through sport and recreation should not be under-estimated. Establishing positive peer norms through play can be a powerful tool to change negative attitudes about sex education, women and those individuals with different cultures and beliefs. Again, sport can be an effective school that influences life.

In relation to HIV/AIDS, coaches can be valuable teachers for prevention, role models for non-discrimination and promoters of advocacy for persons with HIV/AIDS (figure 4.1). Education on HIV/AIDS risk behaviours and the dispelling of myths about HIV transmission and care may be far more effective if provided by a coach in the context of the coaching role than if provided by outside educators or individuals not familiar with or respected by youth. When appropriate, coaches can work with local nurses, social service providers and teachers to link youth to programmes that promote health and education, and provide support that gives hope for the future. However, the coach can continue to be a critical force in realizing behavioural and/or attitudinal change by serving to reinforce information and opportunities provided by others. He or she can act as a facilitator, moving information and opportunity for growth from the external environment to the internal reality of the individual youth.

Figure 4.1   The coach as role model and facilitator of a comprehensive
               community network

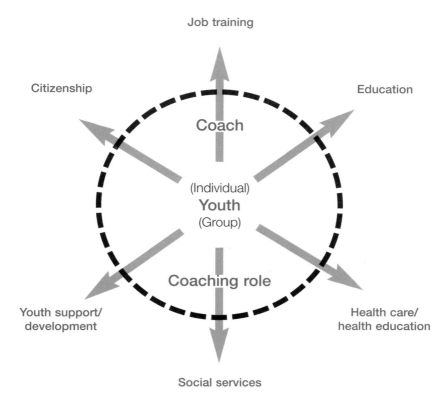

Although elite athletes can play an important role in drawing attention to social issues such as HIV/AIDS, violence and poverty, the real action takes place in small towns and villages, on playing fields and at recreation centres. In these settings, youth has the opportunity to observe character and a sense of respect for others in adult role models. There are also opportunities to link youth to new attitudes and resources that promote a better life. Although certainly not the complete answer, the principles underpinning the Universitas programme[2] and its associated Youth Sport Programme (in collaboration with the IOC) in particular are worth considering. They may well form components of an initiative that we can all use to help craft a more comprehensive response to HIV/AIDS in our communities. What we have done thus far has not solved the problem. Maybe we can use the lessons learned during the 2005 International Year of Sport and Physical Education to explore new and less obvious approaches to fighting HIV/AIDS.

A move to action

To that end, in October 2005 Kennesaw State University, Georgia, United States, developed and hosted an international summit on effecting social change through women's leadership through sport. The key element was the recognition that women have provided leadership in their communities, resulting in positive social change. In particular, women globally have been the strongest force in developing responses to HIV/AIDS in their communities. To do this, they have had to tackle issues of poverty, gender inequity, and lack of health and social services infrastructure. Based on women's proven effectiveness in developing community networks to address HIV/AIDS, it is clear that they have the potential to influence society more broadly, both locally and globally.

The above summit built on the perspective of women's leadership and sport as a vehicle of social change to explore these forces and to come up with a strategy for deliberately moving them forward. One of the tangible outcomes was the announcement of a new centre for social change through women's leadership in sport at Kennesaw State University. The centre is designed to serve as a catalyst for further exploration of the concepts of women's leadership, sport, and social change and development. With collaboration of partners such as the Universitas network and international organizations supporting women in and through sport, the centre represents an initial step in crafting a better tomorrow through our belief in the potential of women's leadership and of sport to facilitate youth development.

Notes

[1] See: www.janacnet.org, accessed 6 Mar. 2006.

[2] See www.ilo.org/ public/english/universitas, accessed 6 Mar. 2006.

IMAGINING THE FUTURE: THE UNITED STATES SPORTING GOODS INDUSTRY IN 2010*

5

Gregg Hartley and Dan Kellams

Introduction

"The future doesn't exist. If it existed, it wouldn't be the future." So said Ned Rorem, the great American composer, celebrating his 80th birthday in 2003. While this insight may encourage us to live more contentedly in the present, it cannot prevent us from wondering what the future will bring when it does come into existence as the present. Is the future something that will just happen to us or can we in some way create it through our own careful planning and hard work?

The truth probably lies somewhere between those two extremes. The most ambitious Americans, such as successful entrepreneurs and politicians, believe that the future can be shaped by their own efforts. We strongly feel that by studying the sporting goods industry today, we can discern a vague outline of it in 2010. The fact is that change is happening so rapidly and unpredictably that the year 2010 can be seen as no more than a blur. It seems to us that the industry is experiencing dislocating change right now and that these forces will continue to transform it in unpredictable ways for years to come.

Consider these findings from our online survey of more than 100 industry chief executive officers (CEOs) and presidents: eight in 10 expect joint ventures and alliances to be important growth engines for the future; more than half expect to acquire other companies by 2010; one in four expects a change in the ownership of his or her own company. Add to this the pace at which information technology is reshaping our businesses; the enormous, still untapped power of the Internet; and the growth plans of the mighty mass merchants Wal-Mart and Target, who are aggressively expanding their superstore concepts and reshaping retailing by the new practices they adopt.

---

* Materials are copyright by the respective sources and SGMA International.

With a great deal of help from many industry leaders, we have been able to identify these and other forces and to at least suggest what they mean for the future of our industry. You may not agree with everything that is said, but the chances are you will find this report both thought-provoking and challenging, as did many of the people who reviewed it in early drafts.

The future may not exist right now, but we know for certain that it will bring even more challenging times than we face today. Those who fail to anticipate and prepare will be left behind along the way. After all, there is no turning back; the past doesn't exist, either.

The industry today

The sporting goods industry has experienced slow growth and extensive consolidation during the first years of the twenty-first century, primarily because of a weak economy, an excess of retail space and manufacturing capacity, and the intense price competition that naturally results from an oversupply of products and retail space. As companies have grown larger, professional managers and professional management techniques, particularly in information technology, have played increasingly important roles. Mounting cost pressures have forced many manufacturers to cease making goods; instead, they "source" them from independent factories in developing countries where labour costs are low. What was once a yawning gap between suppliers and retailers has closed considerably as the two parties work more closely together and as retailers increasingly demand more services. In addition to meeting retailer demands for lower prices and increased services, suppliers have striven, often with success, to create innovative new products and product features. Still, retailers and suppliers alike worry about "the sea of sameness" in retail stores.

During the past decade, the industry has experienced significant consolidation among both retailers and manufacturers. This consolidation is in part a natural consequence of an industry with excess capacity. On the supplier side, stronger companies are buying up weaker ones at good prices for a variety of reasons. They include the desire to achieve economies of scale by eliminating duplicative functions, such as sales staff, to obtain the critical mass required for heavy spending on research and development, and information technology; to build on core strengths; to add product categories or brands to their portfolios; and to offer a comprehensive selection of products to their retailers.[1]

On the retailing side, chain stores have waged a brutal war of geographic expansion, resulting in many weaker chains and independents going out of business or being acquired. The merger of Garts, first with Oshman's and then with The Sports Authority, has created a chain of unprecedented power in the industry, with some 400 stores in 45 states, the closest thing to a truly national chain the industry has seen. The company plans to open as many as 30 new stores annually over the next several years. Several sporting goods chains[2] have aggressive plans to continue opening new territories. Their growing marketing clout is sure to claim more victims among an already dwindling population of independent retailers. The pace of geographic expansion has slowed for athletic footwear specialty stores, which expanded rapidly during the 1990s.

In many supplier companies, professional managers have replaced entre-preneurial leaders who founded companies out of a passion for sports. The industry has adopted many sophisticated management techniques, especially the use of information technology for inventory management. Newcomers to the industry, from packaged goods, electronics or other industries, often remark that sporting goods still have not caught up with many techniques used routinely in more sophisticated industries.

Many manufacturers, seeking the lowest costs possible, have stopped making products themselves (some never did) and instead "source" them from independent factories in emerging countries. As a result, many companies that were once manufacturers are now suppliers, or "vendors". Seeking an edge, suppliers have invested heavily in new product development and have been successful in bringing many performance-enhancing technologies to the marketplace. The competitive requirement to innovate is as intense as the pressure to reduce costs.

Manufacturers historically were out of touch with consumers of their products. They tended to leave customer relationships to their retailers, and often dealt with them through independent representatives. In recent years, the yawning gap between supplier and retailer has closed a great deal. Many suppliers have established internal sales staffs, ending their relationships with independent sales representatives. Suppliers and retailers are increasingly working together to better understand one another and the customer. Retailers are requiring suppliers to take more risks and responsibilities in inventory management and for the success of their products on the retailer's shelves. The practice of suppliers providing exclusive products to major retailers through "special make-ups" or exclusive products has taken root.

Today, both suppliers and retailers worry about what one panellist called "the sea of sameness out there". Every store seems to have the same products, even when they come from different suppliers. This is partly because of excess capacity and partly because suppliers have become extremely nimble in tracking fashions and matching technological breakthroughs by their com-petitors. No product stays new and exclusive for very long. Some retailers criticize suppliers for not investing enough in research and development, while suppliers insist that it is a major priority for their companies. In addition, retailers criticize suppliers for poor "channel management", saying that they sell their products too widely to too many stores of too many different types. In recent years, for example, athletic footwear brands have begun selling certain lower-priced models to discount chains that were formerly off limits, such as Shoe Carnival and Famous Footwear.

The market for sporting goods

Except in the fitness category, the sporting goods industry, including key sports playing, equipment buying, sports apparel and athletic footwear, cannot expect demand for its products to come from an expanding US market. No population growth is expected in the key youth market aged 5 to 19, according to the US Census Bureau. Expectations of growth between 2005 and 2010 range from 60.7 million to 61.0 million. The boom in this population occurred between 1990 and 2000, when it expanded by 12 per cent, from 53.0 million to 59.3 million. Half of all consumer spending on athletic footwear and 55 per cent of spending for sports apparel goes to products worn by individuals aged 24 or under.

On the one hand, team sports, racquet sports, outdoor sports and other activities have lost millions of casual participants, who have turned to other pursuits for fun, including action sports. Even soccer, repeatedly named the "hottest" sport in the US by SGMA International members, has grown no faster than the population as a whole. It had 17.6 million participants in 2002.

In contrast to the massive declines in casual pickup sports, participation in *organized* team sports is growing at many levels. This provides a steady demand for sports equipment, footwear and apparel (although only about one-third of all athletic shoes and sports apparel items are actually purchased for use in sports or exercise). Much of the growth in organized sports has come from girls taking up team sports, both in schools and community leagues. Growth in many local youth sports leagues has also occurred because programmes have been extended to young players, aged 5 and under. Over the years, as casual players stopped playing pickup sports for fun, the entire youth sports scene has tended to focus on more serious players – and millions of kids have found something more fun to do with their spare time. Particularly, many young people have taken up "extreme" or "action" sports, such as skateboarding and snowboarding. Participation in these sports has grown more rapidly than the population as a whole and has opened up new markets for sporting goods. In 2002, participation in inline skating declined for the fifth year in a row to 21.6 million while skateboarding participation rose to 13.0 million, a 40 per cent increase over 1993. These activities do not, however, create a heavy demand for equipment, footwear and apparel found in team sports, although skateboarding and snowboarding fashions have spread beyond the confines of the sports themselves.

Among the four most popular outdoor activities – fishing, tent camping, hiking and hunting – only tent camping has experienced participation growth in recent years. Over longer terms, these activities have, as a group, lost millions of participants. There is no sign of a turnaround here, although many industry groups have launched campaigns to try to halt the erosion in participants. Other sports categories, such as bowling, billiards, water sports and snow sports, have, with a few exceptions (such as snowboarding), suffered declines in participation or have grown more slowly than the population as a whole.

Geographic markets are saturated. As with US retailing in general, the sporting goods industry suffers from excess – too many stores with too much merchandise. This has contributed to debilitating price wars and shrinking profit margins for many companies. It also limits the opportunities for growth by opening new channels or entering new geographic markets. It suggests that the industry faces years of bruising market-share battles with price playing the key role in attracting customers. Facing mature markets in the US, many suppliers are seeking growth in international markets. Although the scope of this chapter is limited to the US market, it should be noted that economies remain weak in the most-developed countries in Europe and Asia. A rapidly growing middle class in emerging nations such as China and India is tempting many US companies to explore opportunities there; but doing business in these countries is a complex undertaking and risks are high.

Consumers have taken on record debt: in the US this is at an all-time high, up to more than 18 per cent of total assets at mid-year 2003, compared to 14 per cent in 1980. Higher interest rates in the future could slam the brakes on consumer spending. Years of price-cutting by retailers have made consumers extremely savvy about bargain hunting. The Internet has made shoppers smarter, more independent and more sceptical than ever of advertising and marketing techniques used by "big business". Concerns arising from the weak economy, war and terrorism have made consumers especially cautious about spending for basic items as they seek to free up money for things that "really matter", such as health, home, family and hobbies. This attitude should benefit fitness products, which are increasingly associated with health, and athletic products generally among families with children deeply involved in sports. A fragmented industry marked by oversupply, inefficient operations and poor growth prospects will have difficulty attracting investors, whose money is needed to fund consolidation, R&D and more efficient operations.

The exception to the low-growth scenario outlined above involves the fitness industry. One of its key markets – ageing baby boomers – is growing and its members have strong incentives in terms of health, vigour and well-being to spend discretionary dollars on health club memberships and home fitness equipment. The population aged 55 and older will grow by 14 per cent, from

66.1 million to 75.1 million, between 2005 and 2010. Over the past 15 years, this has been the fastest-growing age group in health clubs and is a prime market for exercise equipment. A strong market among older Americans – coupled with increasing interest in exercise and health among all members of the population – bodes well for the future of this segment of sporting goods.

The obesity crisis has sparked concerns about the long-term health of the nation and this is beginning to create a sense of urgency about the importance of physical activity. Concern that something must be done is rising in legislatures in Washington and many states – which are, at this writing, strapped for cash. The health care industry is increasingly experimenting with incentives to encourage clients to eat properly and exercise more. Corporations are developing new ways to inspire their employees to live more healthily. A few school systems are responding to pleas from parents and fitness advocates (such as P.E.4Life)[3] to restore physical education programmes, but anecdotal evidence seems to suggest that the pendulum is still swinging toward restricting physical activity programmes in schools in favour of an emphasis on class work. For example, the media continues to report on schools curtailing recess. There is also a growing trend towards requiring fees for students to participate in school sports.

The awakening awareness that Americans are killing themselves through lack of physical activity – and that something must be done about it – stands to benefit the sporting goods industry. The question is whether this awareness will ignite a national movement or continue as a slowly evolving force. Some of our panellists are bullish on the prospects for industry growth because they believe this trend will accelerate over the next several years, leading to a significant change in the cultural attitudes about physical activity. Others believe that much more must be done in terms of education and motivation. Some observers see change occurring, but at a slow pace. They point to the decades-long shift, still under way, in American attitudes about smoking. An evolution in attitudes about exercise has been under way for years, reaching back to the running boom of the 1970s. The year 1996 marked the appearance of the landmark Surgeon General's Report on Physical Activity and Health. Here the Government for the first time confirmed the scientific evidence that physical activity improved health and prolonged life, and made the encouragement of physical activity a matter of national policy.

As indicated by tables 5.1 to 5.3, the past decade or so, and future projections, show a slowdown in the growth of manufacturers' shipments of sporting goods industries, an ageing population and declining casual participation in many team sports. The exception is soccer, which has experienced growth over the past 15 years. Frequent participation in team sports has not grown in the past five years. Many youngsters have turned to individual "action" sports for unsupervised play.

Table 5.1   Slowing down, 1990–99 and 2000–02 (average annual growth rate in manufacturers' shipments of sporting goods)

	1990–99	2000–02	
	(%)	(%)	(US$bn)
Exercise equipment	22	1	3.775
Other sports equipment[1]	4	0	13.72
Sports apparel	7	1	23.225
Athletic footwear	2	1	9.335
All categories	5	1	50.055

Note: [1] Includes equipment for team sports, golf, camping, snow sports, water sports, skating sports, racquet sports, bowling, billiards and other activities.

Source: SGMA International Market Intelligence.

Table 5.2   Key population trends, 1990–2010 (millions in each age group)

Year	Aged 5 to 19	Aged 55 and older
1990	53.0	49.2
2000	59.3	53.8
2005	60.7	66.1
2010	61.0	75.1

Source: US Census Bureau.

Table 5.3   Sports participation trends, 1998 and 2002 (millions of participants, aged 6 or older)[1]

	1998		2002	
Basketball	42.4;	36.6	36.6;	10.2
Slow-pitch softball	19.4;	02.6	17.7;	02.6
Soccer	18.2;	04.5	17.6;	04.7
Baseball	12.3;	03.7	10.4;	03.3
Inline skating	32.0;	05.8	21.6;	03.6
Skateboarding	07.2;	01.6	12.5;	03.9
Snowboarding	05.5;	00.5[2]	07.7;	00.5[2]

Notes: [1] The first number means have played "at least once" and the second means "have played 50 times or more".
[2] Have snowboarded only 25 times or more.

Source: US Census Bureau.

Many blame a weak economy for the sporting goods industry's slow growth since 2000. Moreover, the industry is expected to experience more challenges in the remainder of the decade. Companies dealing with exercise equipment, however, could resume strong growth.

Consolidation for retailers and suppliers

While some panellists[4] agreed that consolidation among sporting goods retailers is a foregone conclusion, others predicted more mega-mergers, with strong regional and national chains absorbing weaker ones. However, predictions say that before the decade is out, the larger sporting goods chains are likely to confront one another in certain markets. There are few under-served markets left in the US and with geographic markets saturated, market share battles will be even fiercer, "leaving retailing the domain of larger and better-managed companies."[5] This is already occurring, reported the newsletter *Sporting Goods Intelligence*, citing figures that show that the 66 largest sporting goods retailers enjoyed a collective revenue gain of 8.2 per cent in 2002, compared to only 2.9 per cent the year before. "We feel comfortable in concluding that the larger retailers have gained on the rest of the market", the newsletter said.

In retailing generally, the giant mass merchants (Wal-Mart and Target) are expected to continue to expand aggressively with their supercentre concepts. Wal-Mart today operates 1,386 supercentres and plans to open 1,000 more over the next five years. While this expansion, in the words of Lee in *Business Week*, 26 May 2003, "is a nonunion dagger aimed at the heart of the traditional supermarket", Wal-Mart is expected to enter many other merchandise categories along the way. The creation of 1,000 more supercentres is sure to send shockwaves through all retailing. Further, the examples set by Wal-Mart and Target in cost-cutting, private branding, information technology, supplier relations and consumer research will trickle down to the sporting goods industry. In its cost-cutting efforts alone, the chain is credited with helping to suppress inflation, said Lee (ibid.). "Over the years, Wal-Mart has relentlessly wrung tens of billions of dollars in cost efficiencies out of the retail supply chain, passing the larger part of the savings along to shoppers in bargain prices."

As chains become more powerful by offering wide selections and competitive prices, new forms of specialty chain stores serving niche markets are expected to appear in sporting goods as they have in general retailing. Just as Gymboree (children's clothing) has launched Janie and Jack (children's gifts) and Chico's (apparel for boomer women) has spawned Pazo (apparel for yuppie women), so will retailers develop boutiques customized for sports-oriented consumers. Jim Corbett, vice president of Fruit of the Loom, visualizes stores dedicated to soccer players or women fitness enthusiasts. Such concepts can be winners because they will focus very tightly on serving specific needs and passions, Corbett said. Architect Peter McCrae, writing in *Sports Edge*, also predicts the emergence of sporting goods stores keyed to specific sports and life-styles.

In the fitness industry, the rise of neighbourhood health clubs, most notably Curves for Women, is an example of successful specialty retailing. These smaller clubs are tailored to serve a time-pressed clientele that is happy to forego many amenities, including showers. Facilities are also developing that specialize in baby boomers, rehabilitation services and sport-specific training. In the meantime, a broad class of independently owned specialty stores will continue to survive and prosper, several panellists said. They include bike shops, skate shops, tennis shops, pro shops, ski shops and outdoor equipment specialists. These stores will provide customized service to a population of enthusiasts; many of the stores will be located in towns surrounding vacation areas.

The emergence of private retail brands is one of the most significant events to occur in sporting goods in the past 20 years, said one of our panellists. Others noted that private brands are a growing force in the lower-priced tiers, but implied that the practice was unlikely to extend beyond the middle tiers, and that even that level of penetration would be difficult for retailers to accomplish. This view seems to ignore what department stores, supermarkets, drug chains and discounters such as Target and Wal-Mart have accomplished in building private brands.

There is a difference between private labels, which are clearly positioned as a store's own product sold at a discount, and a private brand, says Marshall Cohen, industry analyst for The NPD Group. Private brands are marketed similarly to national brands to achieve a distinct integrity and identity, he says, citing Arizona jeans at J. C. Penney, Jaclyn Smith apparel at Kmart and the Mossimo line at Target.

Private labels or private brands now capture a greater share of the total apparel market than do national brands, NPD has found, and the segment has grown by 5 per cent over the past five years – while overall apparel spending has declined. The growing trend towards private labels is not confined to apparel. It is estimated that 50 per cent of all Target products are private label.[6] "Retailers will continue on an aggressive track to increase private label offerings," says NPD's Cohen. "There's not a category out there that won't have private label. I wouldn't be surprised to see a private label automobile." Sporting goods retailers have got the message and acted accordingly.[7] Private label sports equipment is increasingly appearing on the shelves of mass merchants, who are focusing on products and categories where margins are high and volume is sufficient to warrant the inventory investment, several panellists said. The practice is almost certain to spread to sporting goods chains.

Private labels matter to retailers not only because they can deliver higher profits, but also because they are an important way to differentiate. "Over the long term, we are looking to build our own brands," said Mang. "It's part of our program to differentiate ourselves, control our own destiny, develop offerings that suppliers won't help us with." Mang sees a limit to private labels, however. "It's tough enough to be a good retailer without being a supplier too. You would have to build a whole organization to succeed, and that gets pretty expensive just to cut out a middleman's profit." Team dealer buying groups, like retail chains, are also increasing their practice of buying directly from factories. This occurs when "a vendor brand is not strong enough to demand support," said Trevor Swangard, president of the buying group TAG. Executives from supplier companies on our panel said that constant innovation and strong brands were their best defence against losing sales to private brands. So far, that has been the case in athletic footwear, where private labels have made few inroads. Here, however, major retailers are increasingly demanding exclusive models and "special make-ups". Reebok and Limited Too have collaborated on a line of sneakers for young girls that are appearing exclusively in the fashion chain's 260 stores. The deal also makes Reebok the sole athletic footwear provider to the chain.

In apparel, and in all goods, sales of store brands are growing faster than national brands (tables 5.4 and 5.5).

Table 5.4   Private labels growing strongly: Share of consumer apparel spending (percentages)[1]

Private label/brand	36
National brand	34
Designer brand	9
Other/no answer	23[1]

Note: [1] 12 months ending Apr. 2003.

Source: The NPD Group.

Table 5.5   Store and national brands: Growth in unit sales, 2001–03 (percentages)

Store brands	8.6
National brands	1.5

Source: A.C. Nielsen/*Fortune* magazine.

Table 5.6   Future sales and marketing efforts[1]

Effort	Average rating
Create new distribution channels	4.20
Research and development	4.02
Sales training	3.59
Internet B2B services[2]	3.49
Special make-ups	3.15
Consumer advertising	2.74
Produce private label goods	2.77
Co-op advertising	2.74
Direct sales to consumers	2.49

Notes: [1] Average rating on a scale of 1 to 5. [2] Internet business to business (B2B) is a professional provider of Internet services aimed at business. Services include web hosting, email hosting, domain registration and SSL certificates.

Source: SGMA International online survey of 105 member CEOs and presidents.

Table 5.6 shows the replies of companies which were asked to rate the importance of sales and marketing efforts over the next five years.

Table 5.7 gives companies' average ratings on the importance of pressing issues to future success.

Table 5.7   Pressing business issues[1]

Success issue	Average rating
Improving revenue/profits per SKU[2]	3.76
Gaining new accounts	3.75
Adapting systems and processes to customer demands	3.60
Assuring customers are profitable	3.54
Making decisions about information technology	3.09
Meeting industry competition	3.19

Notes: [1] Average rating on a scale of 1 to 4. [2] Stock Keeping Unit (SKU) is retail merchandising jargon for what the aerospace industry would call a part number. A code number is assigned to a particular style or size of good.

Source: As for table 5.6.

Conclusions: The future

Consolidation

Consolidation has also been identified as a major industry force in the future. Suppliers will be a lot bigger to meet the demands of ever more powerful retailers for service and for distinctive products. Some public companies with revenues in the US$100–500 million range may seek to go private as a way to avoid shareholder pressure for growth, said Helen Rockey. By giving up their obligations to shareholders, these companies may be able to remain independent and competitive by reducing their size and narrowing their focus. Some acquisitions in the future will be made for purely defensive reasons, to eliminate competitors, said Trevor Swangard of TAG.

Large suppliers will seek growth by assembling portfolios of niche brands. This strategy will give them access, credibility and exclusivity in retail channels and consumer markets that would be difficult to penetrate with products bearing a global brand (table 5.8). Acquisitions may well cross traditional boundaries. A large retailer might want to pick up a failing apparel or footwear brand or a small niche brand, and take it in house as a private brand. This has already happened in other retailing segments. Massive incursions from outside the industry are not out of the question.[8]

Consolidation also will be expressed in new types of joint ventures between retailers and suppliers. Entrepreneurs with new ideas will continue to be welcomed and will be sought out by larger companies looking for an edge. The corporate development function (concerned with mergers, acquisitions and new ventures) will become more important at many companies.

Retailers engaged in pruning and sharpening their lines also perform a consolidating function, pointed out Dan Jelinek, vice president of sales for

Table 5.8   Growth strategies (percentage of respondents citing strategy)

Growth strategy	Percentage citing this strategy
Seek alliances or partnerships	76
Acquire other companies or brands by 2010	52
Acquire other companies or brands by 2005	42
Seek outside capitalization	42
Undergo a change of ownership by 2010	26
Undergo a change of ownership by 2005	16

Source: As for table 5.6.

Easton Sports. Retailers themselves are constantly working to streamline their vendor lists and product assortments. The independent sales agent – representing a group of vendors – will not completely disappear, although "the need for them will be greatly diminished", said Richard Kazmaier. He sees these representatives as an essential link between small, entrepreneurial vendors and the surviving network of independent specialty dealers.

Asked about joint ventures and mergers in the years ahead, eight in 10 of our survey respondents said they would be seeking alliances and partnerships. About half said they would be acquiring other companies or brands by 2010.

Product innovation

The ability to innovate in terms of product technology, fashion or other differentiating features is seen as essential to success and perhaps even to survival. This was evident both in our interviews and in the online survey. Only continuous improvement in product will forestall retailers from going to private label apparel, said Kevin Plank, president of Under Armour. A good result of consolidation is that there will be more investment in R&D. Other panellists noted that suppliers are becoming increasingly adept at copying innovative products or jumping on a fashion trend. The result is that the life-cycles of breakthrough products are being significantly shortened, and this is curtailing the profit streams normally associated with unique products and fashions.

Steve Furniss of Tyr foresees the emergence of small consulting firms that will provide product design and development services not only for suppliers but also for retailers determined to build private brands. The pressure for innovation may spawn the creation of small groups of specialists serving major companies. Given a choice of several ways to differentiate their products, 81 per cent of survey respondents said they would do so through quality of product innovation, and 82 per cent through brand image. In reply to another question, 75 per cent said new product technology was very important to their future marketing and sales programmes, far outranking such activities as line extensions, dealer support programmes, partnerships and consumer advertising (table 5.9). Furthermore, suppliers clearly see that product innovation is essential for survival (table 5.10).

The successful supplier will have to be excellent at the intricate process of brand management in all its ramifications, including being selective about which products are sold by which retailers to which customers. Our panellists were adamant about this.[9]

As has been indicated throughout this chapter, suppliers will be required to work even more closely with retailers, overcoming any animosity and, in many ways, taking over responsibilities previously handled by retailers. Jelinek,

Table 5.9   Important sales and marketing efforts (percentage replying activity was very important)

Sales/marketing activity	Percentage replying "very important"
New product technology	75
Line extensions/new categories	47
Partnerships/licensing	39
Dealer support programmes	31
Consumer advertising	26

Source: As for table 5.6.

Table 5.10   Differentiation strategies (percentage replying strategy was very important)

Differentiation strategy	Percentage replying "very important"
Image/brand reputation	82
Product innovation	81
Quality of direct service	77
Personal relationships	74
Comprehensive products and services	56
Research & development investment	55
Business advice to clients	18

Source: As for table 5.6.

of Easton Sports, foresees battles between suppliers and vendors over the loyalty of factories. But in the end, retailers will have more options than suppliers, whose principal alternative might be to try to sell direct over the Internet.

Retailers place a high priority on distinctiveness, and suppliers will face increasing pressure for more effective channel management and for providing powerful retailers with exclusive products and special make-ups. They will be asked to take more responsibility for marketing and merchandising their own products to consumers. Retail Forward, the consulting group, predicts that as "brand-sharing" concepts proliferate, retailers and suppliers will tussle over who owns the resulting consumer research data.

Retailers might absorb some suppliers' brands (which in turn will become house brands) through various forms of acquisition or joint ventures. Other weak brands will become providers of private label goods. This could become a precarious existence as retailers and factories learn to work more effectively together and see less reason to use a middleman. Independent specialty stores may enjoy increased attention from suppliers, said Steve Furniss of Tyr. In addition to being more profitable customers than large chains, these stores will be important platforms for testing and promoting new performance products.

Industry marketing campaigns

As the industry players become larger and more sophisticated, ways will be found to cooperate on marketing programmes to increase sports participation by winning back the interest of young people. "It must become a priority for the industry to be much more proactive in getting people to become involved with sports," said Marty Hanaka of The Sports Authority. Larry Franklin, president of Franklin Sports, believes that the two leading industry associations, SGMA International and the National Sporting Goods Association, should play a leadership role in bringing the industry together on this and other issues. Cooperative efforts to promote physical activity, he said, will involve sports and fitness companies as well as government bodies, health care organizations, insurance companies and community-minded organizations. In many cases, these groups will look to sports and fitness companies for guidance. Eventually, business opportunities will emerge from this effort, Kevin Grodzki said. "Concerns about rising costs for health care will somewhere, somehow create new business propositions," he added.

Mastering information technology

Quality of inventory management – that is, the ability to deliver products where and when they are needed – may be the make-or-break factor for suppliers in the future, said Jim Corbett of Fruit of the Loom. When all other factors are equal – price, quality, brand image – what will really matter is the ability to put the item on the shelf or in the hands of the consumer the minute it's needed. Vendors with technological superiority will have increasing advantages, said Matt Mirchin of Russell. His company has "spent millions" to upgrade its system and will continue to invest. "Companies that can't keep up with the technology have the potential to lose out", he said.

Upgrading or adding IT systems is a difficult challenge even for companies that are strong financially. For one thing, choosing the best alternative among many systems and providers is difficult. Further, companies are learning that even when the right system is chosen, things can go wrong if the company doesn't adapt culturally. According to Arndt et al. in *Business Week* (12 May 2003):

"Corporations learned in the early days of e-business that costly new systems by themselves accomplish little. They can sow confusion and resentment among employees who figure they did just fine the old way. To get a true e-bang for the buck, companies must redesign their business processes . . . to take advantage of the new capabilities."

The Internet is widely recognized as a potent force for dealing with both consumers and other businesses, but a force whose full power has only begun to be realized. For consumers, in fact, B2B via the Internet will become even more important as a marketing and sales channel as broadband and WiFi[10] proliferate and as computer-savvy children grow into adults with disposable income. As with IT issues generally, experimentation can be expensive and companies are still groping to discover more specifically what the Internet will mean for their businesses in the future. For now, most observers inside and outside the industry do not expect online sales to grow significantly in the years just ahead. But the Internet will play an increasingly important role in educating and empowering consumers, who will use it more and more effectively for research leading up to the decision to buy (table 5.11).

The Internet can provide a direct link between the consumer and the factory, no matter where in the world each is located. This raises a futuristic scenario in which these two parties – consumer and producer – hold all the power. When factory and consumer talk directly, there is significantly less need for suppliers as they now operate, and many retailers could become the equivalent of self-service showrooms.

Retail spaces will be transformed by technology, where the principal sales and merchandising agent will be interactive computer programs. These programs will be tied to inventory management systems and will track

Table 5.11   Rating important technology issues (importance to the company's future, on a scale of 1 to 4)

Technology issues	Average rating
Internet strategies	3.40
Warehousing systems	3.15
Sales staff teaching systems	3.06
Supply chain management	3.05
Data security systems	3.00
Intranet usage	2.99
Data aggregation	2.96
Corporate structure	2.87

Source: As for table 5.6.

consumer preferences. Suppliers will be required to master this technology and to ensure its continuous improvement. The consumer data generated will be used to construct special marketing programs aimed at specific consumer segments.

Understanding the consumer

Implicit in all that has gone before is the requirement that many suppliers will have to become much better at knowing and understanding their consumers. This will have to occur as the consumer market "splinters into smaller and more diverse groups with different values and attitudes and [as] lifestyle aspirations become more idiosyncratic and buying behavior more complex", writes Retail Forward. "Successful marketers increasingly will segment consumers on the basis of multi-dimensional shopping motivations", the consulting firm said. If suppliers are not in touch with their consumers, all their efforts in product innovation, brand management, retail partners and information technology are likely to fail.

Notes

[1] Brunswick, for example, is one among several companies that has assembled a family of brands in fitness equipment, with Life Fitness, Hammer Strength, Parabody and Omni Fitness. Russell Athletic has embarked on a similar strategy with Moving Comfort, Bike Athletic and Spalding. Nike's purchase of former footwear giant Converse was only the latest in a long series of buyouts as the company assembles a portfolio of brands. When Adidas purchased Salomon, an industry titan with significant strengths in equipment, footwear and apparel was created overnight. Amer Holdings has assembled Wilson Sporting Goods, DeMarini and Precor, which had previously absorbed Pacific Fitness. Also, Adidas purchased Reebok, becoming the second largest world sport goods industry.

[2] These include Hibbet's (356 stores), Dick's Sporting Goods (140 superstores) and Galyan's (40 superstores).

[3] The Physical Education for Life (P.E.4Life) is a non-profit organization that promotes quality daily physical education programmes in America's public schools.

[4] The author here refers to those individuals who granted interviews and/or took part in email exchanges for the purpose of the survey.

[5] Report:"Twenty Trends for 2010" launched by Retail Forward, a consulting group.

[6] For example, Kroger, a supermarket chain, produces 4,300 food and drink items in its own 41 factories, reported *Fortune* magazine. Barnes & Noble has begun selling books published under its own imprint. Rite Aid is creating new brands called Pure Spring and 411.

[7] In 2002 private brands represented less than 3 per cent of sales at Gart's and 10 per cent at The Sports Authority; the goal for the combined company is 15 per cent. Dick's Sporting Goods announced that it planned to increase its share of private label apparel from 6 to 15 per cent. Bob Mang, president of Galyan's, said that private labels could become as much as 25 per cent of the store's apparel business. The company has already introduced some private label fishing gear.

[8] Greg Hege of Porter Athletic also added: "I don't think there is a company in this industry that is not in jeopardy of losing its sovereignty. Someone from the outside could look at our industry and see it as an attractive, growing aspect of health, leisure and entertainment – an industry with a lot of potential that would require a very big company to realize the potential. Then they start buying up companies to make an industry giant."

[9] Here follows a number of key sentences expressed by panellists on the point:
 "The companies that win will be the ones that know very clearly who they are and what their market is." (Jim Corbett, Fruit of the Loom)
"The companies that can build a brand will succeed." (Matt Mirchin, Russell Athletic)
"It's essential that a manufacturer develop an understanding of who it is, get a focus and stick with it." (Kevin Plank, Under Armour)
"It's critical not to compromise brand reputation when selling products at different price points." (Kevin Grodzki, Life Fitness)

[10] WiFi is short for Wireless Fidelity and is meant to be used generically when referring of any type of 802.11 network.

Sources

Research data. Statistics and conclusions on sports and fitness participation are based on continuing national studies by American Sports Data, Inc. The SGMA International online survey of member CEOs and presidents was conducted during August and September 2003. Approximately 1,000 individuals were contacted; 105 completed the survey, a response rate of 10 per cent.

Bibliography

Arndt, M.; Green, H.; Himelstein, L.; Hof, R. D.; Mullaney, T.J. 2003. "The E-Biz surprise", in *Business Week* (New York, NY), 12 May.

Boyle, M. 2003. "Power shift", in *Fortune Magazine* (New York, NY), Vol. 148, No. 3, 11 Aug.

Hof, R. D. 2003. "The future of tech", in *Business Week*, 25 Aug.

Kahn, G. 2003. "Invisible supplier has Penney's shirts all buttoned up", in *Wall Street Journal* (New York, NY), 11 Sep.

Lee, L. 2003. "Thinking small at the mall", in *Business Week*, 26 May.

Macrae, P. S. 2003. "The sporting goods store of the future", in *SportsEdge* (Alpharetta, GA), Aug.

Rubel, T. 2003. *Twenty trends for 2010: Retailing in an age of uncertainty* (Columbus, OH, Retail Forward).

Ryan, T. J. 2003. "Authority always wins", in *Footwear News* (New York, NY), Aug. 2003.

Sporting Goods Intelligence (industry newsletter) (Glen Mills, PA, John G. Horan).

Surowiecki, J. 2003. "EZ does it", in *New Yorker* (New York, NY), 8 Sep. 2003.

The following individuals granted interviews or took part in e-mail exchanges:

Jim Baugh, founder of P.E.4Life

Marshall Cohen, industry analyst for The NPD Group, provided insights and data on the growth of private brands

Jim Corbett, vice president, Fruit of the Loom

Gib Ford, former president, Converse

Larry Franklin, president, Franklin Sports

Steve Furniss, president, Tyr Sports

Kevin Grodzki, president, Life Fitness

Marty Hanaka, chairman and CEO, The Sports Authority

Greg Hege, president, Porter Athletic Equipment Company

Dan Jelinek, vice president, sales, Easton Sports

Richard Kazmaier, president, Kazmaier Associates

Kevin Lamar, president, Nautilus Health and Fitness Group

Bob Mang, president and CEO, Galyan's

Matt Mirchin, president, Russell Athletic

Bob Munroe, senior vice president and general manager, Reebok USA

Kevin Plank, president, Under Armour

Helen Rockey, partner, Sports Ventures

Trevor Swangard, president, TAG

PART II

OPPORTUNITIES AT THE GLOBAL AND REGIONAL LEVEL

EMPLOYMENT OPPORTUNITIES IN THE SPORTS SECTOR: A REVIEW OF THE EUROPEAN SITUATION

6

Jean Camy

Introduction

Today, on average, one European in two engages in a "sport", of whom one in five participates within federated associations, and almost all watch sports events live or on television. Widely organized on an associative basis, sport relies on the public authorities to differing degrees depending on the country and has acquired an increasingly commercial slant in recent years. Beyond its immediate confines, sport has an impact on a series of activities that affect a large number of different sectors: construction of facilities; sports goods; clothing; food; health care services; information and communication.

Sport has been identified as a growth area offering job creation potential. The statistical data available in several European countries[1] in fact show that since 1980, the number of jobs classified under sporting activities (NACE[2] group 92.6) has tripled and that this trend seems to be continuing.

Three main reasons can be put forward:

- the development of sporting activities themselves affect different groups of the population (the elderly, youngsters getting back into society, persons with a disability, etc.) and meet a variety of needs (leisure, health, entertainment, education);

- the indirect effects of raising the standard of living of Europeans, who devote a growing proportion of their income to expenditure on leisure and health (especially leisure activities in the sports field);

- the change in the "supply of sport", which is becoming increasingly professional (the commercial facet of sports activities is growing; associative sport draws an increasing number of professionals).

The question is how this development can facilitate job creation, without weakening associative sport and its effects on strengthening social links. The policy of developing employment in sport in Europe appears entirely in keeping with the introduction of a "European model of sport", which aims for an optimum combination of the intervention of the associative and local and national commercial operators (European Commission, 1999).

The characteristic of what could be called the "European system of sport" stems from a balance between types of operators which is very different from that observed in other parts of the world. These operators have many connections to sport: public authorities are interested in its health, integration and cultural identity functions; companies are attracted to its strong growth market; and because it is still a focus for voluntary team organization and development of social integration, association must retain its full role.

The sports sector in Europe: Definition and organization

When we talk about "sport", we must first and foremost differentiate between "sporting activities" per se (sports sector) and "sports-related activities" (which, together with the sports sector, form the "sports industry").

Figure 6.1   The sports industry: Central activities and peripheral activities

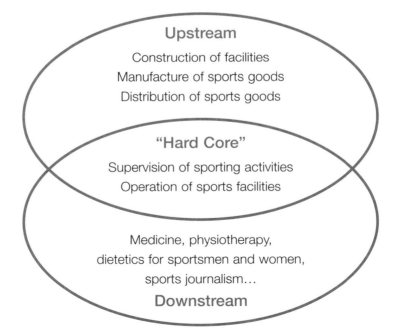

- The "hard core" activities are referred to as "sports activity" or the "sports sector". Sporting activities are confined to the services activities, which are related directly to practising sports, i.e. provision of facilities or equipment and supervision of sporting activities (the services of the sports associations are clearly included in this category). This corresponds to NACE group 92.6, the only class where sport is isolated in the official classification system. The activities under group 92.6 are not homogeneous (presence of sports associations, commercial sports service enterprises, self-employed professional sportspeople).

- The "upstream" and "downstream" activities (corresponding to the sports industry) are referred to as sports-related activities. For example, physical education clearly appears as an educational activity, which may be related to sport depending on differing degrees in various countries. These classes are naturally far more diverse than the first, since they group together industry, trade, education, transport, etc.

Presentation of the sports sector

The sports sector is made up of several segments organized around the production of differentiated services.

Professional sport's main focus is to produce events. Professional football occupies a dominant position in Europe, well ahead of other sports (basketball, motor sports, tennis, golf, etc.). Although professional sport only accounts for around 50,000 workers and about 2,000 businesses (generally small businesses, an increasing number of which have commercial status), it has high visibility because of its media coverage and its high degree of international appeal.

Competitive association sport forms the original and still dominant fabric of the sports sector. It is made up of associations, which in turn come together in sports federations, providing its members with training and competitive sporting activities. Essentially run by volunteers, it is nevertheless witnessing increasing professionalization of its human resources (coaches, managers, hospitality and maintenance staff). It is sometimes difficult to separate competitive association sport from the leisure sports sector. However, we can estimate the number of people pursuing professional activity in this segment at about 250,000, mainly in the 25 European Union (EU) countries, within more than a million associations, in the company of 10 million volunteers and 85 million members.

Sporting leisure pursuits occupy a growing place in the sports sector. They are organized either by associations (an increasing number of which are also present in the competitive sports sector), or by businesses, often very small ones. Each sporting leisure field (fitness, horse riding, sailing, winter sports, racquet sports, etc.) has its own particular features and its own identity. Some of them are faced with problems of the mobility of their staff within the European area (skiing, mountain pursuits, etc.). There are probably more than 400,000 people working in this segment of the sports sector in more than 30,000 businesses, more than half of which are in the commercial sector.

Social sport constitutes the last segment. It is difficult to analyse, as it includes not-for-profit organizations aimed at groups for whom social integration is difficult (e.g. people with a disability, minorities, etc.). We can estimate the number of people working in this sector at anywhere between 50,000 and 100,000, often close to local public services and financially supported by them.

These four segments enjoy relative autonomy, which varies depending on the EU Member State involved. In some of them, guidance of the whole sector is in the hands of the sports association movement (National Olympic Committee, Sports Confederation, etc.), which occasionally has the support of the public authorities. Everywhere, however, there are strong centralizing trends around the poles of professional sport, particularly football, and, less visibly, around commercial sporting leisure pursuits.

However, these segments are socially, culturally and even economically dependent on each other. It seems difficult for each of them to be able to optimize their development, or even to survive, if they do not work in conjunction with the others. In the United States, where the autonomy of each segment is taken to the extreme, relations nonetheless continue to exist between the segments (between professional and competitive association segments, for example).

This means that although the feeling of belonging to a whole – sport – is broadly shared by the enterprises in the sector, the segments and even the groups found there feel that they have important specific features. Some of them have powerful lobbying resources and are seeking to be recognized by the European authorities. This is not only the case with professional football, but also with mountain guides, who sought (albeit in vain) to obtain a sectoral directive of their own in the early 1990s.

Sport-related activities in Europe

While it is difficult to assess the activities falling within the "sports sector" proper, assessing the volume and form of the activities in relation to sport (sports industry) is even more problematic. In fact, the systematic inventory of the activities concerned carried out in the context of a satellite European classification system by the European Observatoire of Sport Employment

(EOSE)[3] shows that sport affects nearly all the main sectors of the official classification system (NACE) without it being possible to isolate them in the context of the statistical information available.

We shall confine ourselves here to presenting the most significant groups by the volume of activity they represent (or by the prospects they offer in this field).

A first group comprises the enterprises specialized in the construction of sports facilities, stadiums, gymnasiums, swimming pools, golf links, and so on (NACE division 45). These specialized enterprises only corner a small proportion of the market even though, increasingly, the large building and public works firms, which have the lion's share, incorporate specialized teams (including consultancy bureaux and architects). This market, which developed considerably in the 1960s along with the growth in the practice of sporting activities, was essentially dependent on public procurement. Even though this remains dominant in the majority of the EU Member States, it is increasingly giving way to private operators. The standardization of equipment meeting the norms of the sports federations is being replaced by a movement of diversification of this equipment integrating the expectations of leisure sports and sports entertainment. In so far as almost all forms of sporting activities require premises, which have been constructed or adapted for this purpose,[4] the renovation and creation of sports facilities and areas is one of the keys to the development of sport.

A second group brings together the manufacturers of sports equipment and goods, and the distribution firms associated with them.[5] Even though it includes few large enterprises, this market is extremely competitive and totally international (at least as regards manufacturing). It is also going through a traditional concentration process in all the markets that have reached maturity. It often calls on the latest technology and its development, increasingly in terms of quality, depends on the development of "self-service" behaviour among sportspeople, i.e. the use of equipment, which partly replaces human supervision.[6] The data available on certain specific products (sports footwear, skis, etc.) show a moderate growth in this economic sector with a decline in the industries subject to competition from Asia.

A third group of activities is that of the specialized media (audiovisual and written press). This field is expanding rapidly, with regard to both television and the production of specialized magazines that support the activity of sportspeople (over a thousand titles). If this is combined with the entire sector of publishing and production of audiovisual educational material, the group should also experience strong growth in the coming years.

We must also present the education and training sector, which includes physical education at school, at all levels of training in all types of establishments, and the training of future professionals in universities and public or private institutes. With regard to training, it can be estimated that the number of institutes and universities is close to 1,500 within the EU (employing over 15,000 people) and that they receive over 250,000 people annually as students or professionals receiving ongoing training.

We also review the activities of the public sports authorities. Whether these come under the central, local or regional government authorities, they represent a group that has developed to various extents in the different EU Member States. It is hardly surprising to see that, depending on whether the national traditions are "interventionist" or "liberal", the public services that central government provides are developing to a greater or lesser extent. France is the country with by far the largest number of government officials within its Ministry of Youth and Sports. On the other hand, at the local or regional authority levels, the differences in situation are not so striking. However, public sports authorities comprise a sector that tends to decline almost everywhere.

Finally, we mention the health sector and its "enterprises" specialized in sport, whether these are hospitals or sports medical services, physiotherapy practices, rehabilitation centres, and so on.

We could give many more examples, however, without managing to cover all the sports-related structures (for example, transport and accommodation which are predominantly non-sports-related, food for sportspersons, etc.).

Sports professions

In compliance with the principles of the ILO's International Standard Classification of Occupations (ISCO 88; ILO, 1988), the sports professions group includes all persons who engage in a sporting activity for remuneration (professional sportspeople) and those who supervise this activity directly. Under this classification, the "unit group" 3475, entitled "Athletes, sportspersons and related associate professionals" belongs to the "major group" of the intermediate professions. Knowledge of the theory and practice of sport and their application is the basic skill of the "sports professions" belonging to this group. In fact, it covers five main types of functions:[7]

- "professional sportspersons", participating in a limited number of sports and, in general, depending on the sporting events which constitute their livelihood;

- "sports officials", i.e. all those who, as referees, judges or timekeepers, directly supervise the conduct of sporting competitions;

- "sports activity leaders", who use sport as a means of getting specific groups of the population (elderly people, the disabled, young people, etc.) involved in team activities;

- "sports instructors", who teach one or more specific sporting activities to groups of the population who learn from scratch or wish to develop their abilities; and

- "sports coaches", responsible for preparing and guiding systematic performance in a given sport.

Sport-related professions

There is also a full range of professions that, although they belong to other large occupational groups, require a high level of specific skills in the field of sport. As for sport-related activities, the EOSE has tried to give as exhaustive a list as possible of these professionals who, to be identified as involved in a "sport-related profession", must show certain characteristics of institutionalization (professional trade unions, specific training, recognized designations, etc.).

These professions are classified in the order of ISCO 88:

- professional managers of sports or sports-related organizations;

- sports doctors;

- physical education and sports teachers in the school environment;

- sports journalists and other specialists in communication through or on sport;

- physiotherapists specialized in sport;

- agents or promoters of events or professional sportspersons;

- sellers of sports goods;

- caretakers of sports facilities and other reception staff;

- sports facilities maintenance workers.

Finally, the two categories of professionals we have just described are not the only ones present within the sports and sport-related sectors. A large number of people who work there come under other occupational categories that are not specific to their enterprise. Moreover, some sports professionals work outside the sports sector (in France, nearly half of them work in public administration).

In the following sections, we shall concentrate essentially on the sports sector per se, and the professions and training courses specific to it.

European sports sector employment

Total job numbers and trends

Given the reservations expressed above, the sports sector (NACE group 92.6) accounts for nearly 800,000 jobs in the 25 EU Member States (table 6.1). These jobs are main occupations but are not always full time. This table also considers all categories of occupations exercised in the sports sector. The United Kingdom

Table 6.1   Employment in the sports sector (NACE 92.6), 2000

Country	No. of jobs	% population
Austria	16 396	0.42
Belgium	14 524	0.33
Cyprus	1 867	0.50
Czech Republic	15 400	0.32
Denmark	13 000	0.46
Estonia	573/1 461[1]	0.09/0.23
Finland	11 290	0.44
France	100 205	0.37
Germany	105 000	0.30
Greece	9 218	0.21
Hungary	5 774	0.14
Ireland	10 421	0.63
Italy	48 802	0.18
Latvia	1 941/2 617[1]	0.18/0.24
Lithuania	3 851	0.25
Luxembourg	458	0.23
Malta	716	0.52
Netherlands	38 700	0.52
Poland	13 369/17 825[1]	0.08/0.11
Portugal	13 105	0.24
Slovakia	4 400	0.17
Spain	64 726	0.35
Sweden	25 500	0.61
United Kingdom	269 872	0.94
Total	**795 128[2]**	**8.71**

Notes: [1] Estimates from different national bureaux of statistics in Estonia, Latvia and Poland for the total population of employment in the sports sector. [2] Total calculation for number employed in the sports sector includes the higher of the two numbers given for Estonia, Latvia and Poland.

Source: This table was compiled by Jean Camy on the basis of data provided by the aforementioned countries' national statistics offices and bureaux, and from the European Commission – DG X, European Network of Sport Science Institutes, European Observatoire of Employment in Sport: *Sport and Employment in Europe*, Final Report, Sep. 1999, pp. 22–23.

alone accounts for 33 per cent of aggregate employment in the sector; Germany and France follow respectively with 13 per cent and 12.5 per cent.

These countries obviously vary significantly in area. Related to their relative size, however, employment in the sector accounts for between 0.11 per cent (Poland) and 0.94 per cent (United Kingdom) of the total active population. Within the EU countries we can distinguish two opposite groups: (a) the countries with a high rate of employment (Ireland, Sweden, United Kingdom); and (b) the countries with a "low" rate: (Hungary, Italy, Poland, Slovakia).

Trend in total volume

It is hard to estimate the aggregate growth of the sports sector because the countries have different national trends in the methods they use to classify statistical information. In the past ten years, however, the aggregate volume of employment, accounting again for distinct differences depending on the country, has grown by about 60 per cent (table 6.2). For example, while numbers doubled in Spain and the United Kingdom, they remained stable and even fell slightly in Austria, Finland and Sweden.

Table 6.2   Growth in employment in the sports sector in EU Member States, 1990–98

Country	No. of jobs		% growth
	1990	1998	1990–98
Austria[1]	9 378	7 790	−17
Belgium	9 210	14 524	58
Denmark	10 796	12 582	17
Finland[1]	7 516	6 967	−7
France	61 854	94 747	53
Germany[2]	–	95 000	–
Italy	48 742	54 978	13
Luxembourg	190	241	27
Netherlands	18 000	24 000	33
Portugal	9 600	14 300	49
Spain	28 200	56 300	100
Sweden[1]	25 414	25 469	0
United Kingdom	110 748	221 449	100
Total	**339 648**	**628 347**	**57[2]**

Note: – data not available. [1] Austria, Finland and Sweden appear in this table to be declining slightly. This is partly attributable to methodological problems (changes in classification of activities during the period examined). In Austria, for example, the same analysis carried out between 1981 and 1991 (strictly comparable classification systems) shows 57 per cent growth in employment, which is entirely comparable to the European mean. [2] Total growth in employment in the sports sector in EU Member States (1990–98) calculated without Germany.

Source: As for table 6.1, p. 92.

Characteristics of employment

The current state of available sports sector statistics makes it difficult to analyse all the 25 EU Member States in a harmonized manner. The range of data below is at times incomplete, but it does provide information on the main characteristics of and the trends in employment.

Part-time employment

Although we do not have data on all countries, the majority appear to have a distinctly higher percentage of part-time work in the sports sector than in aggregate employment. In 1990 and 1998 the percentages of part-time work in the sports sector were 42.7 per cent and 34.2 per cent, respectively (table 6.3). The decline on average is the result of conflicting situations: while most countries experienced a rise in part-time work, there was a fall in Finland, Portugal and the United Kingdom.[8] This decline was sufficient to determine the trend.

Table 6.3   Part-time employment in the sports sector in EU Member States, 1990–98

Country	Part-time jobs 1990		1998	
	No. of jobs	%	No. of jobs	%
Belgium	1 200	13.0	3 200	22.0
Finland[1]	1 400	18.6	1 200	17.2
France	14 400	23.3	27 100	28.6
Germany[2]	–	–	42 500	44.7
Italy	–	–	1 900	3.5
Luxembourg	50	26.3	70	29.0
Netherlands	7 000	38.9	11 000	45.8
Portugal	1 900	19.8	2 500	17.5
Spain	4 900	17.4	13 300	23.6
Sweden[1]	–	–	9 400	37.0
United Kingdom	74 000	67.0	95 700	43.2
Total part-time jobs in the sports sector	104 850		207 870	
Total jobs in the sports sector	245 318		607 975	
% part-time jobs in the sports sector		42.7		34.2

Notes: – data not available. [1] Percentage of part-time employment in recreational, cultural and sporting activities (NACE division 92). [2] West Germany only.

Source: As for table 6.1, p. 92.

Comparative research (Le Roux, 1998) has in fact shown that in France and the United Kingdom, the percentage of people employed part time is significantly higher in the sports sector than in the other sectors. This situation derives from structural characteristics of the job supply (small structures with limited activity or concentrated over certain hours of the day) and the job-seekers (specialists with narrow skills). Beyond the structural differences, however, it is also interesting that the percentage of part-time jobs is not homogeneous when country comparisons are made (from 3.5 per cent in Italy to 45.8 per cent in the Netherlands).

Young people and employment

The proportion of young people (under 25) in the sports sector in Europe is relatively low (around 20 per cent); see table 6.4. The relative stability in the share of young people is mainly attributable to the countries of southern Europe (France and Portugal) but also Finland, where the proportion of young people is falling. This may reflect the strategy adopted in the countries of southern Europe to combat youth unemployment, which consists in prolonging

Table 6.4   Under 25-year-olds in the sports sector of EU Member States, 1990–98

Country	Under 25 years old 1990		1998	
	No.	%	No.	%
Belgium	1 000	10.8	1 800	12.4
Finland[1]	1 701	22.6	1 014	14.6
France	8 100	13.1	9 600	10.1
Germany[2]	–	–	7 500	7.9
Netherlands	3 000	16.7	5 000	20.8
Portugal	4 000	41.7	2 700	18.9
Sweden[1]	–	–	4 300	16.8
United Kingdom	30 200	27.3	75 400	34.0
Total employment of workers under 25 years old in the sports sector	47 600		107 700	
Total number of workers in the sports sector	216 928		496 456	
% workers under 25 years old in the sports sector		21.9		21.7

Notes: – data not available. [1] Percentage employment in recreational, cultural and sporting activities. [2] West Germany only.

Source: As for table 6.1, p. 92.

their training. Although in no European country are young people in a better position than adults with regard to employment, the divergences found between the countries suggest that the various institutional strategies adopted have a direct impact on the distribution of the working population by age group. In France, it was shown that the main cause of the decline in youth employment was training.[9] In fact, in France, as in Belgium and the Mediterranean countries, an internal employment market prevails from which young people remain excluded for a long time (or hold insecure jobs).

The strategies of young people, but also public authorities, are consequently to promote a detour towards training. Whereas in the United Kingdom (and the Netherlands) young people end their studies very early without benefiting from schemes combining training and work (as is the case in Germany), they are penalized less than in France regarding employment access. On the other hand, they are undoubtedly penalized more regarding their working conditions, which seems to be confirmed in the analysis of the percentage of part-time work (which in the United Kingdom and the Netherlands exceeds 40 per cent).

Table 6.5   Women in the sports sector of EU Member States, 1990–98

Country	1990		1998	
	No.	%	No.	%
Austria	–	–	3 400	44.0
Finland[1]	–	–	3 800	54.8
France	25 600	41.4	36 200	38.2
Germany[2]	–	–	42 500	44.7
Italy	11 800	24.2	19 400	34.5
Luxembourg	80	42.1	100	41.5
Netherlands	8 000	44.4	11 000	45.8
Portugal	3 100	32.3	5 800	40.6
Sweden[1]	–	–	12 100	47.5
Spain	7 900	28.0	19 400	34.5
United Kingdom	51 900	46.9	107 000	48.3
Women employed in the sports sector	108 380		241 300	
Total employed in the sports sector	277 334		546 263	
% women employed in the sports sector		39.1		44.2

Notes: – data not available. [1] Percentage employment in recreational, cultural and sporting activities. [2] West Germany only.

Source: As for table 6.1, p. 92.

Women and employment

Contrary to the preconceived ideas about the sector (which claim that it is more male dominated than the others), the sports sector does not present any strong differences from other sectors with regard to the presence of women. However, the increase in the proportion of women is rising rapidly compared to the increase in aggregate women's employment (table 6.5). Here too, there are significant national disparities in the EU countries between those of the north and of the south.

Self-employed workers

The proportion of self-employed workers in the sports sector, which is slightly higher than the mean for employment in Europe in 1990, is falling. The situation in Belgium, Italy the Netherlands and Sweden seems to differ from that in the other countries (table 6.6).

Table 6.6   Self-employed workers in the sports sector of EU Member States, 1990–98

Country	1990		1998	
	No.	%	No.	%
Austria	1 500	16.0	1 200	15.4
Belgium	1 392	15.1	3 617	24.9
Finland[1]	800	10.6	1 200	17.2
France	–	–	13 200	14.0
Germany[2]	–	–	18 700	19.7
Italy	15 400	31.6	–	–
Netherlands	4 000	22.2	4 000	16.7
Portugal	700	7.3	900	6.3
Sweden[1]	–	–	4 500	17.7
Spain	2 400	8.5	9 700	17.2
United Kingdom	–	–	27 000	12.2
Total self-employed in the sports sector	26 192		84 017	
Total employed in the sports sector	130 646		560 546	
% self-employed in the sports sector		20.0		15.0

Notes: – data not available. [1] Percentage employment in recreational, cultural and sporting activities. [2] West Germany only.

Source: As for table 6.1, p. 92.

Self-employed work seems to have been particularly well developed in the sports sector in the early 1990s, although it is now declining towards the European mean for all sectors together. We exercise caution in our analysis, however, because we lack data for France, Germany, Sweden and the United Kingdom in 1990.

Unpaid workers and professionals

The relationship between unpaid work and remunerated work in the sports sector is often problematic. The real difficulty in measuring the contribution of unpaid work makes it tricky to carry out analyses to assess the potential number of jobs it represents. This type of analysis could prove dangerous for the associative sector, which has developed and survives thanks to unpaid work. A few interesting ideas can be taken from the large number of studies conducted on this subject. Regarding unpaid work, we can distinguish between three main groups of countries (Halba and Le Net, 1997): (a) those with a substantial amount of unpaid work in sport (Scandinavian countries and Switzerland); (b) those with an intermediate amount of unpaid work in sport (France, Germany, United Kingdom); and (c) those with a low amount of unpaid work in sport (Italy, Portugal, Spain).

Figure 6.2   Volunteering and employment in the EU Member States, 1998 (percentage for 1,000 inhabitants)

Percentage for 1,000 inhabitants

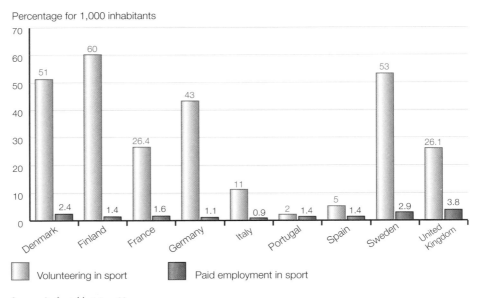

Source: As for table 6.1, p. 92.

Comparing the existing data on unpaid work and employment, the question arises as to whether it is possible to observe competition or complementarities between unpaid work in sport and employment. Figure 6.2 shows that it does not seem possible to derive any precise rule:

- the countries with a substantial amount of unpaid work in sport are also among those where employment is the most highly developed (Denmark, Sweden);

- this is not always true (Finland, Germany); and

- conversely, countries with little unpaid work are not necessarily particularly well supplied with jobs (Portugal, Spain).

Other characteristics of employment in sport

The seasonal nature of sports activities is also a very important dimension in the structure of employment in sport, especially where it is linked to tourist activities. No representative data are available to analyse this dimension. Certain professions in sport correspond to a short career (in particular for 30,000 to 40,000 professional sportspersons). Here too, no data are available to measure the length of careers in sports.

Conclusion and proposals

Having taken stock, it is now a matter of proposing a set of measures and initiatives to contribute to both the development of sporting activities and to employment in the sector, while respecting the main policies defined in a "European model of sport" to bring together public, associative and commercial operators.

Develop the sector by organizing the relationships between the sports operators

Developing sporting activities within the EU involves building a system ensuring complementary relations between associative operators (sports movement), public operators (local and regional authorities, central governments) and commercial operators (sports, entertainment or leisure companies). The specific tasks of these operators must be specified or reaffirmed.

The public expression at European and national levels of a political project resulting from negotiations with all the operators (whether in the form of a law or a declaration)[11] is a prerequisite for developing sporting activities under the necessary conditions of transparency. A suitable tax policy could provide an effective accompaniment to introducing such a framework.

The development of the "spirit of enterprise", the first recommendation of the European Council of Luxembourg on Employment, November 1997 (European Council, 2001), when adapted to the sports context, presupposes that the forms of expression of individual or collective initiatives coming under associative, public or commercial frameworks can find their place:

- The encouragement of associationism must be accompanied by respect for its principles and the rules of democracy; particular effort should be made with regard to adolescents wishing to develop projects themselves in this field.

- Facilitating the creation of commercial structures can be undertaken not only by encouraging the young entrepreneurs in the field of sports services, but also by monitoring the activities with a monopolistic tendency of certain large groups of operators.

- Likewise, it is no doubt necessary to avoid the public services taking charge of missions which would be assumed without difficulty by the other operators and to concentrate their activity on the less-favoured groups of the population and on actions to promote development (including in the form of support for practising sport: "sports tickets", for example).

Boost the skills of the human resources in the associative sector to promote social development

The associative sports movement is undergoing a crisis throughout Europe with regard to its tasks and its organization. It is encountering difficulties in coping with the diversification in the forms of practising sport (from the production of entertainment to leisure sports) and the abuse in its democratic functioning. The solution to these problems undoubtedly involves increased professionalism of the people involved in the sports associations. But it is necessary to watch out for the emerging trend of "transforming the associations into businesses". All professionalism that would lead to the weakening of the associative spirit (to give way to a user or customer logic) would be counter-productive. Adjustment to the trend in demand in an associative framework also involves "training" the volunteer leaders and controlled recruitment of professionals to promote the associative project.

Active participation by the members in the life of the association is a prerequisite for being able to play a role in strengthening social links in the local area. This voluntary participation cannot be obtained without ensuring true democratic debate within the association itself.

The many initiatives taken in the EU Member States to develop employment in the associative sports sector, in particular in the highly suitable context of the Local Development and Employment Initiatives (ILDE) programme, should be conducted in this spirit. While respecting the independence of this movement, the public authorities can use the contract procedure to encourage it in the pursuit of its tasks.

Construct a professional sports sector and sports-related sectors as a prerequisite for improving the quality of employment in sport

The world of sport based on unpaid volunteers has not always sized up the requirements of the move towards professionalization, especially with regard to respect of labour law. Remuneration that is undeclared or outside the rules of the employment contract too frequently disregards any respect held for the basic rights of employees. The uncontrolled increase in the number of part-time jobs, the almost total lack of collective consideration of the seasonal nature of sport or equality between men and women, and the inadequacy of measures for retraining top-level sportspeople are a consequence of the low level of recognition of the potential role of the social partners and social dialogue in the sports sector.

This inadequacy, which the supervisory authorities sometimes try to remedy through regulations, also has consequences for the organization of work and the conditions for the production of services.

As very small (commercial or associative) enterprises are involved, as we have said, the employers and employees are not highly organized. A public initiative should facilitate the emergence of representation of the sector at national and European levels (based on practice in France, the Netherlands and the United Kingdom, for example).

Improve the relationship between training and employment and the capacity for occupational integration in the sports sector

The occupational integration of young people in sports companies and associations often takes place under difficult conditions. Young people finishing university courses are generally ill prepared to exercise a profession in a sports organization. The unemployment rate among such graduates is too high in certain EU Member States, and the proportion of young people trained in sport science and working in the sector is too low.

On the other hand, the sports movement rarely has the means to provide the training to meet the needs. The result is that the number of people engaging in a profession in the sports sector without suitable training is very high in most EU Member States. Better adaptation of training to employment in a sector of very small enterprises entails systematic development of schemes combining training and work, defined and negotiated by the social partners.

Although it corresponds to general principles common to all services sectors, the respect for the social functions assigned to sport must lead to the development of employment in the sports sector being undertaken in accordance with its specific character.

Notes

[1] Data collected and compared in France, the United Kingdom, Italy and Belgium – European Observatoire of Sports and Employment (EOSE), 1999.

[2] Statistical Classification of Economic Activities in the European Community.

[3] See http://www.eose.org/home.htm, accessed 16 Mar. 2006.

[4] Even where these are merely waymarks or rudimentary adaptations.

[5] This is a very varied group, ranging from the manufacture of means of transport for sporting activities (boats, cycles, cars, etc.) to clothing and footwear and sporting goods in the true sense of the term (skis, balls, etc.), and sports equipment (body-building equipment). These activities are divided between NACE codes 18, 19, 34, 35, 36, 50, 51 and 52.

[6] In the growing process of "instrumentation" of sporting activities, instruments for monitoring activity are developing and being paid increasing attention by the general public.

[7] According to the proposal of the EOSE with Eurostat support; see Le Roux and Camy, 1997b.

[8] The fall in the mean undoubtedly stems from the significant fall in the United Kingdom (from 67 per cent to 43.2 per cent). Taking a longer period into account (1980–98), this in fact corresponds to a general upward trend (from 33.9 per cent in 1980 to 43.2 per cent in 1996).

[9] Source from European Commission – DG X, European Network of Sport Science Institutes, European Observatoire of Employment in Sport: *Sport and Employment in Europe*, Final Report, Sep. 1999, p. 26.

[11] In the form corresponding to the specific national characteristics.

Bibliography

Andreff, W. 1999. "The future of sport in Europe", Communication to the Fifth Forum of Sport Science Institutes (Jyväskylä), 3–6 Sep.

—, et al. 1995. *Les enjeux économiques du sport en Europe: Financement et impact économique.* Paris, Dalloz.

Bazzoli, L.; Rodet, N. 1995. "Le rôle des institutions du travail dans la dynamique économique: Vers une analyse institutionnaliste en terme de 'système national de travail et d'emploi' " (first version), in *Actes de la 7ème Conférence de l'European Association of Labour Economists.* Lyon, 7–10 Sep.

Bell, D. 1976. *Vers la société post-industrielle.* Paris, Laffont.

Benoit-Guilleboto, O. 1995. "Les formes nationales d'institutionnalisation des marchés du travail en Europe", in *Chroniques des tendances de la société française et comparaisons internationales* (Paris, Observatoire français des Conjonctures Economiques), Vol. 12, Jan., pp. 179–185.

Boissonnat, J. 1995. "Travailler autrement", in Commissariat Général au Plan: *Le travail dans vingt ans*, Rapport de la commission présidée par Jean Boissonnat. Paris, Odile Jacob/La Documentation Française, pp. 9–33.

Camy, J.; Le Roux, N. 1998. "L'emploi dans le secteur et la filière du sport en Europe: Situation et perspectives", Report of the Congress "Il diploma e la laurea in educazione fisica nella realta professionale attuale e nelle prospettive future", Svoltosi, ISEF Lombardia, 23 Nov. 1997, pp. 27–37.

Castel, R. 1995. *La métamorphose de la question sociale, une chronique du salariat*. Paris, Fayard.

Central Council for Physical Education (CCPR). 1990. *The organisation of sport and recreation in Britain*, Additional note, 1997. London.

Council of Europe, Clearing House, CDDS. 1992. *Les structures du sport en Europe: Situation dans les pays du Comité pour le développement du sport du Conseil de l'Europe*. Brussels.

Council of Europe. 1995. *Le rôle social du sport dans la société: Santé, socialisation, économie*. Strasbourg.

—. 1997. *Les structures du sport en Europe: Situation dans les pays du Comité pour le développement du sport du Conseil de l'Europe*, new edition. New York, CDDS.

Collins, M. 1999. *Going it alone: Small firms in sport and leisure in the English Midlands*. Unpublished paper.

Cooke, A. 1994. *The economics of leisure and sport*. Oxford, Routledge

Coopers & Lybrand. 1994. *L'impact des activités de la Communauté Européenne sur le sport*. Brussels, DG X, European Commission.

Coriat, B.; Weinstein, O. 1995. *Les nouvelles théories de l'entreprise*. Paris, Le Livre de Poche.

Desrosières, A.; Thevenot, L. 1996. *Les catégories socio-professionnelles*. Paris, La Découverte.

Doeringer, P.; Piore, M. 1971. *Internal labor markets and manpower analysis health*. Lanham, MD, Lexington Books.

Dubar, C. 1996. *La socialisation: Construction des identités sociales et professionnelles*, second edition. Paris, Armand Colin.

European Commission. 1993. *White Paper on growth, competitiveness and employment: The challenges and ways forward into the 21st century* (Delors Commission), COM(93) 700 final, 5 Dec.

—, DG X. 1999. European Network of Sport Science Institutes, European Observatoire of Employment in Sport: *Sport and employment in Europe*, Final Report, Sep.

European Council, Presidency Conclusions. 2001. "Conclusions of the Extraordinary Council Meeting on Employment, Luxembourg, 20–21 Nov. 1997."

Exercise Association for England. 1997. "Training and professional regulations", in *Exercise*, No. 14, May/June.

Fontela, E. 1995. *Perspectives à long terme de la croissance et de l'emploi: L'avenir du travail et des loisirs*. Paris, OECD Poche, pp. 27–48.

Freyssinet, J. 1988. "Crise, diversification des formes d'emploi et transformations du rapport salarial", in *Actes du colloque de la Revue Travail et Emploi: L'évolution des formes d'emploi* (Paris), pp. 142–149.

Gadrey, J. 1992. *L'économie des services*. Paris, La Découverte.

Gaspard, M. 1988. *Les services contre le chômage*. Paris, Syros Alternatives.

Gazier, B. 1992. *Economie du travail et de l'emploi*, second edition. Paris, Dalloz.

Gershunyi, J. 1978. *After industrial society? The emerging self-service economy*. London, Macmillan.

Gorz, A.1988. *Métamorphoses du travail, quête du sens*. Paris, Gallilée.

Granovetter, M. 1994. "Les institutions économiques comme constructions sociales: un cadre d'analyse", in *Analyse économique des conventions*. Paris, Presses Universitaires de France (PUF).

Gratton, C.; Taylor, P. 1985. *Sport and leisure: An economic analysis*. London, E&FN SPON.

Halba, B. 1997. *Economie du sport*. Paris, Economica, Blackwell Publishing.

—; Le Net, M. 1997. *Bénévolat et volontariat*. Paris, La Documentation Française.

Hanson, A.; Minten, S.; Taylor, P. 1996. "Graduate employment in the sport and recreation industry: A study of student, graduate and employer perspectives", SPRITO/UK Higher Education Standing Conference on Leisure Recreation and Sport, United Kingdom.

Heineman, K.; Schubert, M. 1994. *Der Sportverein*. Schorndorf, Verlag Karl Hofmann.

Henley Centre for Forecasting. 1990. *The economic impact and importance of sport in the United Kingdom in 1990*. London, The Sports Council.

Horch, H.D. 1994. "On the socio-economics of voluntary organisations", in *Voluntas* (New York, NY), Vol. 5, pp. 219–230.

International Labour Office (ILO). 1998 edition. *International Standard Classification of Occupations* (ISCO 88). Geneva.

Irlinger, P., et al. 1985. *Les pratiques sportives des français*. Paris, INSEP.

Kinnaird, B. 1996. "British ski instructors kept off Alpine slopes", in *BASI* (British Association of Snowsports Instructors) (Glenmore, Scotland), 7 Nov.

Le Roux, N. 1998. "Analyse comparée de l'emploi dans les services sportifs en France et au Royaume-Uni", doctoral thesis, Université Claude Bernard Lyon 1.

—; Camy, J. 1997a. *Nomenclature européenne des activités économiques sportives et en relation avec le sport*. Barcelona, Edition du REISS/EOSE.

—; —. 1997b. *Nomenclature européenne des professions du sport et en relation avec le sport*. Barcelona, Edition du REISS/EOSE.

—; Chantelat, P.; Camy, J. 1999. "Sports and employment in Europe: Situation and perspective", in European Commission – DG X: *Sport and employment in Europe*, 1999, p. 80.

Maurice, M.; Sellier, F.; Sylvestre, J. 1982. *Politique d'éducation et organisation industrielle en France et en Allemagne*. Paris, PUF.

Meda, D. 1995. *Le travail: Une valeur en voie de disparition*. Paris, Aubier.

Menard, C. 1995. *L'économie des organisations*. Paris, La Découverte.

Mietowski, P. 1997. "L'efficacité du modèle britannique de marché du travail", in *Problèmes économiques*, No. 2502 (Paribas), 22–25 Jan.

Organisation for Economic Co-operation and Development (OECD). 1995. *L'avenir du travail et des loisirs*. Paris, Poche.

Perrot, A. 1992. *Les nouvelles théories du marché du travail*. Paris, La Découverte.

Pescante, M. 1993. "Les différents modèles européens de législation sportive", in Association de Comités Olympiques nationaux d'Europe (ACNOE): *La législation sportive en Europe*. Rome.

Pociello, C. 1994. "Le futur comme nouvelle forme d'enjeu", in *Sport et Pouvoirs au XX° siècle* (Grenoble, Presses Universitaires), pp. 139–176.

Sports Council. 1996. *Valuing volunteers in UK sport: A Sports Council survey into the voluntary branch in UK sport*. United Kingdom.

SPRITO. 1996. *National Training Organisation for Sport and Recreation and allied occupations: Bid for recognition*. Lancashire, United Kingdom.

Vimont, E. 1997. "Les emplois britanniques vus à la loupe", in *Sociétal* (Paris), 14 Dec., pp. 28–32.

THE EUROPEAN SOCIAL DIALOGUE IN SPORT

7

Roger Blanpain and Michele Colucci

The origin and format of European social dialogue[1]

The promotion of social dialogue constitutes one of the key elements of European social policies. This follows clearly from Article 138(1) of the European Community Treaty (TEC), which reads as follows: "The Commission shall have the task of promoting the consultation of management and labour at Community level and shall take any relevant measure to facilitate their dialogue by ensuring balanced support for the parties."[2] The notion of social dialogue also includes collective bargaining and the conclusion of agreements between the social partners. Consequently, Article 139 (1) of the same Treaty states: "Should management and labour so desire, the dialogue between them at Community level may lead to contractual relations, including agreements." Social partners are representative organizations of employers and employees, which are cross-industry or sectoral.

European social dialogue in its current form has evolved considerably since its launch in 1985 and it is now well established. European *tripartite* social dialogue takes place within the Tripartite Social Summit for Growth and Employment,[3] established in March 2003, as well as conducting dialogue on macroeconomics, employment, social protection, and education and training. European *bipartite* social dialogue takes place within the cross-industry social dialogue committee and 30 sectoral social dialogue committees. These organizations have affiliates in most or all of the EU Member States.

Quantitatively, the work of the various social dialogue committees has resulted in the adoption of more than 300 joint texts by the social partners, and they have undertaken many transnational joint projects.

In recent years there has been a *qualitative shift* in the nature of social dialogue towards greater autonomy. This is reflected by the increasing adoption by the social partners of "new generation" texts, in which they undertake certain commitments or make recommendations to their national members, and seek to actively follow up the text at the national level.

By August 2004, 30 sectoral committees were in place in the following sectors:

- agriculture (sugar); sea fishing; commerce; textile and clothing; footwear; tanning and leather;

- aviation; civil aviation; road transport; railways;

- banking; insurance; private security; postal services;

- cleaning;

- electricity; telecommunication;

- mining;

- hospitality services;

- inland waterways;

- live performance;

- local and regional government;

- construction; shipbuilding; woodwork; furniture;

- temporary work.

Altogether the above sectors employ more than 60 million people.

Social dialogue has resulted in the adoption of over 40 joint texts by the cross-industry social partners and approximately 300 by the sectoral social partners. It has also evolved considerably in terms of the topics addressed, as table 7.1 shows.

Table 7.1   Number of European sectoral joint texts per topic, 1997–2003

Sustainable development	4
Non-discrimination	5
Working time	7
Health and safety	10
Enlargement	11
Employment	16
Social aspects of EU policies	17
Training	18
Working conditions	28
Social dialogue	29
Economic and/or sectoral policies	30

These texts take a variety of forms, ranging from joint opinions to guidelines, codes of conduct and agreements. Council directives have implemented some of the agreements concluded by the cross-industry social partners and those in the transport sector.

Process-oriented texts

The European social partners make recommendations of various kinds to their members for follow-up, and these recommendations should involve regular evaluation of the progress made towards achieving their objectives in order to ensure they have a real impact. The implementation of some aspects of these texts may require cooperation with national public authorities.

There are two main types of instrument falling within this category.

Frameworks of action

Frameworks of action consist of the identification of certain policy priorities towards which the national social partners undertake to work. These priorities serve as benchmarks and the social partners report annually on the action taken to follow up these texts. Example: *The Framework of Action on the Lifelong Development of Competences and Qualification.*[4]

Guidelines and codes of conduct

Guidelines and codes of conduct make recommendations and/or provide guidelines to national affiliates concerning the establishment of standards or principles. In some cases these are intended to serve as principles or minimum European standards to be implemented at national or company level. In other cases they seek to promote higher standards than those provided for in existing legislation. This category also includes codes of conduct intended to promote the implementation in companies' supply chains of existing internationally agreed standards in the area of labour law established by international conventions.[5]

Joint opinions and tools: Exchange of information

This category consists of social partner texts, which contribute to exchanging information, either from the social partners to the European institutions and/or national public authorities, or by explaining the implications of EU policies to national members.

Joint opinions

This category includes the majority of social partner texts adopted over the years such as their joint opinions and joint statements. It also includes texts that respond to a Community consultation (Green and White papers, consultation documents, Communications), or that adopt a joint position with regard to a given Community policy. Joint opinions explicitly ask the Commission to adopt a particular stance, or to undertake studies or other actions. A pertinent example is the *Joint Opinion of the European Social Partners in Aviation 2001.*[6]

Declarations

This category refers to texts that are essentially declarations – usually directed at the social partners themselves – outlining future work and activities which the social partners intend to undertake (e.g. the organization of seminars, round-tables, etc.). *The Joint Statement and Final Report on the Study on Life-long Learning in the Electricity Sector, signed in 2003,*[7] is a clear example of such acts.

Tools

This category refers to the tools developed by the social partners, such as guides and manuals providing practical advice to employees and companies on subjects such as vocational training, health and safety, and public procurement, often with the assistance of Community grants. Two recent examples include: the *European vocational training manual for basic guarding (private security)*[8] and the *Brochure on tutoring in the construction industry, 2004.*[9]

Procedural texts

This final category consists of texts that seek to lay down the rules for the bipartite dialogue between the parties. This includes the cross-industry social partners' Agreement of 31 October 1991,[10] which made proposals for the revision of the policy-making procedures in the EC Treaty in the social policy field. The Intergovernmental Conference of 1991 incorporated these proposals virtually verbatim into the Treaty on European Union 1992. This category also includes the social partner texts, which determine the rules of procedure for the sectoral social dialogue committees.

Social dialogue in the sports sector

During the past years, the European Commission has supported the creation of a Social Dialogue Committee in the sports sector in order to identify the relevant social partners at the national level, encourage exchanges between them, and form a committee for a sectoral social dialogue. The Committee's goals are to develop a sustainable framework to promote the sports sector, improve working conditions, and promote better education and vocational training.

The sports sector in Europe

It is quite complicated to define the sports sector because it is made up of several segments organized not only around sports activities in the strict sense, but also around a wide range of services.

In the sports world we can identify:

- *professional sports businesses*, which are oriented essentially towards putting on sports events;

- *competitive sports associations*, which represent the dominant element of the sports sector and come together in sports federations;

- *sporting leisure associations* with their own particular features and their own identity in sports such as fitness, horse riding, sailing, etc.;

- *"not-for-profit organizations"* aiming at the social integration of groups such as people with disabilities, minorities, etc.;

These four categories enjoy relative autonomy, which varies depending on the EU country involved. In some cases, they act under the guidance of National Olympic Committees and sports confederations, and often receive support from the public authorities. Professional football, for instance, has powerful lobbying resources and is seeking to be recognized by the European authorities.

The "social partners" in sport

The situation of the sports sector, as just described, has various consequences for social dialogue. First of all, it is very difficult to identify among all the stakeholders the "right social partners", i.e. those who can represent both employers and employees in this particular sector.

In this regard it is opportune to stress that the European Commission itself, in Article 1 of its Decision of 20 May 1998[11] on the establishment of sectoral dialogue committees, stated that:

> Sectoral dialogue committees are to be established in those sectors where the social partners make a joint request to take part in a dialogue at European level and where organisations representing both sides of industry fulfil the following criteria:

a) relate to specific sectors or categories and be organised at European level;

b) consist of organisations which are themselves an integral and recognised part of Member States' social partner structures and have the capacity to negotiate agreements and which are representative of several Member States;

c) have adequate structures to ensure their effective participation in the work of the committees.

In fact, the complexity of the sports world, at professional and amateur levels, has slowed down the creation of social partners. In some cases national legislation set apart the workers' organizations from social dialogue; on the employers' side, there are very few single organizations representing all the employers in the sports sector. In some countries, the professional leagues themselves act as representative organizations when legislation permits. In the world of football, the European Professional Football Leagues (EPFL)[12] have started a tripartite dialogue with UEFA[13] and FIFPro.[14] In fact, representatives of the three organizations have agreed to recognize each other as the appropriate parties to start a "European Football Dialogue". Such a framework between UEFA, the Leagues and the players' unions has been presented as a means to build a better future for European football, in the interests of all stakeholders.

Assessment and prospects

Seminars, conferences, and roundtables have been organized at different levels since 2002, when social dialogue in the sports sector officially started. The results achieved so far have been very poor: problems related to the representation of the parties still remain open and the objectives to be achieved are not clear.

Nevertheless, the impression is that everybody seems to go for a collective agreement at EU level. In order to achieve such a goal, it might be appropriate to have a look at those agreements already reached at national level, where we can identify the following:

- a *global collective agreement*, specific to the sports sector, whether single or articulated. In general, there is a national collective agreement covering the sports sector entirely, or several of these segments, sometimes integrating a number of collective agreements specific to some of these segments. France, the Netherlands and Sweden are in this situation;[15]

- a *fragmented collective agreement*: this is the case with Belgium, where there are three different agreements: one for professional sports, another for association sports attached to socio-educational activities in the round, and one for commercial leisure activities, attached to the services of the individual sector;

- a *single segment agreement*, i.e. reduced to a single segment, usually professional sport, such as one for each given sport: football, basketball, etc., negotiated independently from each other, as seems to be the case in Austria, Denmark, Ireland, Portugal and Spain.

Perhaps at the EU level the first kind of agreement is the easiest to achieve. In France, for instance, a National Collective Agreement on Sport (CCN Sport)[16] was signed on 7 July 2005 by the employers' organizations[17] jointly and six trade unions of sport workers. After seven years of negotiations, the social partners have gathered consensus on this text that contributes greatly to social progress for people working in the sports sector. The social partners will meet regularly to develop a common policy on the issue of professional training in the sector. The signing of this national collective agreement in the sports sector makes a major contribution to the specificity of sport through the adaptation of the common law to sport.

Of course, it is not only a question of content and scope but, above all, a matter of political willingness. In fact there is a high risk that the stakeholders act in an autonomous way and play their own game without forming part of an overall strategy. By doing that, they eventually will fail to take an integrated approach.

Notes

[1] See further: Commission of the European Communities: *Communication: Partnership for change in an enlarged Europe – Enhancing the contribution of European social dialogue* (Brussels, 1 Aug. 2004 COM (2004) 557 final); and Roger Blanpain: *European labour law* (The Hague, Kluwer Law International, 9th edition, 2003), pp. 62–64, 152–172 and 549–589.

[2] "Treaty of Amsterdam amending the treaty on European Union, the treaties establishing the European communities and related acts", in *Official Journal*, C 340, Article 138 (ex Article 118a) (1) 10 November 1997 (see: http://europa.eu.int/eur-lex/lex/en/treaties/dat/11997D/htm/11997D.html, accessed 20 Mar. 2006).

[3] "Council Decision 2003/174/CE establishing a Tripartite Social Summit for Growth and Employment", in *Official Journal*, L70 of 6 March 2003 (see: http://europa.eu.int/scadplus/ leg/en/cha/c10715.htm, accessed 20 Mar. 2006).

[4] In March 2002 the European social partners adopted a framework of action for the lifelong development of competences and qualifications, as a contribution to the implementation of the Lisbon strategy. The social partners play an indispensable role in the development, validation and recognition of vocational competences and qualifications at all levels, and are partners in the promotion of an enhanced cooperation in this area.

[5] As an example, the World Federation of Sporting Goods Industry adopted a "Code of conduct: Guiding Principles" document. These principles are based on standards set up by the relevant ILO Conventions. For more information see: http://www.wfsgi.org, accessed 20 Feb. 2006.

[6] "Civil aviation social partners conclude working time accord": The European-level social partners in the air transport sector – the European Transport Workers' Federation (ETF), the European Cockpit Association (ECA), the Association of European Airlines (AEA), the European Regions Airlines Association (ERA) and the International Air Carrier Association (IACA) signed an agreement on the organization of working time on 22 March 2000, with effect in 2001 (see: http://www.eiro.eurofound. eu.int/2000/04/inbrief/eu0004238n.html, accessed 20 Mar. 2006).

[7] For further information and a full copy of the report see: http://www.eurelectric.org/PublicDoc.asp? ID=29804, accessed 20 Mar. 2006.

[8] L. Spaninks (National Centre for Innovation of Education and Training, Netherlands, CINOP), L. Quinn and J. Byrne (Federation Training Services, FTS): *European vocational training manual for basic guarding (private security)* (Lyon, Apr. 2001). The authors worked in close cooperation with members of the European Federation of Security Service – CoESS – and UNI-Europa, supported by the European Commission: DG Education and Culture and DG Employment and Social Affairs (see: http://wwwunion-network.org/uniproperty.nsf, accessed 30 Mar. 2006).

[9] Construction Industry Federation (see: http://www.cif.ie/asp/section.asp?s=1, accessed 20 Mar. 2006).

[10] Agreement signed 31 October 1991 in Brussels. Terms of Agreement can be found at http://forum. europa.eu.int/Public/irc/empl/esdo_accords_europeens/library?l=/doc/industry_dialogue/911031_do c/_EN_1.0_&a=d, accessed 20 Mar. 2006.

[11] "Commission Decision of 20 May 1998 on the establishment of Sectoral Dialogue Committees promoting the dialogue between the social partners at European level". European Commission, COM(1998) 322 final. For Article 1 and the full Commission Decision, see: http://europa.eu.int/ comm/employment_social/social_dialogue/docs/98_500_ec_en.pdf, accessed 20 Mar. 2006.

[12] The EPFL is the grouping of major European leagues, founded in 1998. For further information, see: http:// www.uefa.com, accessed 20 Mar. 2006.

[13] UEFA is the governing body of European football and has the responsibility for safeguarding the development and interests of the sport at all levels (both professional and amateur) both in the EU and the rest of Europe (for further information see: http://www.uefa.com, accessed 20 Mar. 2006).

[14] Fédération Internationale des Footballeurs Professionels (FIFPro) is the leading worldwide representative organization for professional players (players' organizations). For further information see: http://www.fifpro.org, accessed 20 Mar. 2006.

[15] A global collective agreement can easily focus on some minimum standards, such as wages, and on some sensitive issues like doping and training of athletes.

[16] "Convention Collective Nationale du Sport", established 7 July 2005. For full terms and clauses of the agreement, see: http://www.cosmos.asso.fr/pdf/CCNS.pdf, accessed 30 Mar. 2006.

[17] The Social Council of the Sport Movement (CoSMoS) has as its main objective to defend the employers' interests in the sport movement. For this reason, it represented its members during the negotiations of the National Collective Agreement on Sport. According to article 2 of its Statute, CoSMoS "researches and protects the rights as well as the moral and materials interests of its members". It is eventually charged with disseminating information, organizing professional training and advising its members. For more information, visit the CoSMoS website: http://www.cosmos.asso.fr, accessed 30 Mar. 2006.

PROMOTING SPORT IN AFRICA: AN OPPORTUNITY FOR THE EAST AFRICAN COMMUNITY'S SOCIAL AND ECONOMIC DEVELOPMENT

8

Michael K. Boit

Introduction

This chapter discusses the historical development of sports in Africa. It high-lights sports as an integral part of national development, and attempts to assess the strengths and weaknesses of African efforts to develop sports oppor-tunities and encourage sports participation.

Funding is seen as the biggest stumbling block to developing sports in Africa. Creating a larger market would spur economic growth and hence create a favourable climate for sports development. The East African Community has the opportunity to use this expanded market to promote socio-economic development through sport. Special attention is given to grass-roots develop-ment that forms the nucleus of growth and development of sport in every nation. The role of higher education in the promotion of research and develop-ment is highlighted as a crucial component in the growth and prosperity of any nation. In conclusion, the chapter makes specific recommendations for policy makers from various sectors of national economies.

Economic and sports development

European, Asian and Latin American countries are forming regional blocs to promote culture and a wider market for economic prosperity. The European Union (EU) has established a common currency and is already a world economic power. However, according to World Bank classification, all three East African countries (Kenya, the United Republic of Tanzania and Uganda) are among the least-developed countries (LDCs). This categorization is based on gross national product (GNP) per capita, which is less than US$750 per annum.

This situation raises a complex problem that requires multiple approaches, one of which is sport. Sport has a significant role in economic, social and political development. In the case of the East African Community (EAC), sports will strengthen friendship ties, which go beyond the dichotomy of winning or losing. The entire African continent should form regional blocs to develop both economic and sporting ties. Although there are already regional trade blocs (e.g. the Common Market for Eastern and Southern Africa (COMESA)), these countries need to concentrate on aspects beyond business ventures, such as culture and sport.

The regional alliances in Africa would fall naturally into five major regions: Eastern Africa; Central Africa; Northern Africa; Southern Africa; and West Africa. When regional resources are pooled, trade improves and countries can afford better sports infrastructure, thus raising sports competition standards.[1] Forming regional blocs will boost trade, agriculture, economy, culture and, eventually, sport because it will help to combat poverty, the most severe constraint on sports development in Africa.

Economic prosperity has a direct bearing on sports development. Thirty years of divided efforts have harmed East Africa economically, making most nations perpetually unable to meet a reasonable sport budget. African unity on a regional or continental basis may redeem the continent through economic revival and the creation of harmony, much like the EU. In this regard, the rejuvenated East African Community holds the key to sports development in East Africa.

Corporate sponsorship is needed, but will depend upon economic stability and growth. One of the root causes of economic instability is civil strife, which is directly related to poverty. Civil strife is exacerbated by high unemployment and a struggle for resources, a recipe for ethnic tension and economic instability. A united East Africa can both spur economic growth and absorb ethnic tension through the creation of greater opportunities. A stable economy in turn enables an environment for economic and sports development. The prospect of a wider East African market means that some of the major corporations will generate sufficient funds to take an active role in sports sponsorship.

According to Andreff (2000), professor of economics at the University of Paris and vice president of the International Association of Sport Economists, the lack of valuable sports data is itself an indication of underdevelopment. Facts and figures on sports development are readily available in the United States and in Europe; in Africa, such data are non-existent. Economic disparity is generally one of the greatest disadvantages handicapping African sports stars at world championships and the Olympic Games where African athletes line up with those from Europe and the Americas, reflecting the diversity of facilities, equipment and budgetary allocations. This inequality is evident in technical events or events that require high skills development because they require expensive facilities and equipment. Forming regional blocs in Africa will eventually eliminate the financial handicaps to create a level playing field.

Organized athletics in Kenya date back to 1951 when Archie Evans inaugurated the Kenya Amateur Athletic Association (KAAA). The first East African Athletic Championship, in which Kenya, Uganda and Tanganyika (now the United Republic of Tanzania) competed, took place in 1952. Three years later, these championships became known as the East African Territorial Championships. The 1958 British Empire and Commonwealth Games, held in Cardiff, United Kingdom, marked a significant achievement in East African athletics when two Kenyans won Commonwealth Medals for the first time in history.

The East African Athletic Championships has become a powerful springboard, adequately setting the stage for future success in middle- and long-distance running in East Africa. Although Kenya has sustained a high profile of success in middle- and long-distance racing, the achievement would have been greater if the East African regional championships had survived the post-independent political tensions and subsequent lack of cooperation in regional sports championships. Most sports in the region have remained dormant for many reasons, including economic hardship, lack of sports facilities, lack of technical knowledge and lack of exposure.

Now, out of 26 Olympic sports, the African continent is represented in only four disciplines, including athletics (track and field), soccer, boxing and swimming, mainly by South African participants. For over four decades, Kenya has been taking part in the Olympics in two events: track and field, and boxing. However, electronic scoring may push out African boxers at the Olympics, leaving only track and field. When Kenya and Uganda had regular boxing competitions, there was a respectable standard of boxing in East Africa. Now, the lack of regular competition has caused the two countries to perform poorly at international championships. A unified EAC, however, may turn things around for sports development.

African sports development has been haphazard for the past 40 years. Economic crises and dwindling resources make sports seem like a luxury. Professor Andreff (2000) argues that poverty in the continent manifests itself in less sports practice, poor sports facilities and minimal financial allocation to sport, all of which negatively impacts the quality of sport participation and development. This is because sports development in Africa relies heavily on government disbursement through budgetary allocations.

Andreff gives an example of Tunisia, where the proportion of the budgetary allocation to sport accounted for 1.90 per cent of the total budget in

1986. In 1994, the proportion allocated for sport development by the Tunisian Government dropped to 1.53 per cent of the total budget. Tunisia is a relatively wealthy country by African standards and is also considered a sporting nation; the budgetary allocation, however, reflects an approach common to most African nations when it comes to sports development. According to the 1994 World Bank report, *Adjustment in Africa: Reforms, results, and the road ahead*, the GNP per capita for Tunisia was US$2,050, far above African countries considered the least developed, with GNP per capita below US$600. Lack of investment in sports development is a major contributing factor to lack of interest in sport by the majority of Africans.

Sports funding that relies solely on government contributions is doomed. Future funding needs more corporate sponsorship and less tax-payers' money. Sport cannot compete favourably with health, education, roads and agriculture for a fair share of funds. In developing countries, the largest proportion of sports funding comes from the government. Developed countries' sports funding also comes from club membership fees, gate takings, merchandising (programmes, T-shirts and logo sales), television rights and corporate sponsorships. The ability to generate funds through the above sources depends on a sound economy and a high standard of sport. The EAC is predicted to become an African economic power and be more able to promote sports, allowing it to become less reliant on dwindling governmental support.

Sports affiliation and participation

Andreff (2000) cites a UNESCO survey among the nine least-developed nations. The report found one sports federation member per 800 inhabitants compared with South America, where there was one sports federation member for every 100 inhabitants. This shows that Africans participate in an exceedingly small number of sports. According to the UNESCO survey cited above, the popular sports among Africans are football or soccer (54 per cent), volleyball (15 per cent), basketball (14 per cent), athletics (track and field, at 10 per cent), and judo and wrestling (8 per cent). The establishment of African sports clubs is lagging behind other continents. The sports clubs affiliated to the national sports federations are generally run down and mismanaged, and most of them cannot achieve the intended objectives. The few exceptions that are efficiently run are generally private sports clubs whose membership is out of the reach of ordinary people.

Soccer is the most popular sport in the continent; the majority of sports clubs are soccer clubs. In West Africa, however, the soccer clubs are more highly developed than in East Africa. This is reflected by the standard of soccer performance in countries such as Cameroon, Ghana, Nigeria and Senegal.

None of the East African countries have been able to qualify for the continental championships in spite of massive public support. After several failed attempts, Kenya finally qualified for the Confederation of Africa Championships (CAF), held in Tunisia in 2004.

The major setbacks stem from low funding of sports programmes, inadequate sports facilities, lack of competitive exposure and poor coaching. The coaches for Cameroon, Nigeria, Senegal and Tunisia earn, on average, US$20,000 monthly on top of other benefits. An average soccer coach in England would probably earn over five times that amount. The Kenyan coach who steered the most successful team ever at the Continental Soccer Championships in Tunis, 2004, was paid approximately US$4,600 per month, according to the Chairman of the Kenyan Coaches' Association, William Nyongesa. We can therefore understand why East African countries cannot afford professional coaches. None of the three countries can allocate sufficient funds to finance a reasonable football programme.

The 2003 Castle Breweries Challenge Cup brought together all the teams from the Great Lakes Region, including the Democratic Republic of Congo, and created heated excitement in the region. One can imagine the standard of soccer if other companies were to follow Castle Breweries' example and sponsor tournaments at least three to four times annually. Frequent competitive matches in the region would raise standards and attract major sponsors. In addition, soccer teams from the region would stand better chances of playing at continental and World Championships such as the World Cup in soccer.

This would create a great challenge and a high level of international exposure to the soccer fraternities in the Great Lakes Region. Consequently, it would greatly enhance the teams' likelihood of qualifying for the World Cup or the Olympics. The resulting positive media publicity would provide an alternative to the usual broadcasts on poverty, famine, starvation, and atrocities related to civil strife and genocide. The best strategy is to break the ice by using the Junior Teams to qualify for World Championships. Collaborative joint ventures in soccer would provide the easiest method not only to achieve high standards but most importantly to consolidate the unification.

Sports and education

Even in Kenya, where it is expected that Kenyan athletes will bring home gold medals, primary and secondary schools do not benefit from formal physical education lessons. Instead, the time allocated for physical education in the school timetable is used to teach other classes, or for students' independent study/free time. Extra-curricular activities that include physical education and sport are not considered part of the core curriculum because most institutions do not see its relevance to the world of academia. This has contributed to the underdevelopment of sport in primary and secondary schools. Students who do not participate in sport at primary and secondary school are more likely to remain passive sports participants throughout their lives.

The marginalization and negligence of physical education at primary and secondary schools is one of the major drawbacks to developing sports in the African continent. The other setback is enrolment, which in some countries is often less than 30 per cent. According to the 1994 World Bank report (1994), the African countries whose primary student enrolment was below 30 per cent included Eritrea, Ethiopia, Mali and Niger, among others. This shows that the majority of the children in the continent miss an opportunity to develop fundamental sports skills critical for both leisure and high-level performance because they are not at school.

Andreff (2000) cited another UNESCO study that surveyed the 16 least-developed countries. This study outlined the following findings: one country did not include physical education in the primary curriculum; three countries scheduled only one hour per week at primary level; 15 had only two or three hours weekly allocated to physical education; and only seven had a complete sports time schedule. Since physical education and sports at both primary and secondary schools provide the opportunity for students to discover their talents, it is evident that most African nations make little effort to promote the development of sport.

African institutions of higher learning have yet to exert themselves in the areas of recreational and elite sports; they should build their nation through culture and sport. Generally, most African universities view sport as external to their core curriculum. Hence the development of sport has not been accorded the seriousness it deserves.

Kenya has between six national and six private universities, with 70,000 students. Projections place Kenya's student body beyond the 200,000 mark by 2015. In other countries, such as the United States, with more than 3,000 colleges and universities, the majority of the participants that form the Olympic team are university students. Kenya's current university student population is therefore sufficiently large to form an important reservoir of sport talent in virtually every discipline. With proper talent identification and development, the students should form the majority of the Olympic team by the year 2012. Talent development will soon rely on high-level coaching, research and sports nutrition, all of which will require important technological and educational components. University students, therefore, can have an edge. In the future, sporting success will depend on how efficiently universities adopt technology.

In order to excel in sports, Africa's most important step is to give scholarships in all major sports disciplines, including athletics, soccer, basketball, volleyball, tennis and swimming. That way, Africa can diversify and widen its Olympic participation. The continent's economically superior countries must offer sport scholarships at their national universities as a contribution to both sport and cultural development. The International Olympic Committee (IOC) and other international sports federations, such as the Fédération Internationale de Football Association (FIFA) and the International Association of Athletics Federation (IAAF), should invest more in African sport development by offering sports scholarships directly to African universities. The West African universities would be most suited to offer scholarships for sprinters in track and field, and the field event student athletes. Elsewhere in the continent are the University of Ethiopia and the universities in Egypt, Morocco, Nigeria and South Africa, which are all capable of developing any kind of sport through scholarship programmes. For sports scholarships to achieve greater success, the talent search must include international students from the region in order to raise the standard of performance.

In terms of monetary investment, a track scholarship at Kenyatta University for an international student would cost approximately US$3,800, to cover all educational costs per year. Track scholarships to most American state universities for international students would amount to approximately US$30,000 annually. The IOC has been offering sports scholarships through Olympic Solidarity funds to African athletes. In the future, perhaps the IOC can channel these scholarships through African universities that have the infrastructure and human resources, such as Kenyatta University.

Apart from sports scholarships, the universities should also encourage sports and fitness-related research. National universities should therefore have a department of sport science with well-equipped health and fitness centres, thus enabling talented university students to gain access to high-tech facilities. In this way Africa can become a superpower not only in athletics, but also in a wide range of sport disciplines.

African universities can provide a solution to their countries' downward slide in sports development. Universities have the potential and capabilities to bring about diversification, technology and great improvement in sports performance. Most Africans are talented and versatile by nature, making them capable of excellence in a wide range of sports disciplines. Kenya surprised the world when two runners took up skiing, a sport considered foreign to their domain. To everyone's amazement, they performed with remarkable success. This is a testimony to incredible African sport talent that has remained untapped.

A large part of the United States' success at many world sports championships is the sports scholarship. There is no reason why the African continent cannot use a similar approach. Already, a good number of East African athletes have benefited from American Athletics Scholarships. In fact, since the 1972 Olympics, 12 East African students receiving American university scholarships have won Olympic medals.

This shows that with facilities and encouragement, the entire Great Lakes Region has plenty of athletic talent. World champions and world record holders who did not participate in the Olympics include Henry Rono, who set three world records in less than 90 days, Yobes Ondieki, who became the first person to run the 10,000 metres in under 27 minutes, and Billy Konchela, who won the world 800 meter dash titles twice, are all beneficiaries of track scholarships. There are also several professors in Kenyan national universities who benefited from track scholarships.[2] Many African athletes who have benefited from the American Track Scholarships have gone into highly respectable professional fields.

Judging from the information above, university sports scholarships are a worthwhile human resource investment that African governments, sports federations and Olympic Solidarity should make. In view of the ailing African economy and wasted African talent, investment in sports scholarships is crucial and urgent.

Talent identification

According to World Bank statistics of 1998, the average net attendance ratio for primary school in 25 African countries is 60 per cent. In other words, physical education teachers cannot cultivate 40 per cent of youth talent.

East Africa as a region should set a target to achieve 90 per cent net primary school enrolment by the year 2010. This is not an unrealistic figure because countries such as the Philippines and Malaysia have both attained the 100 per cent mark, while Tunisia has registered 98 per cent according to the 1994 World Bank report (World Bank, 1994).

Talents discovered and nurtured at an early stage of life are more likely to come to fruition, which is why primary school enrolment is an important criterion for talent identification. Once talents are discovered at primary school age, then the talented students must be encouraged to pursue secondary education in order to advance such talents. Attainment of secondary education in Africa is still a privilege for the lucky few. Talented students who fail to meet the competitive high school selection most probably terminate their sport development prematurely. Yet another large proportion of students fails to develop their talents through sheer neglect, mainly due to the lack of qualified coaches. Because of these inadequacies, plenty of exceptional African talent remains undiscovered. The universities can play an important role in training teachers and coaches for both primary and secondary schools.

The East African Community should create subsequent economic growth. The East African countries can then allocate more funds to physical education and sport. The universities in the region should establish physical education programmes and take an active role in sport research in order to raise the level of sports performance in the East African region, and Africa in general. This process will make sport seem less like a luxury, and more like a springboard to jump-start the economy.

Conclusion

The reunification of Kenya, the United Republic of Tanzania and Uganda would widen the market and improve the three nations' economies. Their combined efforts would surpass the output of any individual country in virtually all economic sectors, affording them more financial resources to develop sport infrastructure.

Since the Olympic Games are getting too large and too expensive, forming regional blocs might provide solutions. The Olympic teams could then be selected on a regional basis. In events such as boxing, the selection of competitors is already based on regional quotas. Nations should form regional blocs to harness resources necessary to raise sports performance standards. The East African region is already in the forefront, but only strong determination and commitment by all nations will bring success.

In order for East African cooperation to make an impact in sports, there needs to be more emphasis on the Junior Sports programmes, which will create a large reservoir of youth talent. East Africa could easily become the centre of athletics in the entire continent of Africa, establishing high-altitude centres for local and international training programmes.

The high standards of sport performance and positive publicity should be used to achieve other economic objectives. For example, East Africa could be projected as a top sports and tourism destination. It already has an ideal geographical location, favourable climate, attractive game park resorts and some of the world's best athletes.

Sport has great potential for major international news from East Africa and Africa in general. It can provide a positive alternative to images of war, poverty and famine, and promote local sports heroes. In addition to having role models from abroad, Africans must strive to build homegrown heroes and heroines who could play inspirational roles as mentors in the region and the African continent. But they must first be recognized and paid tribute to as legitimate East African and African superstars.

Every country should make sport development an integral part of strategies for national economic development planning. Concerning universities, East African students need continued support for their participation at World University Games and World Junior Championships. They should compete as one East African body. The team would then be strong and its costs shared, in accordance with emphasizing the EAC as an entity. Various sport disciplines require annual championships, such as the East African University Soccer Championships in Kampala or the East African Track and Field Championships in Nairobi or Dar es Salaam, to foster the development of elite athletes in those sports.

African universities need to emphasize human resources and physical education, recreation and sport science development. The IOC, which has long benefited from Kenyan and Ethiopian contributions, could invest scholarship funding in these high-level institutions to help them develop sports and related curricula. Finally, the EAC should have a department dedicated to the promotion and development of sports in the region.

Notes

[1] Boundaries have divided ethnic groups in Kenya, Uganda and Tanzania for almost a century. For example, there is a Teso tribe in Kenya and a Teso tribe in Uganda, which have similar cultures with a common dialect. The Luo communities have culture and language similar to the Acholi of Uganda. The Sebei and Sabaot communities in Uganda and Kenya are of common ethnicity and culture. The Bugusu of Kenya are culturally and linguistically the same as the Bakisu of Uganda. The Bogot of Kenya and the Suk of Uganda are the same ethnic group divided by an artificial boundary.

[2] Professor Michael Boit, Kenyatta University; Professor David Serem, Moi University; Professor Richard Mibei, Deputy Vice Chancellor, Maseno University; Dr Darius Taruru, Egerton University; and Dr Kipsang Metetek, Principal of Augustana College, Nairobi, to name but a few.

Bibliography

Alesina, A. 1999. "Ethnic and religious division, political instability and government consumption". IMF, Washington, DC; mimeo.

Amin, M. 1972. *Kenya's world-beating athletes: A photohistory.* Nairobi, East African Publishing House.

Andreff, W. 2000. "Sport and economic development", Conference "Play the Game". Copenhagen.

Baillie, P. H. E. 1993. "Understanding retirement from sports: therapeutic ideas for helping athletes in transition", in *Counseling Psychologist* (Sage Publications), Vol. 21, No. 3, pp. 399–410.

Baker, T.; Burgess, A. 1995."Physical fitness and student performance: A plan for developing a research project", University of Pennsylvania School of Nursing, Division of Psychiatric Mental Health; unpublished paper.

Barro, R. 1997. *Determinants of economic growth: A cross-country empirical study.* Cambridge, MA, MIT Press.

Britton, R.K. 1968. *Football for schools in Africa*. London, Oxford University Press.

Collier, P. 1999. "Ethnicity, politics and economic performance", in *Economics and Politics*. Oxford, Blackwell.

Conn, D. 1999. *The football business: The modern football classic*. London, Mainstream Publishing Projects.

De Hoyos, L. 1998. "Africa gives a glimpse at your own future", in *Executive Intelligence* Review, 25 Sep., pp. 27–30.

Dirk, C. L. 2005. "The occurrence of Type-2 Diabetes Mellitus in urban and rural population in Kenya and its association with rural–urban migration"; PhD thesis in progress.

Esterly, W. 2000. "Can institutions resolve ethnic conflicts?" World Bank, Washington, DC; mimeo.

—; Levine, R. 1997. "African growth tragedy: Policies and ethnic divisions", in *Quarterly Journal of Economics* (Cambridge, MA, MIT Press), Vol. CXll, No. 4, Nov., pp. 1203–1250.

Foreman K. 1981. "The use of talent predictive factors in selection of track and field athletes", in *Athletic Congress's Track and Field Coaching Manual*. Champaign, IL, Human Kinetic Publishers Inc.

Goldin, C.; Katz, L. 1999. "The shaping of higher education: The formative years in the United States, 1890 to 1940", in *Journal of Economic Perspectives* (Nashville, TN, American Economic Association), Vol. 13, No. 1, pp. 37–62.

Griggs, R. 1997. "Designs of peace: Redrafting regional boundaries and other prospects", in *Quarterly Publication of the Centre for Conflict Resolution and Media Centre* (Cape Town, University of Cape Town), Vol. 6, No. 1, Apr.

Helms, J. E. 1990. "The intercollegiate athlete: A 1990 profile", in *Counseling Psychologist*, Vol. 21, No. 3, pp. 411–429.

Hemingway, H. 1984. "Rwanda kingdom of traditional East African state, now the Republic of Rwanda", in *Encyclopedia Britannica*. Chicago, Benton Publishers, 15th edition, pp. 737–738.

Hill, T. 1993. "Sport psychology and the collegiate athlete: One size does not fit all", in *Counseling Psychologist*, Vol. 21, No. 3, pp. 436–440.

Holloszy, J. O. 1990. "The roles of exercise in health maintenance and treatment of disease in middle and old age", in M. Kaneko (ed.): *Fitness for the aged, disabled, and industrial worker*, International Series on Sport Sciences, Vol. 20.

Lehwald, H.; Green, L. 1996. "Game adaptation: Essential to health integration within physical education", in *Physical Educator*. Indianapolis, IN, Phi Epsilon Kappa Fraternity Publishers.

National Centre for Health Statistics. 1993. *Healthy people 2000 review*, 1992. Hyattsville, MD, Maryland Public Health Service.

Sachs, J. D.; Warner, A. M. 1999. "The big push, natural resources booms and growth", in *Journal of Development Economics*, Vol. 59, No. 1, pp. 43–76.

Shephard, R. J. 1990. "The cost benefits of exercise: An industrial perspective" in M. Kaneko (ed.): *Fitness for the aged, disabled, and industrial worker*, International Series on Sport Sciences, Vol. 20, pp. 189–204.

World Bank. 1994. *Adjustment in Africa: Reforms, results, and the road ahead*. New York, Oxford University Press.

SPORT AND LOCAL ECONOMIC DEVELOPMENT IN LATIN AMERICA: CASE STUDIES OF PERU AND EL SALVADOR

9

Giovanni di Cola

Introduction

The sports sector includes sporting goods manufacturing, sport-related services, infrastructure development, sports events, athletes, coaches, sponsors, vendors and the media. Globally, it is valued at US$36 billion with a rapid annual growth rate of 3 to 5 per cent. China, however, is responsible for 65 per cent of sporting goods manufacturing. Nevertheless, according to the 2004 survey by SGMA International the majority of economic activity in the sports sector does not occur on the global level.

The sports sector on the local level, while rarely reported, is an effective stimulus for economic activities. Society can foster a "virtuous circle" in which new forms of sport-related services are generated, creating jobs and opportunities to upgrade youth skills.

Local development is an opportunity to connect with the global economy through partnerships: " ...[t]he local community is part of an integrating world. In the end, the local is part of the global and the pattern of globalization is influenced by what happens locally."[1] In the sports sector, this relationship is not only possible but is usually the case. This chapter uses the examples of Peru and El Salvador to describe the process that links local to global in four different stages.

In the first stage, local citizens develop their skills at a sport or physical activity. The sport discipline and the skills necessary to perform it are specific to the community's cultural history or they are related to the environment. During the second stage, local community members use their creativity to build upon their culture and develop local initiatives, such as the Huancayo Race in Peru and the competitive training in selected areas of El Salvador. The third stage involves standardization: local partners develop the event's logistics, "standardizing" them across the region or beyond national boundaries. Taking the Incas races as an example, standardization involves establishing distances, and developing a school to increase local skills and promote the event; for El Salvador, it implies using services to organize Pan-American sport events. Finally, the last stage involves international recognition. During this stage, the events in both El Salvador and Peru can attract international attention, which brings elite athletes, tourists, media coverage, and possible multinational joint ventures and partnerships.

Case study 1: Peru

Peruvians are particularly good at running in the high altitudes of their country's natural, beautiful landscapes. The champions of running events, however, remain unknown to the public; only a fortunate few are invited to other countries to compete in international races.

Beyond the athletic factor, the present relationship between sport, economic activity and local economic initiatives is closely knit. Private business-people, local community groups and municipal authorities have matched their support for sporting events across the country. Peru is a very good example of a country that can use sport as a means to add value to its socio-economic and cultural potential.

Among the races taking place in Peru, two are highly important international sporting events. Peruvians have the ability to use these races to build their local economy and integrate with the global market.

The first, the Inca Marathon, follows the Inca Trail itself, starting at Kilometer 88 and ending at Intipunku, or Sun Gate, of Macchu Picchu. It covers 41 km with an altitude range of 4,253 m. In its second manifestation in 1996, the race was featured as one of the events in the run-up to the United Nations Food and Agriculture Organization's (FAO) World Food Summit in the same year. Local authorities within the Inca region provided technical and logistic support, while a number of national firms offered financial backing.

The second race is the Andes International Marathon, which follows the Valle del Mantaro, at an altitude of 4,000 m, to Huancayo. The people of Wanka organize the event, with the cooperation of Huancayo city council and a group of local sponsors.

Peru's cultural history and high altitude bless its people with exceptional physical strength and anaerobic capacity. During the reign of the ancient Incas, messengers ran in groups of seven or eight, covering distances that ranged from the sea (Puerto Inca) to Macchu Picchu (over 200 km) in just one day.

These epic sporting events depend upon the support of local governments and domestic and foreign firms. They are vital to the country's economy and culture. As a result, improvements in tourism, logistics and services for employment have been enhanced. The international sports and tourism industries have both grown rapidly in recent decades. As the two sectors combine and implement upgraded standards, their growth should continue. Peru can benefit from this expected economic growth by integrating its local economy with the global market through running, a tradition embedded within the country's economy and culture.

In the past, mass-production manufacturing was the main vehicle of national economic development. The leisure/pleasure industry, however, is taking over. The interests of international tourists, especially those of the younger generation, are changing. Most tourists now prefer participating in leisure activities instead of passively enjoying or watching them.

Adventurous, family-fun and participatory sports-oriented types of travel are gaining popularity. Activities on these trips can include golf, marathon running and walking, skiing, rock-climbing, river-rafting, mountain-hiking, cycling, inline and ice skating, tennis, volleyball and basketball, among other sports.

Peru offers many of these activities and is poised to capitalize on its sports-tourism potential. The Macchu Picchu race is an example of an exceptional sports event in Peru. While the country has improved the logistic services in the region, the race still needs technological equipment to ensure its compliance with international standards. When that happens, the event will attract more international racers and fans.

The Huancayo race also encourages economic activity: it has created a local craft industry that produces shoes for the runners of the Mantaro valley and a school to continue the promotion of running events. This school is being built in Huancayo itself and schedules races on the same day as the Andes Marathon. This process is similar to races organized by other sports schools and training centres. The National Olympic Committees (NOCs) and Olympic Solidarity support these types of events and schools.

Peru is a country that is fortunate to have all the various types of climates in the world represented on its territory. This is a great asset for organizing events throughout the year. Developing this potential, which must take the environment into consideration, could bring many other benefits to the country's people. It must stem from a local-level demand to make sure it becomes sustainable, building upon the country's cultural and natural resources.

For the future of young people and sport, these initiatives need to be supported at national and international levels. In the Olympic spirit, local governments and private businesses should collaborate to provide support and develop Peru's socio-economic activities.

Case study 2: El Salvador

El Salvador has an articulated organization of sports that is potentially able to connect with the youth's social and economic needs. The country has the technical capacity to organize Central American sports events. If El Salvador wishes to organize world-class events, its people's rich basket of skills needs to be upgraded. Furthermore, the Ministry of Labour and the National Olympic Movement believe that developing sports can create new jobs and services.

For the above reasons, following the initiative of the UN Secretary-General on Sport for Development and Peace, the Minister of Labour and Social Security carried out a training activity on the issue of social insertion through sports. This was a Cabinet initiative in consultation with the National Olympic Committee of El Salvador (Comité Olímpico Salvadoreno – COES), other sports partners and ILO support. The workshop included 45 participants from both the sport and development worlds, who reviewed the newly established National Youth Policy. During the workshop, participants also identified concrete steps that the Ministry of Labour (MOL) and other sports partners should take. It appeared that enlarging the basis of sport practitioners in the country would affect the development of services and jobs for youth. The participants also indicated that there was a need to address the following policy issues:

- reforming the General Law of Sport with a view to reopening the School of Physical Education and Sports (the body responsible for sports teachers' training);

- reducing the health risks related to the lack of physical and sports activity through massive awareness campaigns;

- establishing an incentive scheme that brings sponsors closer to high-performance athletes.

At the project level, the following ideas and initiatives were put forward:

- unifying actions with local and municipal governments to increase the practice of sport;

- developing the MOL job centres based in three different localities of the country, including services and jobs related to the environment, sport and tourism, and high performance;

- establishing a network of strategic partnerships in order to optimize resources, capacities and the implementation of public, private and academic programmes.

Table 9.1   Jobs identified as a result of the consultation with other sport and non-sport partners

Jobs identified	Training/retraining required	Development objectives
• Recreational facilities manager • Educators and coaches • Guides and sport coaches/community leaders • Sports facilities logistics/experts	• Training in local development and territorial synergies in the areas of: – local governments and national institutions – sport environment and sport tourism – training for educators and coaches – sport/management for federations and for sport centres	• Increased number of teachers/coaches/educators in sport and related activities • Upgrading sport facilities and recreational centres • Managing competitions and sport events

Following the workshop, the COES, with the Secretariat of Youth and the MOL, took steps to work together using sport as a key factor of the country's new youth development vision. At the same time, the MOL and the sport partners made a commitment to review the capacities of workers' recreational centres,[2] run by the MOL and often used by sports federations for training and competitions, to make them more adaptable to local needs and sports-tourism demand.

This is a starting-point for the reclassification of the sites into a sport-service-oriented facility that would create job opportunities and services. Collaboration is being established with the French Regional Centre of Physical Education and Sports (Centre Régional d'Education Physique et Sports – CREPS), Voiron, near Grenoble. The centre specializes in nature, sports and tourism at the local level to "tailor" specific training. This will be jointly assessed by the parties, taking into consideration the local territorial synergies and the environment potential (table 9.1).

This example is typical of local demand (based in El Salvador's four centres) meeting "local offer", such as the one established in Voiron, in a global economy framework. El Salvador needs "à la carte training" to boost local territorial strengths and synergies. Partners should assess the needs locally. They should be relayed to outside entities, with sport-specific capacities and skills.

Conclusion

Collaboration between public authorities and private institutions to develop sport and sports tourism/social events has a double benefit: it encourages sports practice for social inclusion (the Huancayo Race promotes the inclusion of everyone, including children) and it links physical education, respect for the environmental and cultural preservation to benefit the development of society.

Countries such as Peru and El Salvador can use sport to build upon their cultural base and history while promoting development. This approach should be built in four stages:

- local communities develop their own skills;

- skills specific to the community's social environment are developed;

- local community members use their capabilities to develop the event's logistics, "standardizing" them across the region; and

- this last stage is followed by another that involves international recognition.

While in general it is the last stage that is most recognized, the entire process adds value to the community's technical, cultural and economic capabilities. People develop skills and experience when managing the logistics and organization of the sporting event. The event can effectively create growth in the local economy and related industries, and its international brand can be used to attract tourists and foreign investment. This bottom-up approach ensures that the local economy develops to integrate with the global economy and take advantage from it, instead of working against it.

Notes

[1] In 2004 the World Commission on the Social Dimension of Globalization published a report that acknowledged the local and global relationship (ILO, 2004a, p. 67).

[2] The centres are based in Tamarindo, Coatepeque, Chalatanango and Conchalio-La Libertad.

Bibliography

Di Cola, G. 1997. "El deporte: Vehículo de solidariodad y de iniciativas económicas", in *Testimonio*, (Lima), No. 56–57, pp. 23–26.

—. 1999. "Development: Sport and the development of social and economic activities in Peru", in *Olympic Review* (Lausanne), Vol. XXVI-28, Aug.–Sep., pp. 59–61.

International Labour Office (ILO). 2004a. *A fair globalization: Creating opportunities for all*, World Commission on the Social Dimension of Globalization. Geneva, p. 67 (see: http://www.ilo.org/english/wcsdg/docs/report.pdf, accessed 30 Mar. 2006).

—. 2004b. "Common framework on decent work and social insertion of youth through sport in El Salvador' (see: http://www.ilo.org/public/english/universitas/area/salvador/index.htm, accessed 30 Mar. 2006).

—. 2005. "Declaración y compromiso del seminario taller 'trabajo decente e inserción social de jovenes a traves del deporte en El Salvador' " (see: http://www.ilo.org/public/english/universitas/area/salvador/elsalvador_jan05.pdf, accessed 30 Mar. 2006).

United Nations Inter-Agency Task Force on Sport for Development and Peace. 2003. *Sport for development and peace: Towards achieving the Millennium Development Goals.* New York.

Trelles, E. 1998. "The Andean Marathon", in *El Dorado* (Lima, Prom Peru), No. 10, Enero-Marzo, pp. 47–50.

THE DYNAMIC SYNERGY BETWEEN TOURISM AND SPORT, AND ITS EFFECT ON POVERTY REDUCTION

10

Dho Young-shim

Introduction

Persistent severe poverty in developing nations of the world is one of the most pressing global problems we face, requiring immediate and practical redress. There are entire countries, and large regions, in which people live on one US dollar per day or even less. These areas are not only deplorable sites of human misery, but also sources of social instability, virulent infectious diseases, crime, terrorism and war. The problems they generate come to threaten all humankind, even that portion of it fortunate to live in wealthier nations or areas. Therefore, it is a universal concern that economic gaps between rich and poor be reduced. The most effective, socially just and practical means for accomplishing this is to stimulate much greater rates of employment in the most impoverished areas, thereby creating sustainable jobs for the people who live there.

Hosting major sports-tourism events such as the Olympic Games or the FIFA World Cup can serve as a distant aspiration for these countries, and even seem impossibly out of reach. The Republic of Korea demonstrates that this is not necessarily the case. I shall discuss Korea's case later on in detail, but first I present the near-immediate increases in employment offered by tourism itself to impoverished countries and regions.

We must begin with the recognition that travel and tourism are already the world's largest industry, with global revenues approaching four trillion US dollars. They account for approximately 10 per cent of global gross national product (GNP), 10 per cent of all investments, one in every 12 jobs, and 8 per cent of the global trade in goods and services.[1] It is remarkable to consider that while travel and tourism are already so large, they also have one of the highest growth potentials of any industry. The industry is extremely labour-intensive, offering a wide variety of jobs from highly skilled positions requiring advanced levels of education (such as travel agents, hotel managers and transport executives) down to low-skilled entry-level jobs (such as cleaners, janitors, waiters and boatmen), with a wide range in between. A large portion of the money spent on travel and tourism (including the attendance of major sporting events) goes to pay the salaries of the many service-type workers at all levels in the industry. Taxes on their wages and consumer spending provide capital for further infrastructure improvement, making yet more good jobs available. Development of the tourism industry creates a positive spiral effect of general economic development.

Three examples of developing nations in which tourism set off a similar spiral effect include Maldives, Nepal and Cambodia. Despite their extremely isolated geographical position, Maldives were able to build a tourism sector upon their one attraction, lovely beaches and coral reefs. Following the construction of attractive resorts and the launching of an extensive publicity campaign, tourist arrivals soared, leading to the creation of a number of new jobs within the industry. Considering the secondary economic effects, tourism was able to stimulate the entire economy, raising social welfare indicators to unimaginable levels.

Cambodia, a nation that had been devastated by two decades of civil war, also built its tourism industry around one main attraction, the Angkor Wat complex. By developing a culture of value-added tourism (e.g. adventure tourism, health tourism, spiritual-pilgrimage tourism and eco-tourism, similar to the types promoted in Costa Rica, Japan, Korea, Thailand and other countries in Europe and the Caribbean), the country jump-started the industry, leading to high levels of productivity, employment and average earnings. The influx of foreign currency has helped bring new jobs to women and youth, and raise Cambodia's GDP and GNP.

Unlike Maldives and Cambodia, Nepal has always had a reputation as a magnificent place to visit (with sites such as Mount Everest, the Annapurna Range, and many cultural palaces, temples and marketplaces). Eco-tourism initiatives helped trigger Nepal's tourism industry in the 1980s, creating thousands of new jobs that in turn helped lift many urban families out of poverty. Over the past decade, political instability and security issues have harmed the industry, but many observers are confident that as those problems are now being resolved, Nepal's tourism industry has begun to rebound.[2]

International conferences promoting tourism employment

Over the past two decades, widespread recognition by international leaders of the importance and potential of tourism has resulted in diplomatic institutional attempts to lead the way in promoting tourism as a means of job creation.[3] The idea is that tourism, as one of the world's largest industries, can become the first "global peace industry" and work as an engine of economic development and poverty relief.[4]

The Southern African Development Community (SADC) Consultative Conference (Botswana, October 2002) concluded with a declaration that development of the tourism industry holds the best promise for poverty reduction and eradication in African nations. It noted that "there is a window of opportunity to use tourism as a means of showcasing the overall image of the region", and that "tourism can assist in creating an appropriate environment that will attract investments to a wide range of sectors which in turn will lead to sustainable economic development in the region and hence poverty reduction". The declaration strongly recommended that member States engage in the "intensification of the marketing, investment and promotion of tourism", and facilitate the "integration of community-based tourism into mainline tourism promotion and development". Lastly it proposed that more small-scale tourism-oriented projects that directly relate to poverty alleviation be undertaken at national and international levels.[5]

As a further instance of these international diplomatic activities, the United Nations Poverty Thematic Group Conference (Azerbaijan, March 2004) focused on the alleviation of severe property through increasing tourism employment. It noted that since tourism is one of the most diversified economic activities, the United Nations Development Programme (UNDP) sees it as one of the most promising sectors for fostering economic and social growth. It announced practical steps such as:

- establishing viable Tourist Information Centres countrywide that would help link entrepreneurs involved in the tourism sector with potential clientele and communities;

- conducting professional training courses and non-profit training courses for youth from low-income families living in rural areas, thereby facilitating their further employment in the tourism business;

- developing a national strategy on tourism education.

The dynamic synergy between sports and tourism

Major international sporting events have proved to boost the economies of the countries in which they are held, increasing overall GDP, the number of tourists visiting from abroad, and employment opportunities. Tourism has become one of the chief sources of both income- and image-enhancement for most organizers of international sporting competitions. Sports tourism is a growth industry, contributing to the development of both professional and participatory sports, which are now the leading industry in the leisure sector of the global economy.

Using the Olympic Games as an example, before the actual Games hold their opening ceremonies, large-scale, publicly financed construction and infrastructure-upgrade projects provide many new jobs for young workers, both skilled and unskilled. Whatever their current level of development, nations have been very willing to make massive, widespread investment in improving their infrastructure. Once the country is awarded the hosting of a major event, thousands of engineering, technology installation and general construction jobs are created.

During the Games themselves, very high numbers of service-industry jobs, especially those involving the travel and tourism industry, are created for both local residents and citizens of the host nation. Some of these are temporary jobs, but many of them have proved to be sustainable. Young people recruited into these service jobs continue with careers in the same field, using the experience they have gained. Therefore, the hosting of major international sporting events can be seen as a springboard for getting otherwise unemployed young citizens successfully into the labour market and on to rewarding career paths.

These world-class sporting events almost always raise the tourist industry of the host country to a significantly higher level, with long-term gains in both the "international tourism reputation" of that nation and the rate of tourism employment for its citizens. Major sports events are usually accompanied by high levels of tourism in the surrounding areas of host nations and even in neighbouring countries. In contrast, if a country already has an attractive image as a destination for tourists, it will draw an even greater number of international visitors to attend the sporting events that it hosts.

This is what I call the dynamic synergy between international sports and international tourism. The Summer and Winter Olympic Games and World Cup Finals of the past 25 years are all good examples. South Africa has been awarded the 2010 FIFA World Cup Finals, and is confidently expecting a very solid rise in both temporary and long-term travel and tourism employment. The synergy can have powerful and immediate effects for South Africa and the continent as a whole, by providing good jobs and raising income for many sectors of society, which desperately need and deserve it. The World Travel and Tourism Council (WTTC), representing the private sector in the global travel and tourism industry, has already forecasted that tourism will be a significant driver of the African economy in the decade 2000–2010, accounting for 11 per cent of its average GDP. Holding the 2010 FIFA World Cup Football Finals in South Africa will almost certainly boost the role of tourism to an even higher level (Grant Thornton Kessel Feinstein Report[6]).

Some concrete examples of the synergy at work can already be cited. For example, when Spain hosted the World Cup in 1982, its per capita national income was only US$5,380, but ten years later it had risen to US$14,160. The fact that its tourism industry more than doubled in size played a major role. Before the World Cup, Spain had approximately 30 million tourists passing through each year, while by 1992 it was attracting 65 million. The income earned from Spanish tourism rose from US$6.3 billion in 1981 to US$20.4 billion in 1993. Additionally, the United States GNP rose US$4 billion in 1994 solely due to the fact that it hosted the World Cup. When France hosted the World Cup in 1998, it brought the nation's stubborn unemployment rate down from 13 per cent to 11 per cent. Furthermore, an estimated 37 billion television viewers were reminded of the country's already-famous cultural and tourism assets (World Tourism Organization ST-EP Initiative).[7]

Increases in the level of employment gained from travel and tourism (including the hosting of international sporting events) can particularly benefit women, who already comprise 60 per cent of all tourism-industry employees. An increase in service-industry jobs for women dramatically boosts women's social status within less-developed societies, and causes a sharp increase in the well-being of both the employed woman and her entire family. Tourism hospitality is the main economic sector that can offer these benefits, and the only one that employs more women than men – 75 per cent around the globe.

Travel, tourism and sporting-event employment also bring particular benefit to the host nation's youth, as they are usually the ones to get the new service sector jobs. Young people are interested in learning foreign languages and acquiring useful service skills in order to obtain the good jobs that progressively become available.

The development of the tourism industry and the hosting of sporting events provide many other side benefits to developing societies, spreading out like concentric ripples in a pond. They provide both governments and private companies with incentives to improve urban infrastructures, and to offer much greater protection for the natural environment in the areas that visitors will be exposed to. Incentives are created to protect (and where necessary restore and rehabilitate) the nation's historical and cultural monuments and landmarks as valuable assets for humanity and legacies for future generations. All this resulting infrastructure improvement, environmental protection and restoration give rise to many new, well-paying and sustainable jobs for current and future generations.

International tourism and sports also provide strong social incentives for host governments to offer better levels of education to their younger citizens, so that they can successfully get and perform the new service-industry jobs created. Equally, social incentives are provided for the empowerment of women (education, employment outside the home, and a greater voice in making choices) in national cultures where this has been lacking, as more tourism-type jobs are offered. The many fresh opportunities of gainful and sustained employment offer social incentives to ordinary citizens to pursue and accept this education and empowerment, as they see the tangible benefits brought to them. In these ways, the development of international tourism and the hosting of international sporting events serve as a strong stimulant to progressive social development in nations that lack it.

Three factors that lead to economic growth are worth noting. First, it has become generally accepted that the composition of economic growth matters a great deal. Some sectors, in which growth is sustained, absorb labour on a long-term basis. This alters the structure of the labour force by moving workers away from low-productivity towards high-productivity activities. The travel and tourism sector has proved to be a good example of sustainable growth, which has been much more effective in creating employment opportunities than sectors such as agriculture, heavy industry or even light industry (i.e. textiles and garment manufacturing).

Second, the quality of labour is important. If the labour force is skilled, mobile and adaptable to different work environments, it can be gainfully deployed in high-productivity activities. In contrast, an unskilled, inflexible and immobile labour force is not in demand in modern, growth-oriented industries. The travel and tourism industry tends to create jobs that employ skilled, mobile and flexible workers who have high incentives to continue to upgrade their competencies and skills.

Third, adaptability to change is imperative in a technology-driven economic environment. If the infrastructure is fairly well developed and competitively priced, it will attract widely dispersed investments, creating broad-based employment. If not, those few industries that are set up tend to concentrate in one or two locales without making any significant difference to the welfare of the population throughout the country. If the growth composition is flexible to changes in demand and technology (such as in the Republic of Korea), a national growth strategy can adapt to be sustainable. In its absence, initial rapid growth eventually degenerates into long periods of stagnation.

Tourism is the only "hard-currency-earning" product that can be designed, produced, packaged and operated entirely by developing countries themselves. It needs little hard-currency imports up-front, except in the case of building five-star hotels, which usually takes place in a later stage of tourism development. Thus initial development of tourist sites and services can quickly and directly help people in local areas.

The synergy of sports tourism in Korea

The Republic of Korea has been one of the best examples in the past 20 years of how the dynamic synergy between international sports and international tourism works. The country is in fact itself one of the world's best models for the successful development of impoverished countries. In only 40 years it has moved from the official list of least-developed countries to being a member of the Organisation for Economic Co-operation and Development and one of the world's top-ten trading nations. Korea's success has been called an economic miracle, but in fact it was merely the result of properly designed and implemented governmental policies (some generated by the United Nations and related international bodies, others developed in Korea in a homegrown fashion, along with plenty of inspired hard work by the populace). Leaders of many countries have visited Korea to study the Korean models to see how they might adapt them to their own conditions. The Republic of Korea has always been pleased to share the "open secrets" of its path to economic growth and social stability. Only 4 per cent of national income now comes from inbound tourism; it is hoped to raise this figure towards the goal of 8 per cent (still well below the global average of 12 per cent).

Korea's tourism industry has been a part of this success story, with slow but steady sustainable growth and appropriate development. The country has already become a leader in hosting major international sports and tourism events, and has actively cooperated with other nations regionally and globally for the development of international tourism and sports-tourism. Seoul's hosting of the 1988 Summer Olympic Games was a milestone in improving Korea's international image, economic reputation and political relations with other nations. It was in effect the launch of Korea's modern international tourism industry. In terms of tourism business and services employment, that great event provided a dramatic and long-lasting boost.

During the World Cup period, there were 1,430 international media reports on Korea (not including those reporting on the actual matches themselves) from 88 different media outlets. They emphasized the orderly cheering by Korean citizens, the lack of violence or other security problems, the excellent functioning of the infrastructure and Korean-built technology equipment, the sophisticated level of Korea's modern social culture, its hospitality and the fascination of its colourful traditional culture. The Korean national and local governments organized a total of 101 cultural events during the World Cup period, attracting over 15 million visitors, 800,000 of whom were foreign tourists. This greatly enhanced Korea's national image, brand value and international status. Its "brand power score" (an index widely used by marketing professionals) moved 72.5 points to 81.9. The Korea Trade and Investment Promotion Agency estimated that the nation's "export brand power" increased by 3 per cent, translating into approximately US$30 billion. Furthermore, considering that this was the first FIFA World Cup ever held in Asia, the hosting was virtually flawless.

According to a report issued from the Korea Development Institute (KDI), the equivalent of US$2.83 billion was spent in preparations for the World Cup (of which US$1.33 billion was in infrastructure investment). Yet KDI estimated that the economic benefits generated by the World Cup would total US$14 billion and US$4.42 billion worth of added value (direct benefit from investment), plus projected economic output worth US$9.5 billion.

The private Hyundai Economic Research Institute estimated that the World Cup matches held in Korea generated a domestic consumption effect worth the equivalent of US$5.42 billion. It noted that it usually costs an estimated US$10 billion to increase public awareness of the top 100 business brands by 1 per cent, but after conducting post World Cup surveys it was estimated that the global enhancement of Korea's national brand power was worth US$54.75 billion. The increase in national brand value leads to higher national competitiveness, which in turn raises employment levels, exports, national income and development of related service industries (such as tourism), and gives a boost to the entire economy.

Outcome of the 2000 Summer Olympic Games in Australia

The 2000 Summer Olympic Games were hosted by Sydney, Australia, and results from a subsequent study by the Australian Tourist Commission (ATC) revealed that they had significant benefits for the Australian tourism industry, and the country as a whole. The study concluded that:

- The Games attracted an additional 1.74 million visitors, generating over US$3.5 billion worth of foreign exchange earnings between 1997 and 2004.

- The ATC's media relations programme generated an additional US$2.1 billion in publicity for the country between 1997 and 2000, not to mention advancing Australia's brand reputation by ten years.

- The ATC's partnerships with major Olympics sponsors, such as Visa, McDonalds, Kodak and Coca-Cola, generated an additional US$170 million in publicity for Australia.

- In 2000, the rate of international visitor arrivals to Australia increased by 11 per cent, which can be credited to the "Australia 2000 – fun and games" campaign that the ATC launched in late 1999 to encourage tourists to visit Australia in 2000.

- The likelihood of potential travellers to visit Australia increased significantly because of the Olympic Games, as indicated by the 700 per cent increase in traffic to the ATC's website[8] during the Games.

- The International Congress and Convention Association (ICCA) predicted that Australia would be ranked the number one country for meetings held in 2001, overtaking both the United States and the United Kingdom.

- An additional US$56 million in export earnings in 2001 was expected from the ATC's "New Century, New World, Australia 2001" campaign to attract business to Australia as a result of the Games.

- The ATC hosted 50 of the world's most influential tourism-industry leaders from 11 countries in Sydney for the Olympics.

- At the conclusion of the Games, the ATC launched campaigns with 200 industry partners worth US$25 million to quickly convert interest and awareness into actual visits. The last three months of 2000 saw an additional 189,000 international visitors to Australia (up 15 per cent compared to the same time last year), increasing foreign exchange earnings by US$320 million in these three months alone.

- Research indicates that 88 per cent of the 110,000 international visitors who came to Australia for the Olympics are likely to return to Sydney as tourists.

- Australia's inbound tourism is expecting strong growth, approximately 7.8 per cent over the decade 2000–2010 (partly due to the effect of the Sydney Olympics Games). About 1.5 million projected international visitors to Australia over the period are expected to visit because of the promotional impact of the Olympics.

Other sporting events have also had similar kinds of economic effects on a region. The Australian Open (tennis tournament) was held in Melbourne (in the state of Victoria) in January of 2004. Including the "induced tourism effect", the total economic impact of this event on the Victorian economy is estimated at US$203 million. Its tourism industry enjoyed 325,000 additional visitor-nights, including almost 18,000 visitors from overseas. Nationally, it is estimated that 2,500 full-time annual employment positions were generated. The Melbourne Commonwealth Games in March 2006 involved an estimated 15,000 national and international volunteers, and attracted some 90,000 tourists.[9]

The World Tourism Organization's ST-EP Initiative

The World Tourism Organization is now a specialized agency of the United Nations (UN). UN Secretary-General Kofi Annan previously worked to facilitate tourism in Africa, and shares the conviction that the tourism industry is a primary means for alleviating poverty in the world's developing countries. The World Tourism Organization has instituted poverty-alleviation programmes for developing countries, in particular the ST-EP (Sustainable Tourism for Elimination of Poverty) Initiative. At the 2002 World Summit on Sustainable Development (WSSD), convened by the UN in Johannesburg, South Africa, ST-EP was launched by the World Tourism Organization in collaboration with United Nations Conference on Trade and Development (UNCTAD). The ST-EP Foundation opened its headquarters in Seoul in September 2004 with US$5 million in patrimony provided by the Government of the Republic of Korea, as a gesture towards spurring sustainable tourism as a tool for alleviating poverty and preserving environmental, social and cultural resources. The World Tourism Organization also contributed an initial half million dollars to ST-EP.

ST-EP will focus on long-term projects to encourage socially, economically and ecologically sustainable tourism businesses that alleviate poverty, and create jobs and development in the world's poorest countries and regions. It is both a manifestation of the UN Millennium Development Goals (MDGs) to halve extreme poverty by 2015 and practical implementation of the World Tourism Organization's Global Code of Ethics for Tourism.

The ST-EP Foundation will employ four main strategies to accomplish its mission:

- strengthen international cooperation and forge new relations by creating a ST-EP Council of international leaders and celebrities to interact with governments, international organizations, NGOs, corporations and donors, and an Advisory Group to provide professional knowledge for the ST-EP beneficiaries;

- implement and develop ST-EP projects, conducting research to foster high-quality human tourism resources that will provide support for developing countries to establish tourism development plans;

- conduct various promotional events, such as campaigns and award ceremonies for the branding of ST-EP, to which Korea can contribute through its highly advanced e-promotion technology. An exposed and noticeable brand will help other organizations or non-governmental organizations (NGOs) to take part in its projects;

• secure funds for the ST-EP Foundation. In the initial stage, the WTO, Korea and other interested countries will contribute, and corporations and individual donors will be induced to follow suit. ST-EP looks forward to becoming a self-sufficient foundation by taking advantage of promotional events and branding to earn funds. Its goal is for its patrimony fund to reach US$100 million by 2015.

Worldwide interest in and awareness of ST-EP will be increased through promotion and branding, as it conducts research on effective ways to develop projects in target regions and assist those in need. Holding local sports events and cooperating with major international sports events are integral parts of these plans. The hope is that ST-EP will have a significant effect on the alleviation of severe poverty around the world through increased employment in the tourism industry.

The ST-EP programme and the IOC have already teamed up to take on the mission laid out by the World Tourism Organization. The Year of Sports and Tourism was a UN-based initiative held in 1999. In that same year, the World Tourism Organization and the IOC worked together to establish a Cooperation Agreement to combine their efforts.

On the occasion of World Tourism Day in 2004, IOC President Dr Jacques Rogge and World Tourism Organization Secretary-General Francesco Frangialli issued a joint statement entitled "Sport and Tourism: Two Living Forces For Mutual Understanding, Culture and the Development of Societies", declaring their "wish to renew their commitment to reinforce their partnerships and collaboration", and that:

> [S]port and tourism share common goals: building bridges of understanding between different cultures, lifestyles and traditions; promoting peace and goodwill among nations; motivating and inspiring young people; and providing entertainment and enjoyment to relieve the pressures of daily life for large sections of the population. Tourism and sport are interrelated and complementary. Sport (as a professional, amateur or leisure activity) involves a considerable amount of traveling to play and compete in different destinations and countries. Major sporting events, such as the Olympic Games, football and rugby championships and auto racing have become powerful tourism attractions in themselves – making a very positive contribution to the tourism image of the host destination. Both are powerful forces for development, stimulating investment in infrastructure projects such as airports, roads, stadiums, sporting complexes, hotels and restaurants – projects that can be enjoyed by the local population, as well as visitors who come to use them. And once the infrastructure is in place, these two mutually beneficial industries of tourism and sport become the motor for sustainable economic growth, the creation of employment and generation of revenues.

Conclusion

On the basis of these significant declarations, I believe that the nearly unlimited potential of the dynamic synergy of international sports and international tourism will come to fruition through the ST-EP Foundation and other related initiatives in this first decade of the twenty-first century. Sports and tourism will work together to provide employment, promote positive national images, spark fresh infrastructure development, boost sales of many products and a wide range of value-adding services, and therefore reduce poverty worldwide and promote understanding and peace. Solid experience has shown that they provide many more of these benefits when teamed up than each of them operating alone.

There is a plethora of beneficial conditions that result from the synergy between sports and tourism: participants will benefit by enjoying fun, good health, cultural exchange and new friendships. The benefits for the host country will include increased tourism revenue and employment, an upgrade in its national image, and a fresh sense of national unity and international solidarity. The tourism industry will benefit by the added attention it receives and by the boost in travel brought on through the synergy of sports and tourism. The global sporting goods business, companies that upgrade sports and tourism infrastructures, and the entire leisure industry will gain a strong boost as more people travel outside their native borders to play with others of like mind, increasing the opportunities for tomorrow's imaginative entrepreneurs.

The global tourism industry and sports-tourism in particular are inextricably linked, and combined have the potential to reduce poverty in developing nations and regions, by providing both high-quality employment and opportunities for enhanced cross-cultural understanding. Tourism is without a doubt our best, most viable and most effective "peace industry", and its spread will serve to reduce violent conflict and the poverty that feeds into it. In our present tragically suffering world, where terrorism and other senseless violence appears every day on the TV sets in our living-rooms, I want to give fresh hope to our youth, feeding their dreams of a peaceful and cooperative world where such bloody images are only sad historical memories. I truly believe that international sports and tourism can work ever more closely together to give young people that sort of hope, all around the globe.

Notes

[1] World Tourism Organization: *Yearbook of Tourism Statistics* (Madrid, 2004); see: http://www.world-tourism.org, accessed 20 Mar. 2006. This publication contains statistical data on international inbound tourism to 204 countries and territories for the years 1999–2003.

[2] This optimism was based on various media reports on these nations' tourism industries; in Nepal the *Nepali Times* (see: http://www.nepalitimes.com/, accessed 16 Feb. 2006) and in the United Kingdom *The Guardian* (see: http://www.travel.guardian.co.uk/, accessed 16 Feb. 2006).

[3] Such attempts include the creation of the International Institute for Peace through Tourism (IIPT). The IIPT held Global Summits on Peace through Tourism in Jordan, Switzerland and Thailand in 2000, 2003 and 2005 respectively,

[4] As stated in the IIPT's Amman Declaration on Peace through Tourism (see: http://www.iipt.org/globalsummit/ammandeclaration.html, accessed 16 Feb. 2006).

[5] SADC Institutional Reform for Poverty Reduction through Regional Integration, 28–29 October 2002, sect. 18.

[6] See Executive summary (http://www.polity.org.za/pdf/WorldCup2010.pdf, accessed 16 Feb. 2006).

[7] The World Tourism Organization ST-EP Initiative to use Sustainable Tourism for Elimination of Poverty through ecotourism, sports tourism and rural tourism programmes at community level.

[8] See: http://www.australia.com, accessed 20 Mar. 2006.

[9] Taken from the document "Results of Study by Australian Tourist Commission", published by the International Olympic Committee (IOC).

PART III

THE CONTRIBUTION OF SPORT TO YOUTH DEVELOPMENT

THE ATHLETIC COACH AS INVITATIONAL LEADER

11

Betty L. Siegel and Mike Spino

Overview

In most athletic events, the primary objective for coaches is to win; however, to take this one-dimensional approach is to ignore the more far-reaching benefits of effective coaching. Indeed, the most effective coaches are those who act as change agents in the lives of their players and in their communities. The outcomes of play are diverse and instructive, especially those that go beyond questions of winning and losing. For instance, assisting players in character development or teaching decision-making skills is not always reflected in a game's final score. More than sport tactics, then, this chapter addresses how we might expand our understanding of what coaches do, whom they influence, and how their talents can be used for larger purposes.

Besides, the athletic coach can play a significant role in helping local communities understand these issues and move toward positive change.

Through an expanded coaching education programme, our athletic teachers can become the leaders of the sport and development "movement", converting animosity to friendship and conflict to peaceful harmony. Athletic coaches, especially from developing nations, played a significant part in the United Nations (UN) International Year of Sport and Physical Education 2005, forging a link between both local and national sport initiatives and the humanitarian efforts at the heart of the UN's Millennium Development Goals (MDGs).

An expanded definition of coaching

Anyone with experience in international coaching projects knows that most students will never produce Olympic-calibre athletes and teams in their coaching careers, but nevertheless they can – and often do – become supremely important and influential individuals in their nations. It is these students, also, who often work tirelessly as athletic coaches in their local communities, shaping the characters of generations of athletes by serving as leaders and mentors. While those in the upper echelon of sports administration may have the more powerful influence, it is the athletic coach, free from the demands of politics, who will most likely have the most lasting effect on individuals and communities.

Millions of people look to coaches for direction and encouragement. Coaches can mould the behaviour of athletes at an early age, helping to shape their basic belief systems, character traits, and values. They have the ability to motivate players to believe in themselves, to prepare thoughtfully for the future, and even to make life-affirming decisions about difficult personal issues. Whether a nation prospers or decays can be influenced by how a coach teaches young people to interact with each other through play. For this reason, it is essential to offer workshops and training sessions that expand the capabilities of the athletic coach and facilitate a working relationship with social workers, nurses and other helping professionals. Such programmes encourage us to expand our sense of what success means for both coaches and athletes, both on and off the fields of play.

The potential for an expanded understanding of the coach's role in socio-economic and human development was poignantly stated during a presentation at an international coaching conference in 2003 by an ILO official. Because almost 30 per cent of nations have never won an Olympic medal, there are countless coaches in these countries that are categorized as "losers" on the world sport scene – in fact, during Olympic broadcasts, such coaches and their players seem hardly to merit a mention. Yet it is precisely these kinds of coaches that become heroes or heroines of both their local communities and their countries. Once again, by expanding our definition of the responsibilities and capabilities of the athletic coach, we can begin to redefine success in sport.

With proper training, within this expanded definition, the coach can become more adept in his or her abilities to transfer wisdom, teach life skills, and encourage an interest in both education and community involvement. In the final analysis, these personal tools may become the most significant aspect of the coach's teaching repertoire. One could even go so far as to say that the properly trained coach possesses the background to shape the future through the individual lives of his or her athletes.

An invitational philosophy of coaching

If it is in their relationships with their athletes that coaches can have the most profoundly positive influence, then we must begin to move beyond the "win-at-any-cost" philosophy, which can be damaging to young athletes, driving them away from the more beneficial aspects of physical activity and competition. In the United States, 35 per cent of boys drop out of organized sporting activity before the age of 12. Girls usually leave the playing field six times as much as boys, making them an even more vulnerable population. Clearly, the "win-at-any-cost" philosophy can only exacerbate this unfortunate trend, especially if it is pursued without regard for the athletes themselves as capable and valuable individuals.

To focus on the positive influence that coaches can have on the lives of their players is really to highlight the leadership aspects of the coaching profession. In this regard, the theory of Invitational Leadership, defined in the book *Becoming an invitational leader* by Drs Betty Siegel and William Purkey, seems particularly useful as a model for athletic coaches. *Invitational* leadership means precisely that – leadership as a means of inviting others to succeed. Many of us tend to think of leadership as something that is exerted by one individual *onto* others – that is, the leader, having earned a position of dominance and power, begins to issue orders and direct his or her subordinates. No matter how kind and generous they might be toward their associates, such leaders are of the command-and-control variety. By contrast, invitational leadership involves a generous and genuine turning toward others in empathy and respect, with the ultimate goal of collaborating with them on projects of mutual benefit. The emphasis shifts from command and control to cooperation and communication, from manipulation to cordial summons, from exclusiveness to inclusiveness.

This philosophy has profound implications for the practice of coaching, for the invitational leader is unique in asking others to meet their goals *as a condition* of his or her own success. This is not merely a by-product of this particular leadership style. On the contrary, encouraging others in their quest for self-fulfilment is embedded in the principles of invitational leadership. An ethical theory, invitationalism is centred on four basic principles:

1. Trust (i.e. individuals are the highest authority on their own personal existence and, given the opportunity, will find their own best way of participating in human interactions).

2. Respect (i.e. people are responsible and should be treated accordingly).

3. Optimism (i.e. people possess untapped potential).

4. Intentionality (i.e. human potential can best be realized by places, policies, processes and programmes specifically designed to invite optimal development, and also by people who are intentionally inviting with themselves and others).

For coaches, to lead invitationally would be to honour the *mutual* commitment between themselves and their athletes, rather than merely to issue a series of orders and directives. In addition to treating athletes with dignity and respect, the invitational coach will invite his or her players to succeed on their own terms, teaching, in Stephen Covey's words, "in ways that release human potential rather than trying to control behavior" (Covey, 1991).

The intentionally inviting hierarchy

Inviting behaviours can be taught to coaches, but in order to be understood fully, they must be systematically defined and clearly articulated. In addition, coaches are most likely to adopt such behaviours if they can predict their effects on the overall learning posture of their athletes. Together with Dr Judith Stillion, director of Kennesaw State University's Institute for Leadership, Ethics, and Character, Dr Siegel has outlined a nine-step hierarchy of inviting behaviours as a guide to educators in all fields who wish to become intentionally inviting leaders.

The first step in the hierarchy is caring. While the word "caring" can denote many dimensions of feeling, in this context it is meant to convey interested concern at a rather low level. Behaviours illustrating this level might include such things as giving an unexpected compliment or making supportive comments during practice. When a coach exhibits caring, athletes learn that their existence is affirmed and that they are noticed and at least minimally valued.

The second step in the hierarchy is that of respecting differences. Coaches who set up the rules for their teams with an eye towards promoting respect of each athlete's right to develop are setting the model for respect of differences. Other aspects of respecting differences include knowing when an athlete may require more rest or more specialized training than others and finding ways to accommodate those needs. Athletes who learn early on that their coach respects differences among them learn at a very basic level that they are accepted. In the vocabulary of transactional analysis, the athletes learn that their own individual make-up is "OK", a lesson that has powerful implications for later positive mental health.

Both of these first two levels make up the personal dimension of the hierarchy. It is called the personal dimension because good coaches almost always come into the profession with these abilities. They are caring people who naturally respond to athletes as individuals. Although these levels are basic to the hierarchy, they are perhaps the most difficult ones to teach, for they have to do with traits intrinsic to a good coach's personality and character.

The third level of the hierarchy is that of providing success experiences. This level makes up the pedagogical dimension of the hierarchy and most closely approaches what Skinner (1984) calls the "technology of teaching". All the things prospective coaches learn about creating team objectives, methods of delivering instruction and training, and modes of communication go into this level. In fact, some coaches, especially those new to the field, believe that this is the highest level to which they need aspire in their work. When coaches invite growth by providing success experiences, athletes learn "I am able".

Of course, not all experiences in sport can be success experiences. Athletes must learn early on that failure is part of the experience of sport, but good coaches will build in a critical ratio of success to failure experiences and will de-emphasize failure when it does occur. Further, inviting coaches must be able to turn each failure into a growth experience for athletes. To do so is to help athletes retain their self-confidence even in the most trying circumstances.

The next two levels in the hierarchy make up the validation dimension. The fourth one, recognizing accomplishments, does not imply that coaches must put undue emphasis on final results, but rather on recognizing movement in the expected direction. Coaches who wish to move to this level of the hierarchy will find themselves saying things like, "You're really trying hard" or "That's much better than you did last week." The emphasis here is on the process rather than the product, the experience of learning rather than the results of the game or match. How many times do athletes become discouraged because their coach demands perfection? To *encourage* athletes most effectively involves meeting them where they are in their abilities and applauding their efforts at each stage of their development.

Of course, a coach cannot ignore final results, and that is why the fifth level goes a step beyond recognition to rewarding outcomes. Even if an athlete is involved in a losing effort, inviting coaches will focus on the positive aspects of that athlete's performance. All humans need approval for proper moral and personality development, as well as for social reinforcement. When an athlete's efforts in competition are validated, that athlete learns that his or her skills and talents are valued and valuable. Such validation also helps athletes to build positive self-concepts, causing an increase in the motivation to succeed.

There is probably little disagreement that most coaches should be concerned with each level of the hierarchy to this point. However, from this point on there may be less consensus. Many coaches, looking at the title of the next dimension – the psychological – feel that they are moving beyond the realm of the requirements of successful coaching. Indeed, many feel inadequately prepared to address this level of the hierarchy. Proponents of invitational theory would argue that coaches cannot avoid attending to this dimension. If this is true, it would seem helpful, if not imperative, that coaches learn to recognize and consciously address the four levels within this dimension.

The first level within the psychological dimension – the sixth level – is helping athletes to relate positively. The human being is a psychosocial entity, and almost all psychological theories recognize the importance of social experience to positive development. Maslow's hierarchy of needs (1968), for example, stresses the importance of belonging and self-esteem in the total adjustment of the individual. Coaches can choose to structure instruction systematically so as to promote their players' ability to relate positively, or they can choose to ignore this level of invitation. Those who choose to incorporate it can do so in a number of ways by promoting teamwork both on and off the field of competition. In working and socializing together outside of practice and competition, athletes may learn powerful lessons concerning how to relate positively to other human beings – and this can only have a positive effect on the results of competition itself. By encouraging athletes to collaborate in this way, invitational coaches lay the foundation for the remaining levels of the psychological dimension.

The next level within the psychological dimension – the seventh level – is that of promoting adequate coping. Coaches who allow athletes to throw temper tantrums, complain about or ridicule their fellow players, or exhibit other types of bad sportsmanship are not creating optimal invitational conditions. Young athletes must be taught to cope realistically with difficult situations, as well as their peers, for such knowledge is necessary in becoming mature, responsible adults. Coaches can promote such knowledge by offering instruction on sportsmanship, coping skills and stress management alongside instruction on their individual sport. A coach might also ask his or her players to write down their thoughts about their experiences in competition – their fears and hopes – in order to help them better comprehend and cope more successfully with their feelings.

The last level in the psychological dimension – the eighth level – is encouraging involvement. When a coach invites through encouraging proper involvement, athletes learn that they are responsible. Much of the criticism of recent years concerning narcissism in Western culture – and its influence on other cultures around the world – is a result of the failure of our citizens to make a responsible commitment to the larger society. (Note that the hierarchy implies that one has to be truly independent before one can make responsible commitments to others.) Coaches who invite by encouraging involvement help their players to think through what their larger obligations are beyond the immediate question of winning or losing competitions. Thus, they enable their players to come to know themselves more deeply and understand the ways in which they can give back to their culture.

The ninth and final level of the hierarchy is that of celebrating the total uniqueness of the individual. It has been labelled the autonomous dimension because it assumes each athlete's absolute independence to grow based on prior learning. When coaches are able to communicate to their players that they authentically recognize and rejoice in their unique capabilities and personalities, those players learn that they are free to become all that they are capable of becoming. This dimension assumes the inclination of coaches to recognize and affirm their players as people in the process of becoming. It involves willingness to structure tasks in such a way as to invite and reward divergent rather than convergent thinking. It also promotes a feeling of satisfaction in those coaches who have the ability to take pleasure in observing and being a part of their players' unique and special ways of growing.

Coaching as a form of service

This expanded definition of the leadership involved in coaching includes a significant ethical component. More than ever, it seems, the news media is full of stories of ethical violations by athletes and coaches – from steroid use in baseball and by Olympic athletes to fights between players and fans at professional basketball games. Yet the athletic coaches in our local communities can go a long way towards countering this trend and returning integrity to the world of sport.

This might best be accomplished by coaches who are aware of their potential to create positive change – among their athletes, as well as in their communities and nations. Part of any training programme for athletic coaches should, therefore, focus on the elements of ethical leadership and positive psychology. In a fascinating interview recently with *Edge* magazine, Martin Seligman, Fox Leadership Professor of Psychology at the University of Pennsylvania, discusses his work to "create a positive psychology whose mission would be the understanding and building of positive emotion, of strength and virtue, and of positive institutions" (Seligman, 2004). Significantly, this goal can best be accomplished, he argues, by those who pursue a "form of happiness" defined by "knowing what your highest strengths are and deploying those in the service of something you believe is larger than you are". Happiness, or what Seligman calls the "good life", is therefore linked to meaningful, ethically motivated work dedicated to the greater good – *not* merely to selfish forms of pleasure and play.

Coaches must learn to speak and act in accordance with a philosophy of service, where ethical commitment and community involvement become goals as important as winning championships or medals. We might define the new leadership roles of coaches as having much in common with what management expert Robert Greenleaf (1996) calls "servant leadership".

To slightly alter Greenleaf's terms, *those served* could be read as *athletes*, while the *servant–leader* could be read as coach and mentor. Greenleaf clearly believes that leadership is closely aligned with teaching and mentoring, as one of the major requirements of leaders is that they move others towards service. His is a model that could serve us well in the world of sport. In his thinking, it is not enough that leaders concern themselves merely with organization and management – or, for our purposes, issues like game strategy and recruitment – rather, they must inspire and instruct by example. Servant leadership is thus based upon an ethical relationship between those who serve – *athletic coaches* – and those who are invited, or led, into a life of service – *athletes*. From here, the influence of coaches will grow exponentially, as our young athletes will be introduced to principles of citizenship they will carry far into their lives and careers.

Coaching as a heartfelt commitment

To talk about coaches as servant–leaders is to understand coaching as the work of the heart as well as the head. The work of our athletic coaches, as we have seen, can have a lasting impact on the future of our communities, particularly if these coaches work with young athletes. As the philosopher Neil Postman so eloquently reminds us, "children are the living messages we send to a time we will not see", and so our coaches, like our teachers, are working in a very real sense on behalf of the future. Our athletic coaches are educators, after all, and their responsibilities go far beyond the requirements of athletic performance.

Still, how can athletic coaches think about the future in this abstract way, given the day-to-day requirements of instruction and training? Again, the answer lies in developing an overall invitational philosophy of coaching that places value not in end results only, but also in the process of forging relationships with athletes and serving the greater good. In his essay "Teaching in the face of fear", master teacher and lecturer Parker Palmer (1997) writes about what is necessary to "improve the quality of . . . teaching", and his words apply equally well to coaching, especially if we consider our athletic coaches as some of our most important teachers themselves.

Caught up in the pressures of competition, our coaches must take time to reflect on what brought them to coaching in the first place. A love of sport is obviously a prime motivator, but no doubt they will discover that it is precisely the "human dimensions of our craft" that provide the most satisfying rewards of their work. Parker's words, especially his notion that teaching is intimately connected to "inward sources" like "identity and integrity", can inspire our coaches to shift their attention to their roles as agents for positive change.

Conclusion

If we are to succeed in the world of sport in facing the challenges set by the UN's MDGs, we will need the leadership of the highest-level coaches from many nations. When the Secretary-General of the United Nations appointed former Swiss President, Mr Adolf Ogi, as the Special Advisor for Sport and Development, it seemed a recruitment call for coaches to step forward. Now is the time to organize community-oriented facilitation training for coaches to learn that their roles need not be limited to their sports. Certainly, their work will always involve teaching others the intricacies and strategies of their games, but it must also come to include a wide range of other responsibilities – or, say, possibilities – for the potential for coaches to have a positive impact on the lives of their communities and nations is great.

Colleges and universities can play a vital role in supporting an invitational philosophy of coaching education. In the United States, particular sports – namely, football and basketball – are closely identified with academic institutions. At Kennesaw State University, we are proud to have won national sport championships in a number of sports, and have full-time coaches with a passion for teaching and mentoring their athletes. Institutions of higher learning in the United States and Europe also have invaluable resources – in terms of both people and money – that might be used in outreach programmes to developing nations.

Exchange programmes or targeted coaching workshops could bring American, Asian or European coaches to poorer nations for training in invitational leadership, as well as further instruction in specific sports, whether they be more universal games like running and soccer or those closely identified with the culture and traditions of individual countries. There is also the possibility of introducing new – and therefore neutral – games to cultures in order to assist in conflict resolution, much like the successful Play for Peace programme that used basketball as a way to bridge the divide between Catholic and Protestant youth in Northern Ireland.

Whether on the local or the global level, we might say that training coaches in this expanded way means teaching them how to expand their focus from success (winning competitions, preserving the sport) to significance (learning one's obligations to community, realizing one's potential for leadership, defining an ethically motivated life). This is a high standard for any field, but it becomes possible if there is broad consensus on the necessity for expanding our conception of what coaching entails. Once concepts such as ethics, public service, and moral leadership become a central part of our understanding of coaching, we really can begin to see how the International Year of Sport and Physical Education had a direct bearing on the UN's MDGs.

Coaches who are working for the greater good should not be isolated cases, but instead part of an umbrella organization of coaches, ranging from the local to the national to the global.

Those termed "coach" in almost all nations are viewed as protectors of their nation's heritage, flag bearers for a better future – and working together across national boundaries, coaches can help to unite our world in remarkable ways. In the expanded definition of coaching, winning might still be the primary objective, but the playing field is much broader – and success means, quite simply, that everyone wins.

Bibliography

Covey, S. 1991. *Principle-centered leadership*. New York, Summit Books.

Gould, D.; Petlochoff, L. 1988. "Participation motivation and attrition in young athletes", in F. L. Smoll, R. A. Magill, M. J. Ash (eds): *Children in sport*. Champaign, IL, Human Kinetics, 3rd edition, pp. 161–178.

Greenleaf, R. 1996. "The strategies of a leader." in D. M. Frick and L. C. Spears (eds.): *On becoming a servant leader: The private writings of Robert K. Greenleaf*. San Francisco, Jossey-Bass Publishers.

Maslow, A.H. 1968. *Toward a psychology of being*. New York, NY, Van Nostrand Reinhold.

Palmer, P. 1997. "Teaching in the face of fear", in *National Teaching and Learning Forum*, Vol. 6, No. 5.

Purkey, W.; Siegel, B. L. 2003. *Becoming an invitational leader*. Atlanta, Humanics Press.

Seligman, M. 2004. "Eudaemonia, the good life", in *Edge* magazine, No. 135, 25 Mar. (see: http://www.edge.org/3rd_culture/seligman04/seligman_index.html, accessed 31 Mar. 2006).

Siegel, B.; Purkey, W. 2002. *Becoming an invitational leader*. Georgia, Kennesaw State University.

Skinner, B. F. 1984. "The shame of American education", in *American Psychologist*, Vol. 39, No. 9, Sep., pp. 947–954.

Women's Sport Foundation. 2002. *National Action Plan for Women's and Girls' Sport and Physical Activity 2001–2002*. London.

SAFE AND HEALTHY SPORT: A TRAINING PACKAGE FOR YOUTH

12

Laurent Rivier

Introduction

The sporting world is turning more and more to professionalism, reaching unprecedented intensity levels and becoming an economic phenomenon in its own right. Many ethical questions and concerns about adequate medical protection and insurance for those taking part in sport activities are provoking discussion and debate. It is important, therefore, to inform people widely about the benefits and dangers of these practices, to keep abreast of current regulations and indeed to imagine revision of all these fields.

Overall assessment of safe sport

Taking part in sport should be a conscious activity that can only develop healthily within the limits of the physical and psychological abilities of the individual. Athletes expose their health to various dangers by training as hard as possible in preparation for a competition. When athletes respect their limits, use appropriate equipment and surround themselves with good advisers or coaches, they can manage these dangers. They also must pay particular attention to diet and staying hydrated. A healthy champion can develop symptoms of overexertion if the training regimen pushes the body beyond its ability to adapt. All parts of the body can be affected: inflamed tendons, cartilage loss, torn muscles and heart. Increased production of free radicals speeds up the ageing process. Antibodies cannot be produced in quantities large enough to fight infections. Athletes who strive for the best performance choose to expose their body to instability and imbalance. They must always be aware of their own capabilities and limits.

Science confirms the validity of this recommendation, as long as sport is not practised to excess. The intense effort and stress that competition places on athletes can have negative consequences, sometimes causing physical and mental illnesses. An athlete can guard against these dangers with adequate preparation and training. It is clear, however, that striving for the ultimate sporting performance can be extremely dangerous. Among the excesses that result from this frenzied search for success are over-training, under- or over-eating, the bad habits of untrained coaches and sports administrators, and even pharmacological manipulation. In the end, it is a question of deciding appropriate limits and using available expertise.

Knowledge about human physiology, sports medicine and sport psychology has increased rapidly over the past few years. Since they are linked to the development of new techniques and the use of equipment that was previously unavailable to athletes, it is not surprising that sporting performances are reaching new heights. However, these extraordinary feats can only be achieved if considerable or even excessive demands are made on the human body for periods ranging from a few weeks to several years.[1]

SAFE Sport instruments and means

The Foundation Sport, Science and Society FS3 SAFE Sport programme is targeted to reach young boys and girls, as well as all persons who interact with them in sports activities (sports teachers, trainers, doctors, political leaders, sponsors and so on). It will consist of five modules: four of them, called "teaching modules", deal with corruption, doping, violence and sport practised in a sustainable way; the fifth, called the "trans-disciplinary module", will cover all aspects but in a condensed form, to be presented as an introduction.

Our concept gives 8–14-year-olds first priority. In the following years, teenagers aged 15 to 20 will be the next group to be approached and properly informed. Eventually, in collaboration with sports association and federation managers, sponsors and media journalists, we will contact people involved in sports education, trainers, sports officers and larger groups of sportsmen and women.

The corresponding educational tools for each age group will be created specifically for that purpose and will be adapted according to each main region of the world. The main messages of teachers, professionals and athletes, recognized for their role of ambassadors, will be based on the educational values of sport. This message emphasizes the following issues.

Fair play and sport ethics

Sport instils many values in children. They learn to respect the adversary and accept a code of behaviour – the game's rules. Sport teaches children to accept defeat, be dignified winners and offer their talents and loyalty. It teaches them to use discussion and listening to solve problematic situations, enabling them to say "no" when they have to. In this way, children can appreciate the pleasure of a sporting encounter regardless of the result or outcome. These values can be learned at an early age and will last a lifetime.

Medical ethics

Athletes must have confidence and trust in their doctors, who in turn must care for or treat their patients. The framework and limits of sports doctors' activities are defined by medical ethics. These ethics allow them to help athletes achieve optimal physical and psychological performance without going too far. Doctors cannot accept cheating because this is usually detrimental to an athlete's long-term health and is blatantly contradictory to the educational role they should play in respect of their patients.

A professional athlete's career can last many years, but top-level sport can lead to irreversible accidents or serious illnesses if it is practised excessively. To prevent these occurrences, doctors should carry out regular medical examinations after a medical certificate is issued. In this way, they can monitor an athlete's health. They should never replace the coach or be dependent on the sports administrator. Although doctors enjoy total freedom to prescribe for non-athletes, they must respect the rules when dealing with athletes and, in particular, only prescribe authorized medicines. This is not antagonistic but complementary, since medical ethics are meant to protect athletes from the abuse and side effects of the products they use. Clearly, a doctor who observes alarm signals from the athlete's body should inform the patient. He should never mask those signals through inappropriate analgesic treatment or local anaesthetic because long-term damage to the athlete's career might be more important than short-term results.

If, contrary to all expectations, a doctor decides to treat an athlete with so-called "prohibited" products, he may do so on the condition that the athlete withdraws from all competitions in order to undergo treatment, gives up the licence and notifies the relevant authority of the treatment.

The following paragraphs describe three SAFE Sport modules.

Corruption[2]

Corruption does not usually affect the SAFE Sport targeted public (8–14 years of age). At that age, a lack of respect for the rules is more common, which when done voluntarily is considered cheating. Cheating can also be explained when one person wishes to push another to transgress rules for his or her own benefit. Cheating at the individual level, in this respect, can be used to explain corruption.

The aims of this module are to identify the various sports actors who contribute to developing corruption mechanisms, whatever their level of practice. Psychological and sociological dimensions will be covered, and the actions proposed to teachers and trainers will concern not only the athletes and the children they have to care for but also themselves, in such a way that they will be able to intervene within sport clubs and associations. Special attention will be given to young athletes in order to help them develop their own way of thinking and to help them be aware of the dangers of bad behaviour.

Doping

This module aims to demonstrate to young athletes that it is essential and indispensable for sport to be based on fair competition and respect for the health of each competitor. Information on the procedures used in anti-doping controls will be included, together with the influence of the various actors surrounding the athlete (family members, doctors, sports organizations at the local and national levels, international federations, lawyers, political authorities, media, sponsors and public opinion).

Violence

Aggressiveness is one of the internal characteristics of a number of sports. This can be moderated by the sports practice itself and the establishment of rules to prevent it. However, all these measures are sometimes not good enough to contain violent behaviours, such as hooliganism. Other forms of violence do exist, and these concern relationships between various sport actors and the degree of society's tolerance when confronted by these behaviours. Violence is not limited to physical aggression, but can take many forms, including physical violence, violent and sexual abuse, moral violence and institutional violence.

This module shows the different forms that violence can take in the context of sports activities in particular, and explains the corresponding rules. It will also develop strategies aimed at avoiding the exposure of children and teenagers to violence resulting from physical or psychological damage.

Sustainable development

Sustainable development, according to one definition, demands that we seek ways of living, working and being that enable all people worldwide to lead healthy, fulfilling and economically secure lives without destroying the environment and endangering people's future welfare. Agricultural expansion and urbanization have resulted in an unsustainable demand for land, marine and coastal resources. This has led to increased degradation of natural ecosystems and life-supporting systems that permit human civilization. Caring for natural resources and promoting their sustainable use is an essential response of the world community to ensure its own survival and well-being.

In 1999, the International Olympic Committee adopted Agenda 21 of the Olympic Movement. These recommendations should support sports organizations in the following sound sports practices: improvement of socio-economic conditions (cooperation, integration, health, consumption); conservation and management of natural resources; and reinforcement of the main actors (women, youth and elders). Sport must respect these ideas and support sustainable development objectives.[3] This module will transmit them by giving practical lessons to young sportsmen and women, and to their entourage (trainers, sport managers, parents).

Conclusion

Adequate education for promoting good sports practice and health is essential for future generations. Based on several key modules, the Foundation for Sport, Science and Society has constructed a holistic approach aimed at fighting the dangers in modern sport, such as violence, doping, corruption and gigantism. By building teenagers' personalities, it is possible to persuade adult athletes to offer the best and credible examples of correct behaviour. One of SAFE Sport's most important objectives is to develop young sportsmen and women who adhere to each module's principles through the will to belong to the world of safe, healthy and sustainable sport. Trainers, sport leaders, doctors and sponsors surrounding them should also arouse a similar conviction.

Today's sports problems cannot be solved by one single programme. SAFE Sport is being set up to create universal coverage in order to complete what is already in place or prepare for the future. Sports problems are complex, requiring several approaches working in parallel and coming from various sources in order to convey efficiently the correct message. We will be happy if we can contribute to bringing this message to the great athletes of tomorrow.

Notes

[1] When an adult reaches the latter half of life, muscles slacken and athletic performance gradually declines. Muscle loss is offset by increased fat. From age 35 onwards, the maximum oxygen capacity of VO_2 falls by 15 per cent every ten years, and from age 45 maximum strength declines by 1 per cent per year. The body also becomes heavier and not conducive to physical exercise. Growth hormone is credited with combating the effects of ageing. Regular physical activity triggers its production. For example, growth hormone levels can increase by a factor of 20 to 30 after a good training session. Consequently, experts believe that a sensible blend of strength, resistance and stamina training can slow the ageing process.

[2] The use of condemnable means to force someone to act against his or her duty and/or conscience.

[3] The idea of sustainable development in sport emerged in 1990 and was linked to the environment during major sport events (Albertville 1992 and Lillehammer 1994 Olympic Games). Many countries have adopted it as a political goal since it was first introduced in 1992.

Bibliography

Key texts

- Charter for Children's Sporting Rights (1988)
- Council of Europe: European Convention on Spectator Violence and Misbehaviour at Sports Events and in particular at football matches (1985)
- Council of Europe Code of Sport Ethics (1992)
- European Olympic Committees (EOC): Good Governance Principles in Sport (2001)
- Magglingen Declaration and Recommendations (2003)
- MINEPS IV Paris Declaration (2003)
- Olympic Movement Agenda 21 (1999)
- United Nations Environment Programme (UNEP): Triple Bottom Line Economic, Social, Natural Capital – UN "Global Compact" (2001)
- UNESCO Active Living Framework (2002)
- UNESCO International Convention against Doping in Sport (2005)
- World Anti-Doping Agency (WADA): World Anti-doping Code (2003)

Specific titles

Ayats, R.; Durbec, A. 2000. *Doping or no doping*. Lausanne, Panathlon Club.

Baddeley, M. (ed.). 2002. *Sports extrêmes – sportifs de l'extrême, la quête des limites.* Geneva, Georg.

Biddle, S. J. H.; Fox, K. R.; Boutcher, S. H. 2000. *Physical activity and psychological well-being.* London and New York, Routledge.

Brunet-Guedj, E.; Moyen, B.; Genéty, J. 2000. *Médecine du sport.* Paris, Masson, 6th edition.

Burke, L. M.; Desbrow, B.; Minehan, M. 2000. "Dietary supplements and nutritional ergogenic aids in sport", in L. Burke and V. Deakin (eds.): *Clinical sports nutrition.* Sydney, McGraw-Hill, 2nd edition, Ch. 17.

Cascua, S. 2002. *Le sport est-il bon pour la santé?* Paris, Odile Jacob.

Chappelet, J.-L. 2003. "Managing a safe and sustainable sport", in *Proceedings of the First Sport and Development International Conference*, Magglingen, Switzerland, 16-18 Feb., p. 45–61.

Drinkwater, B: L. 2002. "Women in sport", Vol. VIII of *The Encyclopaedia of Sports Medicine*, published by the IOC Medical Commission in collaboration with the International Federation of Sports Medicine. Maldon, MA, Blackwell Science.

Foundation Sport, Science and Society (FS3). 2001. *Safe sport*. Lausanne.

Got, C.; Alazard, J.-C. 1986. *Le sport sans risques: Prévenir les accidents par le choix des pratiques et du matériel*. Paris, Vigot.

Heipertz, W.; Böhmer, D.; Heipertz-Hengst, C. 1990. *Médecine du sport: Abrégé à l'usage des médecins, enseignants, entraîneurs, étudiants et sportifs* (translated from German by J. Etoré). Paris, Vigot.

Houlihan, B. 1999. *Dying to win: Doping in sport and the development of anti-doping policy*. Strasbourg, Council of Europe Publishing.

Maffulli, N.; Chan, K. M.; MacDonald, R.; Malina, R. M.; Parker, A. W. 2001. *Sport medicine for specific ages and abilities*. Edinburgh, London, Sydney and Toronto, Churchill Livingstone.

Micheli, L. J., et al. 1998. "Sports and children: Consensus statement on organized sports for children", in *Bulletin of the World Health Organization* (Geneva), Vol. 76, No. 5, pp. 445–447.

Monod, H.; Flandrois, R. 2003. *Physiologie du sport: Bases physiologiques des activités physiques et sportives*. Paris, Masson.

Müller-Platz, C. 1999. *Leistungsmanipulation: Ein Gefahr für unsere Sportler*. Cologne, Sport und Buch Strauss.

Riché, D. 1998. *Guide nutritionnel des sports d'endurance*. Paris, Vigot, 2nd edition.

Rivier, L. 1999. "Une zone grise dans le dopage des sportifs: Les substances ergogènes", in *Médecine et Hygiène*, Vol. 57, No. 2274, 27 Oct., pp. 2034–2041.

Singler, A.; Treutlein, G. 2001. *Doping – von der Analyse zur Praevention*. Aachen, Meyer and Meyer.

Thill, E.; Thomas, R.; Caja, J. 1994. *Manuel de l'éducateur sportif: Préparation au brevet d'état*. Paris, Vigot, 9th edition.

THE ROLE OF SPORT IN THE SOCIAL DEVELOPMENT OF YOUNG PEOPLE AND THE WIDER COMMUNITY: THE YCSCA

13

Geoff Thompson

Introduction

An unmotivated and uninspired child in a classroom with special needs becomes a disaffected adolescent, socially and culturally isolated. While young, this child is excluded from school and thrown onto the streets with nowhere to go and nothing to do. Once on the streets, the disillusioned youth belongs to a new culture – a gang culture, competing for territory and economic status. Youth culture now challenges our current institutions, instilling and replacing elitism with new boundaries and identities. Anti-social behaviour leads to crime and violence, which costs society billions of pounds and threatens our very quality of life.

Youth culture has been the experience and work of the Youth Charter for Sport, Culture and the Arts (YCSCA). During the past 12 years, this non-governmental organization (NGO) has worked with thousands of disaffected young people on street corners, in schools, care homes, secure units and prisons. The YCSCA has used sport and the arts to provide young people with the opportunity to develop in life.

Today's young people are facing a range of more complex situations than those experienced by their parents. Traditional education systems develop youth to a level where a relatively static employment market could easily absorb them, but many socio-economic forces threaten this system's very existence: unemployment growth; drug dealing; excessive consumption; intolerance; family disintegration; diminishing education standards; and general social conflict. The development of a voracious consumer society has swept aside the non-work horizons of an annual holiday, moderate sports opportunities, general hobbies and social intercourse in a local pub. Retailing giants have focused all this pressure on members of the 7–25 age group, who are also our society's future.

None of this has gone unrecognized: policies, strategies, schemes and programmes all abound within organizations such as the United Nations, the European Union and national governments, and have specific guidelines on youth policies. What appears to be lacking, however, are ways in which organizations can realize these policies and ideas using a strategic and coordinated framework. Nowhere can one find how such schemes will be practically undertaken to obtain the required result. Now, more than ever, an internationally coordinated approach is required to help young people develop and achieve in life. At present, there appears to be a number of isolated projects, resulting in duplicated efforts and misplaced human and financial resources. International organizations should use efficient information coordination, as well as experience, to build on the undoubted success of those who have identified and used an effective approach.

The youth of our world today are in desperate need of help; the instability of their future has never been so acute. More than ever before, the future of society and civilization depends on building individuals who are responsible, act with integrity and above all play a part in the development of their communities. The number one priority is to ensure that young people embrace their social responsibility as citizens.

The YCSCA aims to help young people, primarily between the ages of 7 and 25 years, by providing them with the opportunity to develop and achieve in life. Through sport, technology and the arts, youth is enabled to take an active and responsible part in society. The YCSCA has accomplished these aims by partnering over 500 other international organizations and NGOs. These include the Fédération Internationale de Football Association (FIFA), the International Olympic Commission, Manchester United Football Club, the United Nations and the World Health Organization.

The YCSCA's approach is built on the foundations of integrity, quality, equity, values and determination. It has empowered young people, communities, government agencies and the business sector, and now focuses its efforts to achieve a positive impact across social inclusion, regeneration and renewal agendas.

Case studies

Moss Side and Hulme, Manchester: Building bridges, building hope

In 1992, in a neighbourhood of historic social deprivation, a 14-year-old schoolboy named Benji Stanley was shot dead on the streets. The YCSCA responded to the national debate on the phenomena of youth gang culture and violence by meeting with the young people of the Procter Youth Centre, whose dream was to improve a run-down kick-about area next to their youth club. The YCSCA, in partnership with Hulme Regeneration, created a project raising

£100,000 from both the public and private sectors. John Kennedy Civil Engineering built an outdoor multi-sports arena catering for 37 different sporting activities, which also attracted additional funds from SportsMatch, the Sports Aid Foundation Trust and Hulme Regeneration. New and second-hand sports and gym equipment were provided by Forza UK and the Foundation for Sports and the Arts, which improved the choice of activities for users as well as establishing new-found trust between the young people and the wider community. Additional funding was raised locally to train 100 community sports leaders through the Central Council of Physical Recreation's Community Sports Leaders Award. This allowed trained volunteers to work within the community.

This project was the first truly multi-agency approach that demonstrated the role that sport and the arts could play not only in improving the social conditions for young people and the wider community, but more importantly in developing confidence and trust between the many local, public and private sector, and voluntary agencies. The project was officially launched by actress Susan Hampshire OBE and attracted personal support from former Sports Minister Ian Sproat, as well as Youth Charter for Sport (YCS) and vice-presidents.

The overall impact and success of this approach helped establish a platform and model that led to social inclusion programmes and regeneration projects that have seen over £5 million invested in the area over the past 12 years. The YCSCA's Sports Social Impact Model has since been replicated by other local authorities and youth-related organizations in neighbourhoods and communities throughout the world, demonstrating the role that sport and the arts can play as a social tool in the community impacting the areas of health, education, social order and the environment.

Tour of Los Angeles, 1994: The spirit of the streets

Following the Los Angeles (LA) riots in 1991, a group of 20 Angelenos representing one of the most diverse multi-cultural groups of young people to leave American shores visited the United Kingdom. The purpose of their visit was to develop the leadership skills and experience that would help them return to their communities better equipped to deal with the strife of everyday life. The tour group visited the area of Hulme and Moss Side, Greater Manchester, and shared their experiences of gang culture and violence. Their inspiration and contribution to the then troubled city inspired the "Spirit of Hulme and Moss Side Tour of Los Angeles". While touring downtown LA, 17 young people from Greater Manchester were exposed to sporting, cultural, artistic, social, political and economic values. Furthermore, they would look at the role that sport was playing in one of the most socially disadvantaged neighbourhood communities where anti-social behaviour and gang culture were sadly the way of life.

The Moss Side Millennium Powerhouse was the legacy of the Spirit of the Streets Tour. The group members wished to see a centre designed and operated by local youngsters in partnership with the wider community, while providing them with a sense of ownership, identity, commitment and belonging. The aim was to refurbish the then Moss Side Youth Centre into a twenty-first-century sports, arts, education, training, IT and employment enterprise. This approach has now been developed into the YCSCA's Social Centre of Excellence Regeneration Project.

As part of the social and cultural legacy of the 2002 Commonwealth Games, the "Spirit of the Streets Tour of South Africa" has provided a life-changing experience that will bring similar legacies and benefits to ten communities in the United Kingdom and the Commonwealth through the Citizenship in Action initiative.

In June 1995, 106 leaders were enrolled on the Junior Sports Leaders Award (JSLA) and Community Sports Leaders Award (CSLA) courses. The CSLA course delivered by the Leisure Services Department of Manchester City Council successfully trained 12 CSLA graduates, who completed their course in May 1996. They are still working as volunteers providing sporting activities.

Work with individuals – Pathways to life

Over the past 12 years, the YSCSA has worked with young people in schools, communities, secure units and young offenders' institutions and prisons. The Youthwise Personal Development Programme, Social Centre of Excellence and Webwise IT Project have all been inspired by the experiences, contributions, successes and failures of the young people we have worked with. Some examples are given below.

From exclusion to inclusion

Adesuwa McCalla was a young woman with lots of ability, talent and ambition, but going nowhere. She hoped to work in the media and went on endless work placements in television and radio, but still found herself unemployed, with nothing to do.

Selected as one of the participants in the "1994 Spirit of the Streets Tour of LA", Adesuwa visited Los Angeles to gain a greater insight as to how she could develop herself and benefit her community. Upon returning to Manchester she became one of three participants in the Spirit of LA Tour who helped establish the YCSCA Headquarters at Salford Quays in 1996. During that time, Adesuwa developed the social skills required to help her realize her dream to attend the world-famous Howard University in Washington, DC. With a plan developed, she began to make applications, as well as secure the necessary grant funding for her scholarship. With no grants available, YCSCA identified resources from its social enterprise fund and also secured travel from British Airways. Adesuwa was committed: she sold some of her sportswear, further assisted by her mother adding to the much-needed funds. Adesuwa finally gained acceptance, with the YCSCA providing ongoing support. Although she encountered many initial obstacles, she also put to good use all the social skills and obvious talent and ability that she was capable of realizing. Adesuwa graduated with a first-class honours degree in International Law and now works for MTV in New York. More importantly, she is now sponsoring two other young women in realizing their potential.

From incarceration to inclusion

Sipho Tshabalala's story is a remarkable one for a young man growing up in Soweto, South Africa, during and after the apartheid era that offered little opportunity. Like many youths who helped liberate the Rainbow Nation, he was to find his energies and political indoctrination developed and forged through soccer. As a keen supporter of the Orlando Pirates, his youthful energies were exercised within the many local rivalries between those who supported the Keiser Chiefs (the rival team). It was a local derby match between these two teams that was to change Sipho's life. Following initial friendly exchanges, violence occurred with Sipho defending himself and wounding a Pirates supporter, who later died of injuries he inflicted. Sipho was to spend five years in the infamous Leekwop Prison, but was to show that this tragic accident could be turned into a positive opportunity. He developed the Prisoner Development Programme, secured resources and established an IT centre. In addition, he remarkably organized a national apology to the victims of those in Leekwop Prison who had committed these crimes against them.

On release, Sipho began a post-rehabilitation programme with assistance from the YCSCA South Africa desk. Through his experience, he assisted project and programme developments like the hosting of an Irish youth group, the Youth Day celebrations in 2001, and the Selekelela High School project. Sipho's dedication and hard work led to his eventual hiring as the personal assistant to the CEO of the South African Football Association. Sipho continues to assist the YCSCA South Africa desk and is a remarkable example of one person's ability to overcome personal tragedy.

Conclusions

- One of the few activities common to youth throughout the world and acceptable within each country is sport. The idea is to use sport as a means to develop citizenship values in young people and to help them not only determine their goals, but achieve them through the contribution that they can and should make to their communities.

- Priority for receiving this help should be given to those communities throughout the world that are severely affected by social exclusion, deprivation and conflict, and are seeing an increase in criminal activity. Presently there is no mechanism that is able to detect the priority areas and channel support towards them.

- There needs to be a coordinated effort to help the youth of the world within a proper international framework that allows for the flexibility of different approaches, innovations, projects and programmes to be presented, delivered, organized, supervised and successfully achieved. This help must be given with total respect for national and social customs, inherent in the identity of the country involved, while providing social and economic outcomes that are internationally recognized as providing each country with responsive and responsible adults.

- Only the capacity to understand and to establish a dialogue among the communities can generate satisfactory needs assessment, which in turn leads to cost-effective and impact-oriented projects.

- However, there must be a mechanism that would allow YCSCA and similar entities to be given visibility and a means to act appropriately and expediently.

Bibliography

Blake, G. No date. "Sport the great integrator", Leisure dissertation. Roehampton, University of Surrey.

Centre for Leisure and Sport Research. 2002. *Count me in: The dimensions of social inclusion through culture and sport*, report for the Department for Culture, Media and Sport. Leeds, Leeds Metropolitan University, Mar.

European Commission. 2001. *A new impetus for European youth*, White Paper. Brussels, COM(2001) 681.

Richards, G. 1970. *Youth at risk report – Outward Bound course for the socially handicapped.* Canberra, National Outdoor Education and Leadership Services.

United Nations. 2002a. *Creation of Youth Advisory Committee to Congress of Non-Governmental Organizations* (CONGO). New York, NY (see: http://www.un.org/esa/socdev/unyin/opportunities.htm, accessed 22 Mar. 2006).

—. 2002b. *Traités multilateraux: Pour une participation universelle – thème 2002: development durable.* New York, NY.

United Kingdom, Department for Culture, Media and Sport. 1999. *Policy action team 10 – a report to the Social Exclusion Unit – The contribution that arts and sport can make.* London, House of Commons.

—, HM Treasury. 2002. *Promoting sport in the community.* London, Apr.

IDENTIFYING JOBS, CORE AND SOFT SKILLS FOR EMPLOYABILITY

14

Giovanni di Cola

Introduction

This chapter focuses on three different aspects of the ILO Youth Sport Programme (YSP) that have actually helped mainstreaming sport into development: (1) assessing needs at local and national levels with both sport and development partners, including experiences of country needs; (2) identifying job opportunities and services for youth in the world of sport and beyond as a result of a dialogue established within a network between sport institutions, social and development partners; and (3) developing youth employability skills starting with the sports sector which comprises both soft and core skills.

The ILO Youth Sport Programme: Needs assessment, from project to policy level

The ILO has developed the YSP, which contributes to inserting youth within the sport community through partnership.[1] The YSP has two levels of interventions: the policy level and the project level.

At the policy level, the YSP has helped the Albanian authorities and the United Nations Country Team to review the Youth National Policy. This assistance facilitated the full integration of sports partners into the development process.

At the project level, workshops carried out in 2004–2005 in Senegal and El Salvador identified areas for joint work and partnerships with the Minister of Sports of Senegal, the Minister of Labour of El Salvador and, as main national counterparts, sports federations in Senegal and the National Olympic Committee (NOC) in El Salvador. The detailed results of Senegalese activities are described below; information about El Salvador can be found in Chapter 8.

Since July 2004 activities have also been carried out at the project level in Mozambique. Women are being trained at Boane's Olympicafrica sport centre in a cooperative where children's school uniforms are manufactured. This is the starting point of a cooperative agreement between the International Olympic Committee (IOC), the NOC of Mozambique and a local development agency.

The development community often looks at sport and development as conflicting parameters. Development leaders, in most cases, perceive sport as merely a recreational tool rather than a value-based engine that can develop core skills for youth employability. Sport, as explained in other chapters of this book, is more than competition, money and, certainly, doping. The ILO's YSP aims to positively acknowledge sport-specific skills and values,[2] as well as making sure that local needs are taken into consideration in the global economy.

Sports institutions that can both assess their socio-economic needs and pool efforts, resources and capacities for partnerships are a great asset to any global community. In this respect, the YSP's priority target is youth, namely young women and men who need to acquire and upgrade skills and capacities for employability. That way, they can be inserted into society from a social and economic point of view.

YSP outcomes by country

Albania

A national network of sport and development partners was established in Albania to deal with issues of common interest:

- youth and sport in the development agendas;

- advocacy, sensitization, information sharing, media and volunteerism;

- human rights, equal opportunities and gender;

- youth and sports supporting local/community development;

- youth sports and arts;

- preventive health and working conditions;

- youth sports and job opportunities, service providers and physical well-being;

- youth sports and education, training and coaching; and

- youth sports and infrastructure.

The partners identified a set of activities within each area as part of a national strategy for youth development, supported by the entire United Nations (UN) system agencies. Many of these activities involved using sport in socio-economic development. They included a wide range of initiatives:

- linking specific sport events to tourism development at the local level;

- using sport as a vehicle to develop educational tools for schoolchildren;

- reducing health-related problems at work by encouraging sport and fitness for workers; and

- coaching education and certification so that coaches develop skills needed for dealing with socio-economic issues.[3]

Senegal

Senegal's key need is an inventory of sports-related jobs. This is a result of both the explosion of new services surrounding sport infrastructures and facilities, and the need to properly reorganize sport jobs, including coaches, social educators and teachers. This inventory offers the opportunity for a joint venture in the direction taken on employment with the Ministry of Labour. It also forms a broader review of the "legislation cadre" of sports in the country.

Senegal has the technical capacity to produce small sport manufactures (volley-nets, balls, etc.). At the project level, the country needs to turn this capacity into services that would generate sustainable income and decent jobs for youth. The projects should be systematically strengthened with a microcredit insurance scheme to ensure sustainability.

Partnerships could form around a pool of sport federations and by sport category (water, martial arts and others). Each federation can enhance its capacities by providing services to each other. For example, the fishing federation could repair boats used for rowing; or karate schools could provide regular education in rural areas. This process would turn services into jobs and income-generating activities into the sustainable development of services and skills training. Coaching should be reinforced throughout to accompany this trend.

In a workshop carried out in Senegal at the end of 2004, the Minister of Sports emphasized the need to conduct an inventory of the new sport-related jobs and occupations. For example, the sport facilities in an urban area involved such tasks as catering, coaching, security, and maintenance and building infrastructures, among others. This exercise would lead to identifying training needs that differ from the current and traditional programmes in the education system, and not only in sport science and physical education. It would also contribute to reducing the gap between employers' needs and skills development and labour market opportunities.

During the same workshop, different sports federations, such as the well-established Senegalese Sport Federation and the newly established Rowing Federation, discovered that they could create new synergies and service exchanges through boat logistics and maintenance. Amazingly, the Senegalese Labour Federation found that new activities resulting from this kind of partnership could be an opportunity to appropriately retrain unoccupied workers in the fishing sector.

Mozambique

Following an assessment conducted with the IOC in June 2003, about 20 women were trained to work in and run a cooperative in Mozambique. The women produced almost 200 school uniforms for children (552 pairs in total). The cooperative was set up by the project within the first two months of the activities, following the training.

The creation of the cooperative responds to a need expressed by the population of Mabanja, outside Boane Sport Centre (around 50 km from Maputo). The NOC of Mozambique realized that without increased income and the opportunity to strengthen local capacity, the population could never manage the Boane Centre. In other words, it would never become self-sustained, developing sport at all levels. The ILO was therefore called upon to provide expertise in capacity building and cooperative development, among other positive measures.

The training has also linked the rural area of Mabanja with the local development agency of Matola, opening a perspective for a new market and economic synergies. The group of women will act as a resource for social mobilization on HIV/AIDS prevention.[4] Clearly, the project has local-level implications only, but it can expand its reach further through a training/facilitation module scheduled to take place over the next months. Furthermore, the national authorities, recognizing that national policies were not targeting youth, took up the issue of sport for strategic human resource and skills development aimed at that age group. As in the case of Albania, the United Nations Country Team (UNCT), collaborating with the Ministry of Youth and Sports beyond the Ministry of Labour, embraced the sport sector as an integral part of the country's poverty-reduction strategies. Further training and the establishment of a network of sport and development partners at the national level by the UNCT, with the support of the NOC and the ILO, has led to the identification in Boane of different job categories (table 14.1).

Table 14.1   Examples of jobs identified as a result of the consultations carried out in Mozambique

Jobs identified	Training/retraining required	Development objectives

• Sport centre managers
 	
• Educators and coaches
 	
• Community leaders
 	
• Sports facilities logistics maintenance personnel
	• Training in local development and territorial synergies in the areas of:
	  – local governments and national institutions
	  – sports environment
	  – sports tourism
	  – training for educators and coaches
	  – sport/management for federations and for sports centres
		• Increased number of teachers/coaches/educators in sport and related activities
		
		• Upgrading multipurpose sports facilities and recreational centres
		
		• Managing competitions and sports events at the local level

Strategic linking

The main outcomes of the exercise described above are both the identification of new types of job and the need to conduct an inventory of job categories in all developing countries.

The institutional shift that the YSP and its common framework have provided in Albania especially is quite impressive. For example, the Ministry of Youth and Sport appointed the new director of "Sport for All" during the YSP process. The director also recognized the importance of the network of sport and development partners, used both by the Ministry itself and the UNCT in advancing socio-economic issues.

In Mozambique, the Ministry of Youth and Sport and the Minister of Labour, supported by the UNCT-Mozambique, and more recently by UK Sport and the Youth Sports Charter, started to work on sport socio-economic-related issues, including girls' education, skills training for youth and HIV prevention, while also exploring new avenues for collaboration with private sponsors. As indicated, the YSP process in Mozambique wants to link properly not only to national development strategies, but also to the UN Development Assistance Framework (UNDAF) and the Poverty Reduction Strategy Papers (PARPA).

This is an opportunity to use sport's values, skills and technical resources and to mainstream them into national development policies. Every opportunity to access local needs towards sports partnerships should be explored. In this context, international conferences, networking, and research and development are becoming part of a broader effort to process information towards changes. These changes will improve people's lives as well as empower youth to deal with socio-economic challenges and decent work.

The result of the exchange between sports parties and the development community is that policy may come before project activities. Experience has shown, however, that policy issues are generally interrelated with project-level issues. The project cycle embeds the processes of monitoring and evaluation. Like a matrix for partnerships, it must take into consideration the following areas: objectives; targets; means of action; activities; direct implementation; partnerships; and evaluation. The partnership should not be set up without the following:

• a matrix that provides a list of partners (local, national and international);

• contributions (financial, human resources, technical capacities and equipment);

• links with national policies; and

• basic indicators for monitoring and evaluation, such as ownership, accountability and sustainability.

Since a full set of indicators concerning the evaluation and impact of the MDGs on sport activities already exists, there is no need to elaborate a new set of them.

A desk review, undertaken at the request of the ILO's In Focus Programme Skills, Knowledge and Employability, has identified sport-specific skills that can be added to core skills for employability necessary to perform a job at the local, national or international level. Table 14.2 lists the sport-specific skills, as described in the Report of the United Nations Inter-Agency Task Force on Sport for Development and Peace (United Nations, 2003, p. 8).

Table 14.3 refers to the outcome of a desk review of various sport projects. These projects include, on one hand, a pool of sport-related projects funded by

Table 14.2   Skills and values learned through the sports sector

• Cooperation	• Fair play
• Communication	• Sharing
• Respect for the rules	• Self-esteem
• Problem-solving	• Trust
• Understanding	• Honesty
• Connecting with others	• Self-respect
• Leadership	• Tolerance
• Respect for others	• Resilience
• Value of effort	• Teamwork
• How to win	• Discipline
• How to lose	• Confidence
• How to manage competition	

Source: United Nations, 2003.

Table 14.3   Sport-specific skills in the employability framework

Sport-specific skills[1]	Reference projects: EU[2] and UN[3]	Relevant factors for employers: competencies[4]	Relevant factors for employers: qualities[5]
Interpersonal communication	EU: Denmark Title: *Life manager* Project aim: train Baltic sport associations on intercultural and interpersonal communication, leadership, team building, etc., based on the Danish experience (Train the trainers module)	• Negotiating • Persuading • Establishing, maintaining and using networks • Sharing information	• Empathizing • Being assertive
Teamwork	EU: Latvia Title: *Summer and Winter sports games in Berzes krasti* Project aim: use the values of sport activities to teach youth social skills such as teamwork, respect for rules and tolerance	• Cooperation • Coaching, mentoring and giving feedback	• Able to work as an individual • Working in a multicultural environment
Problem solving	UN-NGO: Moving the Goalposts KILIFI (MGTK), Kenya Title: *Football, social support and peer-led education for rural teenage girls* Project aim: within the framework of tackling poverty through more access to education and health, poor Kenyan women and girls are introduced to football in order to develop motivation, confidence and self-awareness. More importantly, this sport will give the girls the chance to be leaders, strengthening their decision-making capacities, critical thinking and how to find a way out of problems through solutions	• Develop creative and innovative solutions	• Showing independence and initiative • Showing mediation capacities

/cont'd

Sport-specific skills[1]	Reference projects: EU[2] and UN[3]	Relevant factors for employers: competencies[4]	Relevant factors for employers: qualities[5]
Leadership	EU: Sweden Title: *Sport leadership: an investment in the future* Project aim: create an international leadership training programme for young people, based in local communities with a large number of immigrants. Special attention devoted to recruiting girls	• Develop critical thinking • Solid decision-making capacities • Self-management	• Showing self-confidence capacities • Showing understanding and sympathy
Discipline	EU: Hungary Title: *Heroes for a healthier and sportier future* Project aim: demonstrate the importance of certain sports values within the learning and education process, such as discipline, order, and persistence	• Prioritizing	• Respect for duties and obligations • Determination • Commitment • Focusing on personal effort
Fair play	EU: Germany Title: *Children in sport clubs in good hands* Project aims: within the framework of sports clubs, associations and schools, children will be involved in sports activities and will develop core values such as fair play, respect for one's opponent and the rules, and tolerance		• Respect for rules • Transparency • Honest behaviour when competing
Tolerance	1. EU: The Netherlands Title: *Support-it* Project aim: promote tolerant behaviours and stimulate youngsters to participate in preventing intolerant behaviours	• Mediate conflicting situations	• Respect diversity

Tolerance	2. UN: Danish Gymnastics-GlobalEduSport-Asciana	
	Title: *Training of children in children's centres in Kabul through sport*	
	Project aim: use sport for peace and stability. Children involved will develop important social skills such as mutual tolerance, tools for conflict resolution and health awareness	
Healthy lifestyle	1. EU: Austria	• Develop positive energy
	Title: *Learning while being active*	• Sound nutritional habits
	Project aim: promote a healthy lifestyle. Sports activities will show the positive influence they have on children and youth's physical, social and mental development. Simultaneously, the project will promote core skills such as fairness, tolerance, team spirit and performance	• Move for health
		• Avoid drug, alcohol and tobacco addiction
	2. UN: NGO Vivario and Luta Pela Paz, Rio de Janeiro, Brazil	
	Title: *Fight for peace*	
	Project aim: use sport to channel aggression into positive energy. The methodology teaches respect for rules, discipline, self-confidence, competition and dedication to sport. It fosters the culture of peace through classes on human rights, family, culture and violence. It also provides access to the job market by arranging internships and employment opportunities for project youth	

/cont'd

Sport-specific skills[1]	Reference projects: EU[2] and UN[3]	Relevant factors for employers: competencies[4]	Relevant factors for employers: qualities[5]
Equal access and justice	1. UN: United Nations Volunteers (UNV) – 15 May School, Viet Nam. Title: *Youth participation project at 15 May School* Project aim: improve child and youth participation through education and vocational training. Particularly, the project addresses children with behavioural problems, restoring self-respect and confidence while providing opportunities to the most disadvantaged people in Ho Chi Min 2. EU: United Kingdom Title: *Young enabled sailors (YES) – Educational opportunities through disabled sailors* Project aim: YES will demonstrate that sailing is one of the few sports in which disabled and non-disabled people can participate on equal terms, both for leisure or competition *Sport discipline used: Sailing*	• Independent judgement ability	• Objectivity • Lack of prejudice
Solidarity and friendship	EU: France Title: *Artisport 2004/Athens and the Olympic spirit* Project aim: carry out cultural and artistic production on the basis of reflections and values of the Olympic ideals, such as peace, democracy, justice, fair play, solidarity, friendship, equality, etc. Parallel sporting championships in Olympic disciplines will take place		• Sharing values • Team spirit

Peace building[6] and conflict resolution	UN: NGO Civil Peace Service – Rwanda Title: *Football for peace* Project aim: encourage football as a sport discipline in order to teach responsibility, improve capabilities in conflict resolution and fight ethnic discrimination dividing the Rwandan population	• Consensus decision making • Encouraging and maintaining dialogue	• Understanding opponents • Respect for rules • Non-discriminatory behaviour
How to win and how to lose	EU: Poland Title: *Aware – more skilful* Project aim: show children and youth the importance of honest competition, as well as core values such as noble rivalry in accordance with fair play rules, accepting defeat, enjoying victory, and striving to be better		• Fair play • Respect opponents • Commitment to effort
How to manage competition[7]	EU: Poland Title: *The Village Sport Animator* Project aim: strengthen the competencies of a group of young people dealing with the organization of sports events at the local community level. These youth received further training on issues such as organizing popular events, development of mind through sport, sport and health, and the use of computers in their work	• Managing and training • Leadership • Commitment • Physical literary (the ability to control one's body movement)	
Non-discriminatory and socially inclusive	1. EU: Greece Title: *Sport through arts within the framework of the 2004 Athens Olympic Games* Project aim: addressed to teachers and physical education instructors, it tries to find new solutions through sports values to all types of	• Peace culture • Dialogue among opponents	• Respect for diversity • Tolerance

/cont'd

Sport-specific skills[1]	Reference projects: EU[2] and UN[3]	Relevant factors for employers: competencies[4]	Relevant factors for employers: qualities[5]
Non-discriminatory and socially inclusive	discrimination, such as racism, social exclusion on the basis of origin, gender, faith, sexual orientation and age. The project will create a model of interactive education on Olympic values		
	2. EU: Sweden		
	Title: *Sport as means of educating underprivileged young people*		
	Project aim: significantly contribute to social integration of young people from poor neighbourhoods. Local clubs organize non-formal education activities to strengthen tolerance, fair play and personal development		
	3. EU: Greece		
	Title: *Equal opportunities*		
	Project aim: involve equally able-bodied and disabled people in sport initiatives to raise awareness of the Paralympic Games. Theatrical performances for children will focus on diversity, tolerance and social inclusion		
Volunteering	UN: United Nations Volunteers (UNV) in Ghana, Madagascar, Sierra Leone and South Africa. Title: *Youth and Sport for Development and Volunteerism* Project aim: use sport to mobilize youth as community volunteers and recipients of skills and knowledge, and promote volunteerism to contribute to achieving the MDGs	• Take care of others	• Commitment to contribution • Understand vulnerability

Notes to Table 14.3

[1] *Report from the United Nations Inter-Agency Task Force on Sport for Development and Peace*, 2003.

[2] European Commission DG for Education and Culture: "Pool of sport and service-centred partnership" (2004) includes a selection of 250 projects co-financed by the EU and implemented in collaboration with sports partner organizations at the European country level. The general aim of the projects reflects the importance of sports values and skills for employability, and their knowledge transfer to children and youth as well as to all community members.

[3] Sport and Development International Platform (see: http://www.sportanddev.org, accessed 24 February 2006) includes a selection of 158 projects funded and implemented by relevant UN agencies, NGOs, and other sports partners (such as international sports associations and federations, national and local sport clubs). Activities, all related to the use of sport as a means for social and economic development, also address serious issues such as poverty, unemployment, violence, crime and all types of discrimination. Some projects have been implemented in war-torn countries such as Afghanistan, in post-conflict situations such as Namibia and Rwanda, or in cities as in Brazil where urban violence and antisocial behaviours are affecting communities.

[4] The *Employability skills for the future* report (Commonwealth of Australia, 2002) clearly defines the difference among the terms "skills", "competencies" and "qualities". Specifically, a competence is used to refer to an "observable behaviour performed by a specified level and therefore provides a basis for the assessment of performance".

[5] The Commonwealth of Australia report (2002) also defines qualities as those capabilities of an individual in most instances, although "characteristics" is sometimes used to describe workplace/job-specific requirements.

[6] It is worth recalling here the importance of sport in peace-building activities. In fact, it is the respect for the rules of the game by opponents that avoids discrimination throughout the same game. Two famous examples are those between India and Pakistan at cricket or between the US and China during the famous ping-pong match in the 1970s.

[7] Specific training on leadership and managing big events and competitions is carried out by the MEMOS programme.

the European Union in 2004 on the occasion of the European Year of Physical Education and Sport; and, on the other, a list of UN sport and development-related projects inventoried for the preparation of the UN Inter-Agency Task Force referred to above. The aim of the desk review was to identify sport-specific skills that can complement core skills for employability, thus contributing to reinforce youth training needs for labour market insertion.

Sport-specific skills are considered basic ethical requirements for all competitors accepting the sport rules of any discipline, for example volunteering, teamwork and team building, tolerance and accepting rules. These skills are unique and add value to generic employability skills. These sport-specific skills eventually fit both the ILO framework and other internationally and nationally recognized skills frameworks for employability (Commonwealth of Australia, 2002).

In fact, the ILO Human Resources Development: Education, Training and Lifelong learning Recommendation, 2004 (No. 195) establishes a framework of skills for employability. Article 2 of the Recommendation defines the four key elements of the framework:

(a) the term *lifelong learning* encompasses all learning activities undertaken throughout life for the development of competencies and qualifications;

(b) the term *competencies* covers the knowledge, skills and know-how applied and mastered in a specific context;

(c)   the term *qualifications* means an expression of the vocational or pro-
      fessional abilities of a worker that is recognized at international, national
      or sectoral levels;

(d)   the term *employability* relates to portable competencies and qualifi-
      cations that enhance an individual's capacity to make use of the
      education and training opportunities available in order to secure and
      retain decent work; [*employability*] is also the term used to compare the
      sport-specific skills with the internationally recognized skills for
      employability.

Using the above information, an additional comparison between generic
employability skills, as perceived in selected countries, and sport-specific skills
selected by the ILO, table 14.4 shows a more comprehensive picture of how
generic and sport-specific skills match and complement one another.
Analysing the differences, we find that both from a professional and personal
point of view, young workers entering the labour market with sport-specific
skills would be well equipped with creativity, team-building and, most of all,
peaceful and tolerant behaviour vis-à-vis cultural diversity. The last skill is
absolutely necessary for youth entering the labour market in a global economy
with such large discrepancies and diversity.

Table 14.4 shows how sport-specific skills can complement core skills for
employability. One would eventually like to determine how much they could
improve the work environment. Workers need the opportunity to acquire and
shape these skills, according to their own needs and the labour market,
through sport activities and related training. We should assume that the sport-
specific skills could significantly improve the work environment because they
fit nicely with the internationally recognized skills shown in table 14.4.
However, the analysis would take us much further. For example, if we take
row 2, "Communication", we discover that sport skills such as interpersonal
communication and the respect for rules and others are stronger than the ones
adopted by the countries selected in the review.

The same applies to the "technology" cluster in row 7 reinforced in
sport-specific skills by the notion of "using equipment". It is well known that
using sports equipment for performances is one of the best assets of the
sporting industry in relation to technological change and industrial clusters. A
long list of successful experiences of former coaches and trainers began by
introducing technology (in skiing, Grand Prix motor races, sailing, etc.) to
their athletes with which they started businesses on performance management
with satellite applications, in partnership with universities and research
centres. Nowadays, the cultural cluster is even more important and is fully
combined with the aspect of tolerance. Amateur or professional sport does

Table 14.4   Comparative table of generic employability skills with sport-specific skills

Australia: key competencies	United Kingdom: core skills	Canada: employability skills profile	United States: workplace know-how	Sport-specific skills selected by the ILO
1. Collecting, analysing and organizing information	Communication	Thinking skills	Information Foundation skills: basic skills	Volunteering Taking care of others
2. Communicating ideas and information	Communication Personal skills: improving own performance and learning	Communication skills	Information Foundation skills: basic skills	Interpersonal communication Respect for rules Respect for others
3. Planning and organizing activities	Personal skills: improving own performance and learning	Responsibility skills Thinking skills	Resources Foundation skills: personal qualities	Managing competition (events organizer)
4. Working with others and in teams	Personal skills: working with others	Positive attitudes and behaviour Work with others Adaptability	Interpersonal skills	Teamwork Team-building Multidisciplinarity
5. Using mathematical ideas and techniques	Numeracy: application of numbers	Understand and solve problems using mathematics	Foundation skills: basic skills	Managing performance, and training
6. Solving problems	Problem solving	Problem-solving and decision-making skills Learning skills	Foundation skills: thinking	Problem solving Mediation skills
7. Using technology	Information technology	Use technology Communication skills	Technology systems	Using technology and sport equipment
8. Cultural understanding	Modern foreign languages	Manage information Use numbers Work safely Participate in projects and tasks		Healthy lifestyle Fair play Tolerance

Source: Commonwealth of Australia, 2002, comparative table integrated with the ILO column showing core skills resulting from the sport sector (ILO/Universitas Programme, 2005).

not need to go through training filters that would leave some prejudice behind. The same may be said of healthy lifestyles and fair play.

Soft skills

Soft skills are a set of skills that influence how we interact with each other. The term includes such abilities as effective communication, creativity, analytical thinking, diplomacy, change readiness, problem solving, leadership, team building and listening skills. The goal of soft skills training is to give students the opportunity to learn and practise new patterns of behaviour and in so doing to enhance human relations.[5]

A Namibia-based sport- and development-related project provides an example of sports skills development benefits (although these are recorded as "soft" skills rather than core skills for employability). Project officials of Physically Active Youth (PAY), supported by the Canada Commonwealth Games and the University of Toronto, used development through a sports programme to provide a combination of academic tutoring and physical activity to disadvantaged youth (i.e. teenagers more likely to fail or drop out of school). The programme's physical activities test both strength and academic knowledge, while teaching values such as cooperation. PAY links directly to school systems and promotes youth involvement through an elected youth advisory board.

The project has had an immediate and positive impact in Namibia for 40 students at risk, offering them two hours of daily activity and several field trips. Thirty-seven of the 40 students, who otherwise would have failed or dropped out, passed their tenth-grade exams. These students can use the skills they learned and the self-esteem they gained to improve the life of their communities. Through this experience, PAY has also increased their future employment prospects.[6]

A second example is a programme that promotes adherence to the Code of Ethics and Good Practice at the European level to ensure the high quality of physical education programmes in all schools in the best interests of the children. The Code, which contains the principles embodied in the Council of Europe's Code of Sports Ethics, consists of a series of guidelines for all people responsible for children, namely parents, guardians and teachers. Teachers and adults interacting with children in physical education should carry out this work with integrity and respect towards children. In particular, they should take into consideration the principles listed in table 14.5.

Certain situations may cause children physiological stress within the physical education context:

• pressure to excel or win, or other inappropriate expectations;

• excessive criticism of a child or team;

Table 14.5   Soft skills as developed in physical education activities

Teacher–child relationship	Behaviour of physical education teachers and personal standards
• Open, positive and encouraging	• Maintain the highest standards of personal conduct and support the principles of fair play
• Free from verbal, physical, emotional or sexual abuse	• Be responsible for setting boundaries between a working relationship and friendship with children
• Respectful of the needs and developmental stage of the children	• Realize that children or outsiders could misinterpret certain situations or friendly actions
• Aimed at the promotion of enjoyment and individual progress	• Never exert undue influence over a child in order to obtain personal benefit or reward
• Carried out in a context where children's rights are protected	• Be watchful of all situations, particularly bullying (mobbing) which may occur: – child to child – group to child – adult to child – child to group

- inappropriate use of sanctions, discipline or rejection;

- displaying dislike of a child or disapproval of skills/performance ability;

- failure to provide support, encouragement and approval for effort and achievement;

- failure to involve a child/children as fully as possible in the activity;

- the use of inappropriate language.

These should be avoided, and instead should consist of benchmarks.

Likewise, the following practices are injurious to children's health and welfare and should also be avoided:

- pushing a child to perform at a level that is beyond his or her capacity related to age or maturation level;

- making demands on children that lead to burn-out;

- knowingly permitting an injured child to participate in a physical activity;

- failure to take into account standard safety precautions or adequate precautions to protect a child from environmental hazards;

- failure to take into account a child's ailments or relevant weaknesses.

The result is that sport can be used to reinforce ethical behaviour as much as it can be used to address and identify abusive situations that children may have suffered independently of the practice of sport. As shown in table 14.5, this is an important issue as it may be used not only in crisis and post-conflict situations but also to combat child labour and to ensure decent working conditions for all workers.

Conclusion

Although not exhaustive, the analysis in this chapter indicates that sport and sport-related activities may address some of the problems of youth insertion. They may offer an opportunity for skills development. Coaching and physical education can contribute to effecting social change, as well as addressing the issue of equal opportunities. Sports institutions are different from both the ILO's tripartite social partners (governments, employers and workers) and UN development agencies. The two groups have separate mandates and, therefore, partnership is fundamental to develop joint activities and policies. Sports organizations have a record of excellent partnerships, serving as a good collaborative framework to carry out effective programmes. A partnership matrix, the ILO Common Framework for Sport and Development, brings (technical and human) resources together through relevant training processes and modalities similar to those described above. Development, in general, can benefit from sports partnership if ethical solid ground is agreed by the partners.

The skills development process within the Youth Sport Programme opens doors to other research areas within the world of sport: women's leadership and empowerment in the sport sector; governance of sport federations and authorities; and coaches as invitational leaders for social change. It is indeed necessary to strengthen and expand a global alliance that promotes social and economic youth insertion such as the ILO's Youth Employment Network (YEN), using sport as a way to connect with other institutions.[7]

It would also be useful to collaborate with universities and the world of sport towards a modular training package (master's or post-graduate studies) based on the above sport-specific skills and core specific skills for employability. This training would complement courses already in place, which concentrate on sport administration and federation management, with sport sciences. This multidisciplinary approach would definitely be an asset for youth because it could easily adapt to the labour market's changing situations and opportunities.

The combination of values and skills embedded in sport and sport disciplines is able to determine training for job opportunities. Apart from a few exceptions, like Tunisia, where more than 60 sports occupations have been inventoried, African countries, in general, lack a structured classification of sport and sport-related economic activities occupations. Senegal and Mozambique, among other countries, need to carry out such classifications. The reason is twofold: to learn more about the present situation in the sport sector and its environs; and to discover the potential employment opportunities and skills for youth linked to the sport sector in the African continent.

Soft and core skills for employability are part of a holistic approach to youth development. Soft skills offer an avenue for further research to be conducted on training needs for children and youth. Children need the creativity, communication and analytical thinking that soft skills entail so that they can continue to adapt their behaviour and develop throughout their entire life.

Finally, as reported in other chapters of this book, particularly Chapter 6 on employment in the sports sector in Europe (Camy), the experience of the European Observatoire of Sports Employment (EOSE)[8] is particularly interesting. The EOSE, established in 1994, upgraded the state and size of the European labour market in sport and sport-related sectors; reported on the situation of vocational education and training (VET) in sport and sport-related sectors in the EU and candidate countries; and contributed to developing social dialogue in all European countries by strengthening employers' and workers' organizations in the sport sector. An initiative whereby the ILO would take the lead to conduct similar work in developing countries would be most welcome and should be able to count on the support of sport partners.

Notes

[1] For more information on the ILO Universitas Programme and its activities, see: http://www.ilo.org/universitas, accessed 24 Feb. 2006.

[2] For more information on the YSP, see note 1.

[3] For more information concerning the Albanian National Plan for youth development, see: http://www.un.org.al, accessed 24 Feb. 2006.

[4] For more details concerning the project activities in Mozambique, see: http://www.undp.org.mz, accessed 24 Feb. 2006.

[5] Source: US Air Force HRD.

[6] In his report on the PAY project, Professor Bruce Kidd of Toronto University outlines several benefits of sports programmes. For disadvantaged youth, sport can enhance school retention, academic performance, health and well-being, and a sense of purpose and achievement. It also makes the same adolescents less likely to engage in risky behaviour. Sport can especially enhance women's self-esteem, "boundary maintenance" and their affirmation in non-traditional roles. Moreover, sport makes youth feel physically safe, personally valued, socially connected, and morally and economically supported, which, as Kidd points out, are conditions necessary for an easy transition to adulthood. For the presentation at the Atlanta Summit (October 2005), see Kennesaw State Athletics: http://www.kennesaw.edu/sports, 2005, accessed 24 Feb. 2006.

[7] See Youth Employment Network (http://www.ilo.org/public/english/employment, accessed 24 Feb. 2006).

[8] The EOSE was created within the European Network of Sport Sciences in Higher Education (ENSSHE) recently renamed ENSSEE: European Network for Sport Science Education and Employment, supported by the EU.

Bibliography

Andreff, W.; Szymanski, S. 2006. "Sport in developing countries", in *Handbook on the economics of sport*. Cheltenham, Edward Elgar.

Commonwealth of Australia, Department of Education Science and Training. 2002. *Employability skills for the future*. Barton.

European Physical Education Association (EUPEA). 2002. *Code of ethics and good practice guide for physical education*. Ghent.

ILO/Universitas Programme. 2003. *Employment and social dialogue in the sport sector*, Report of the first ILO Workshop on Sport and Development. Geneva, 23 Apr.

Madella, A. 2002. "Le professioni dello sport. Il mercato del lavoro nello sport in Italia: caratteristiche e tendenze", in *Scuola dello Sport* (review of sport culture). Rome, Vol. XXI, No. 55.

United Nations. 2003. *Sport for development and peace: towards achieving the Millennium Development Goals*, Report from the United Nations Inter-Agency Task Force on Sport for Development and Peace. Geneva, July.

—, General Assembly. 2004. "Sport as a means to promote education, health, development and peace", resolution 59/10 adopted by the General Assembly, Agenda item 47, 59th Session, 8 Dec.

World Commission on the Social Dimension of Globalization. 2004. *A fair globalization: Creating opportunities for all*. Geneva, ILO.

ANNEXES

TABLE OF RECOMMENDATIONS
FOR ACTION

I

Subject areas	Recommendations
Policy decisions in sport (Chapter 1)	• Promote sport in developed and developing countries to maintain good health, to contribute towards education and the social agenda, for economic performance and for sustainable development
	• Sport participants at all levels should act ethically, striving to avoid the unwanted effects and identified future threats surrounding sport discussed in Chapter 1, to allow for sport to be a successful vehicle for sustainable development and serve as a means to an ends regarding the health, social and economic welfare of countries
Opportunities in physical education and sport science (Chapter 2)	• Identify specific new services and related career opportunities in the areas of sport science
	• Facilitate international discourse on core elements in the training of professionals, including physical education teachers to ensure quality physical education
	• Assemble information on various distance-learning programmes into a database (similar to the European Observatoire of Sports Employment)
The Paralympics (Chapter 3)	• Paralympic sports opportunities have infinite potential to promote a positive image and improve health throughout all regions of the world
	• Paralympic sports yield positive social perceptions, environmental change, and individual athlete empowerment that can collectively increase the rates of employment and access to education while improving the quality of life for athletes and others

/cont'd

Subject areas	Recommendations
Sports in relation to HIV/AIDS (Chapter 4)	• Coaches can be seen as effective role models and facilitators in communicating information and issues surrounding HIV/AIDS to youth
	• Women can also be seen as effective actors in developing community networks to address HIV/AIDS. The international summit on effecting social change through women's leadership through sport at Kennesaw State University in October 2005 recognized and discussed women's effectiveness in generating social change and tackling challenging issues, among others, HIV/AIDS
US sporting goods industry in 2010 (Chapter 5)	• Merging and consolidation will dominate the conduct of the sporting goods industry
	• A few niches will allow the market of sporting goods to expand in response to specific customer needs
	• Focus on services available in East Africa for bids and training of high-level athletes with the use of university networks
Employment opportunities in the sports sector in Europe (Chapter 6)	• The public expression at European and national levels of a political project resulting from negotiations with all the operators (whether in the form of a law or a declaration) is a prerequisite for the development of sporting activities under the necessary conditions of transparency
	• Construct a professional sports and sports-related sector as a prerequisite for improving the quality of employment in sport
	• Improve the relationship between training and employment and the capacity for occupational integration in the sports sector
European social dialogue in the sports sector (Chapter 7)	• The completion of a global collective agreement at the European Union level, specific to the sports sector, whether single or articulated, would be the best option to conclude the process started in 2002. A collective agreement, in fact, would include the stakeholders as part of a unique strategic approach
Employment opportunities in the sports sector in Africa (Chapter 8)	• Creating a wider market in the East African Community by strengthening the ties between Tanzania, Uganda and Kenya; this would release financial resources to develop sports infrastructures
	• Use East Africa's geographical location, favourable climate and attractive game park resorts to make it the centre of athletics
	• Emphasize human resources, physical education, recreation and sport science development in African universities; dedicate a department to the promotion and development of sports in the region

Local development and employment opportunities in the sports sector in Latin America (Chapter 9)	• Encourage collaboration between public authorities and private institutions to develop sport and sport tourism/social events • Countries such as Peru and El Salvador should use sport to build upon their cultural base and history while promoting development • Use sports events to generate revenues and increase economic growth in local economies and related industries by attracting tourists and foreign investments
Tourism and sport, and its effect on poverty reduction (Chapter 10)	• Services to be enhanced for tourism sector workers' training and skill development • Preparation of world and regional sporting events creates job opportunities and drives value-chain sport business
Safe and sustainable sport (Chapter 11)	• The sport movement should account for the three major priorities of the Olympic Movement's Agenda 21: improvement of socio-economic conditions; preservation and sustainable management of resources; and reinforcement of the role of women, young people and indigenous populations • Sports managers must act as ethically responsible professionals, remembering to consider what values are being promoted
Social development of young people (Chapters 12 and 13)	• International organizations should use efficient information coordination as well as best practices based on effective approaches • Establish dialogue between communities to generate satisfactory needs assessment
Sport-specific skills of employment for the youth (Chapter 14)	• Strengthen global alliances to promote youth social and economic insertion, such as the one established with the support of the UN, the ILO and the World Bank • Encourage collaboration among the UN agencies at the country level, the universities and the world of sport to develop a modular training based on core and soft skills for employability • Encourage partnership creation to develop activities and policies among sports institutions and UN agencies using sport for development
International sports federations (Annex II)	• See Chapters 5 and 7

/cont'd

Subject areas	Recommendations
Women, leadership and the Olympic Movement (Annex III)	• Promote research outcomes to assist the Olympic Movement to encourage women's leadership • Conduct training for women entrepreneurs in Continental Olympic Associations of National Olympic Committees, and in management of International and National Federations
Youth insertion and vulnerability reduction through sport in Mozambique (Annex IV)	• See Chapter 14

THE GENERAL ASSOCIATION OF INTERNATIONAL SPORTS FEDERATIONS: A MIRROR OF SPORTS

11

Don E. Porter

The General Association of International Sports Federations (GAISF)[1] is an umbrella organization. Almost 100 International Sports Federations have joined GAISF in order to coordinate, cooperate and communicate in the general interest and development of sport. Since its inception in 1967, GAISF's membership has grown steadily from about a dozen member federations to 100 members today. These include a wide range of sports – summer, winter, outdoor, indoor, individual, team, bat, ball, martial arts (some 100 varieties), short and long track events, water and mind games. Each International Federation maintains autonomy within the governing body for its particular sport.

GAISF provides the International Federations with a forum where they are able to discuss positive and negative aspects of the sports world, and share common concerns. Its mission is to unite, support and promote its member International Sports Federations and organizations for the coordination and protection of their common aims and interests. This also includes assisting and representing the International Federations in realms of common interest within the Olympic and Sports Movement and non-governmental organizations, but excludes Olympic issues.

GAISF's constituent groups are the Association of Summer Olympic International Federations (ASOIF),[2] the Association of International Olympic Winter Sports Federations (AIOWF) and the Association of Recognized IOC International Sports Federations (ARISF),[3] each having a clearly defined role within the Olympic Movement. GAISF reasserts the intrinsic and high-quality values of an independent body, equipped with the trust and competence necessary to be a highly recognized and valued supporter of world sport.

GAISF also establishes and maintains close relations with the many multi-sport games and regional games held around the world. These relationships help GAISF coordinate and protect the common interest of the International Federations that participate in those games. Another spin-off of GAISF has been the creation of the World Games. Initiated in 1981, with 16 non-Olympic sports from 40 countries, it has now expanded to 25 sports, with over 100 countries taking part. The World Games offers opportunities for athletes to participate in multi-sport events, somewhat similar to the Olympics, even though originally the Games did not advocate the nationalistic side of sport. It also includes a number of current Olympic sports, including badminton, table tennis, softball, tae kwon do and baseball.

In addition to an annual gathering of the General Assembly and Congress, GAISF also coordinates an annual international sports convention to discuss key issues facing the sports industry, called "SportAccord". The event brings together 100 International Sports Federations, affiliated to the GAISF, ASOIF and AIOWF, and members of the sports industry and the International Olympic Committee's Executive Board. GAISF, through its Council, now meets regularly with the IOC Executive Board and, during its General Assembly, its constituent groupings (summer, winter, Olympic, non-Olympic, Masters, World Games) have the opportunity to meet independently, as well as jointly.

Among GAISF's many initiatives to benefit sport participation, organization, administration and development is the "Sporting Goods To Go" project directed towards seeing that boys and girls are given the opportunities to participate in sport.

"Sporting goods to go": Helping developing countries to use sport and develop youth skills

Millions of young boys and girls worldwide aspire to be competitive athletes, but through the lack of financial support, facilities, equipment, coaching and other factors, they will never reach the level of national or international competitors. GAISF initiated a project in 2002 with the aim of finding ways to help youth gain easier access to sports equipment. Partners which joined this project include the Sporting Goods Manufacturers Association – International (SGMA),[4] the International Olympic Committee (IOC),[5] the Association of National Olympic Committees (ANOC),[6] the World Olympians Association (WOA),[7] the International Paralympic Committee (IPC),[8] a number of humanitarian/charity organizations (e.g. Gifts-In-Kind, World Vision) and several United Nations agencies. This coalition has utilized "Sporting Goods To Go" to allocate government and NGO resources for sports initiatives. The coalition also provides support from its combined resources and influence to bring sports equipment and technical support to those who need the challenges and goals that sport provides.

Thus far the coalition has generated a wide range of support from major international organizations that understand the importance of sport as a base of unity and competition. These organizations also realize the importance of alliances to ensure that adequate sports equipment is accessed and delivered to where it is needed most. Ongoing and recent conflicts show that even humanitarian efforts, which aim to stabilize a country, should include recreational, physical education and sports activities. In many respects, over the years, sport has become a useful entity because it captures the imagination of youth and enables them to compete, set goals and accept challenges.

Many International Federations work closely with their National Federations to assist and support youth development programmes. They use their development budgets to help provide needed playing facilities with either direct financial support, or by incorporating support from GAISF sponsors and suppliers. While many governments today face economic problems and limited budgets, the "Sporting Goods To Go" coalition can be of assistance in promoting coaching and sports equipment for free. GAISF and its partners are utilizing "Sporting Goods To Go" to coordinate an effort that it is hoped will bring forth the necessary impetus to see that sports equipment is provided to those millions of young boys and girls who wish and need to have sport in their lives.

Notes

[1] See http://www.agfisonline.com, accessed 27 Jan. 2006.

[2] See http://www.asoif.com, accessed 27 Jan. 2006.

[3] See http://www.arisf.org, accessed 27 Jan. 2006.

[4] See http://www.sgma.com, accessed 27 Jan. 2006.

[5] See http://www.olympic.org, accessed 27 Jan. 2006.

[6] See http://www.acnolympic.org/en/index_en.html, accessed 27 Jan. 2006.

[7] See http://www.woaolympians.com, accessed 27 Jan. 2006.

[8] See http://www.paralympic.org/release/Main_Sections_Menu/index.html, accessed 27 Jan. 2006.

WOMEN, LEADERSHIP AND THE OLYMPIC MOVEMENT*

Ian Henry and Anita White

Introduction

This document is an executive summary of the findings of a joint project undertaken by the Institute of Sport and Leisure Policy at Loughborough University and the International Olympic Committee (IOC), directed by Dr Anita White, Visiting Professor at Loughborough University and Katia Mascagni, Project Manager, Department of International Co-operation and Development at the IOC. The work was conducted by a team of researchers, directed by Professor Ian Henry, from the Institute of Sport and Leisure Policy, evaluating the impact of IOC policy in respect of the roles that women play on the Executive Committees of National Olympic Committees (NOCs) in each of the five continental Olympic Associations.

Context and purpose of the project

In 1997, as part of its Women and Sport policy, the IOC established targets for women's membership of NOC Executive Committees. These were for women to hold at least 10 per cent of executive decision-making positions in NOCS by December 2001, rising to at least 20 per cent by December 2005. The IOC has regularly collected statistics on the numbers of women on NOC Executive Committees and measured progress towards the achievement of the targets. The purpose of the research project was to provide information and evaluate progress on the implementation of the IOC policy in relation to women's leadership in the Olympic Movement. The research project thus evaluates the processes of recruitment of women to decision-making structures, their career paths into Olympic leadership, their impact on the activities of the organizations themselves, and the nature of training and support required by both the women members and the sports

---

* Copyright IOC/Institute of Sport and Leisure Policy, Loughborough University, United Kingdom.

organizations to ensure that the benefits of wider involvement in decision-making by women are realized. In so doing the project has explored the views of both women Executive Committee members and NOC Secretary Generals on the implementation and impact of the policy.

Methods

The research, undertaken between January 2002 and December 2003, consisted of four elements:

Questionnaire survey of all women members of NOC Executive Committees

There were 146 usable responses, estimated as a 49.7 per cent response rate[1] of all female members representing 46 per cent of countries. The geographical distribution was as follows:

Africa	37 from 27 different countries (responses from 51 per cent of countries)
Americas	26 from 17 different countries (responses from 42 per cent of countries)
Asia	19 from 12 different countries (responses from 29 per cent of countries)
Europe	57 from 27 different countries (responses from 56 per cent of countries)
Oceania	7 from 7 different countries (responses from 50 per cent of countries)

Questionnaire survey of Secretary Generals of all NOCs

There were 89 usable responses representing a 48.2 per cent response rate[2] of all Secretary Generals. The geographical distribution was as follows:

Africa	25 countries (47 per cent response rate)
Americas	17 countries (42 per cent response rate)
Asia	10 countries (24 per cent response rate)
Europe	34 countries (71 per cent response rate)
Oceania	3 countries (21 per cent response rate)

Detailed interviews with women members of NOC Executive Committees

Thirty interviews were conducted with women executive members: four from Africa, eight from the Americas, eight from Asia, eight from Europe and two from Oceania.

Detailed interviews with Secretary Generals

Twenty five interviews were conducted with Secretary Generals: eight from Africa, four from the Americas, seven from Asia, five from Europe, and one from Oceania.

Main findings from questionnaire survey of all women members of National Olympic Committee Executive Committees

- The women recruited to the NOC Executive Committees were very well educated (78 per cent of those responding had degrees and/or teaching qualifications; 29.5 per cent had postgraduate degrees, and 8 per cent PhDs); a significant proportion had experience as elite athletes (46 per cent had been international athletes, and 20 per cent had been Olympians); 61 per cent were in employment; and 70 per cent were married/cohabiting, most of whom had children.

- Recruitment of women to NOCs was very recent, reflecting response to the establishment of targets; 71 per cent had been appointed since 1996 when the targets were announced.

- Two-thirds of the group reported that they had been elected to the Executive Committee, with the remainder co-opted. In several cases election had followed after a period of co-option.

- 59.4 per cent of women reported that their NOCs had established a Women's Committee though in many instances they were relatively recently established.

- 64 per cent of women perceived their work as being primarily or solely concerned with general matters rather than primarily with women and sport, although 49 per cent served on Women's Committees.

- More than half the respondents (52 per cent) reported having received training since joining the NOC, which is notable given the voluntary nature of the work. IOC regional seminars had been well received. The sample expressed interest in a range of potential training activities, including generic issues such as sports administration and management, language proficiency and skills in dealing with the media, as well as aspects relating to women and sport specifically.

- Most female respondents argued that significant benefits were associated with the introduction of women to Executive Committees (though a minority reported no positive impact). The benefits cited include the promotion of women's influence in the NOC; stimulation of specialist provision for women; having more women on sports leadership training courses; more female candidates appointed to other committees on sports and administrative functions; and as a generally increased profile for women in sport.

Main findings from questionnaire survey of Secretary Generals of all NOCs

- The Secretary Generals also reported that women's membership of Executive Committees had grown since the announcement of the targets in 1996 and that they came disproportionately from elite athlete backgrounds.

- 64 per cent of respondents indicated that their NOC had taken special measures to recruit women to their Executive Committees following the introduction of the targets. These measures included reserving places specifically for women, revising their statutes, encouraging National Federations to nominate women candidates, setting up a taskforce to nominate suitable women candidates, inviting potential women candidates to attend special functions, and directly approaching suitably qualified women.

- The most regularly cited difficulty experienced in attracting women to work on the Executive Committees of the NOCs was the "structural" issue of getting women nominated and elected from a constituency of National Federations whose representatives were predominantly and traditionally male. Secretary Generals tended to suggest that difficulties were the product of "problems" with women (lack of availability of qualified women, reluctance because of family commitments, etc.) rather than as a result of "problems" with the strategy adopted by the NOC to recruit women (e.g. lack of flexibility in working or recruitment patterns, etc.).

- The Secretary Generals described those women who were members of the Executive Boards as being among the most active members of the Executive (51.4 per cent in the most active quartile and 78.2 per cent in the upper 50 per cent).

- As with the responses from the women's questionnaire, Secretary Generals indicated that the work of a majority of women Executive Committee members (71 per cent) was largely or solely concerned with general rather than women's issues. Like the women respondents, the Secretary Generals suggested that women's committees had as yet had little impact. The mean proportion of women as chairs of NOC commissions was low at 21.3 per cent.

- There was a strong association between those countries which had adopted policies on women and sport, and those in which programmes to promote women and sport were run.

Main findings from detailed interviews with a sample of women members of NOC Executive Committees

- The interviewees nearly all regarded the IOC targets as a positive force for change and did not see themselves as "tokens". However, targets on their own may well not be enough to reduce inequalities as although they may deal with the effects of inequity by opening access to leadership positions, they do not directly address the circumstances or attitudes which cause such an imbalance in the first place.

- Given the high levels of qualification and competence of many of the women interviewees, considerable frustration was expressed about apparently less well-qualified male members of Executive Committees being given preference for posts of responsibility.

- Some women in full-time employment with family responsibilities found themselves in very pressured situations, particularly where traditional gender roles and patterns of domestic labour were maintained in the home. They relied heavily on support from families and partners, and there was some evidence of personal sacrifices being made in terms of personal relationships.

- In the vast majority of cases, recruitment to NOC Executive Committees, and subsequent effectiveness, was fostered by the support and encourage-ment of senior NOC members, both male and female.

- The solution of dealing with NOC targets by co-opting women, or encouraging individuals to stand for election, means that the structure of National Federations may remain relatively untouched by such changes and thus the National Federation delegates to the NOC Assembly are likely to continue to be predominantly male.

- Interviewees suggested that their impact/effectiveness on Executive Committees increased disproportionately where there was more than one female member and therefore more than one female voice on the Executive Committee.

- The value of the IOC Women in Sport seminars and other international links for many respondents was very clear. Not only did such events provide a source of new ideas in policy terms, but they also provided support networks for women who might otherwise be isolated if they were among a small minority on the NOC Executive.

- Training needs reported were very similar to those specified in the questionnaire responses. However, it is important also to acknowledge that forms of support other than training (e.g. mentoring, networking and internet resources) may be required if women are to be successfully recruited and retained.

- Women are not a homogeneous group and the data from the interviews suggest that differences across socio-economic, ethnic, religious and geo-graphical boundaries imply the need for very different approaches in different cultural contexts.

Main findings from detailed interviews with a sample of NOC Secretary Generals

- Although the establishment of the targets had served to raise consciousness of the issue of women's involvement in Executive Committees, the target had not been met by all of the interviewees' NOCs. Even where it had, 10 per cent had been regarded as the maximum or norm rather than a minimum level to be achieved. One NOC president indicated that he felt that unless sanctions were incorporated in the system the NOCs would continue to treat the matter less seriously.

- Several Secretary Generals highlighted the structural problem of the make-up of NOCs in that the majority of the membership is made up of delegates from National Federations, who are largely male. This leaves relatively few women who are delegates to the NOC Assemblies to stand for membership of the executive.

- Expectations placed on women recruited as role models often implied high standards as elite performers, and/or high levels of academic qualifications, which were not necessarily applicable to male candidates.

- The competences sought in respect of women (as opposed to qualifications and sporting experience) were not clearly articulated and hence the training needs of new women members were difficult to establish.

- Although the great majority of respondents recognized traditional gender roles as barriers to female participation in the work of the Executive, few looked for flexible policies through which to respond to these barriers.

- There are dangers in treating "women" as a homogeneous group since differences among women may reflect significant sources of disadvantage (e.g. urban–rural, regional differences).

- The respondents were positive about the decentralization of Olympic Solidarity Funding and the potential of Solidarity Funds to be used effectively to support women's development. However, there was evidence that in practice this had been happening in only limited ways.

Conclusions

The success of the targets

Perhaps the most obvious point to make is that the introduction of targets has had a clear and positive impact on the proportion of women in NOC Executive Committees. The rapid growth of the numbers of women in such positions, from a very low base, immediately after the announcement of the targets is clear both in numeric terms from the questionnaire data, and also from the observations made by women and the Secretary Generals during the interviews. Thus the target approach can be said to have had success in raising awareness of gender inequalities, bringing talented women into the Olympic family, and improving Olympic governance by setting an example and providing moral leadership to the world of sport in terms of equity in representation.

The data collected provide a clear indication of the quality of the cohort of women recruited. They were very well educated as a group, many brought valuable transferable skills from their professional work, and many were former elite athletes. They were also very active and hard working, as evidenced by the fact that Secretary Generals indicated that 51 per cent of the women on their Executive Committees were in the top quartile in terms of the most active members, with 78 per cent in the top half. Thus the introduction of the targets policy has helped to unlock the source of a skilled, educated and committed workforce, which has considerable potential to grow.

The use of targets of 10 per cent and 20 per cent has the merit of providing a simple, understandable, measurable and transparent policy goal. Perhaps the only area of confusion in relation to the goal was that relating to the difference between quotas and targets, and respondents almost universally used these terms interchangeably. Notwithstanding this fact, and the implication that quotas are compulsory, there was little sympathy generally for the imposition of penalties for failing to achieve "quota" or target numbers.

The importance of the leadership of the IOC in respect of addressing the issue of inequitable representation on decision-making bodies should not be underestimated. Some respondents felt empowered in making demands on other sporting organizations not covered by the IOC policy simply by virtue of the IOC's position on this matter. Thus the notion of targets as a reasonable expectation in the sporting world was legitimated to some degree by the fact that the Olympic Movement had adopted such an approach.

The limitations of targets

There are perhaps three principal limitations of the target policy evident from the data. The first is that they affect only part of the system of Olympic and sports administration. As one respondent put it, there is a hierarchy from clubs at the base to regional, national and international federations, and to NOCs, Continental Olympic Associations and the IOC. One interviewee pointed out that the NOCs are failing to recommend women for consideration as potential candidates, and thus the IOC itself has restricted room for manoeuvre in terms of appointing more female members. By focusing solely on NOCs and International Federations (the latter not investigated in the current project), important elements of the system are ignored. Co-opting or even electing one or more women onto the NOC Executive is unlikely to have a lasting effect if the predominantly male electorate for the Executive (in the form of the National Federation nominees to the NOC Assemblies) is left unchanged. Thus the policy only addresses certain points in the pyramid with the result that it may not foster organic growth of the number of women in decision-making positions. A long-term sustainable solution to the involvement of women in executive decision making is thus likely to require work at the level of clubs and regional/national federations, in addition to the NOCs and International Federations per se.

The second limitation of the target approach is that even where the targets themselves are achieved, this has not necessarily led to the adoption of policy initiatives that foster women's participation in sport or in executive decision making. There is a danger that some NOCs see the achievement of targets as an end in itself rather than a means towards a more effective Executive Committee. Many NOCs have set up Women's Committees but few respondents have reported much impact as yet. Guidance and advice on ways of ensuring the effectiveness of Women's Committees could be useful both to NOCs and the committees themselves.

The third limitation of the targets is that the universal percentages do not take account of the social and cultural conditions in different countries. In some countries women's equality is well accepted and advanced in all aspects of life, while in others women still face significant inequalities. NOCs operate both in the context of the values of the Olympic Movement and also within the cultural conditions that exist in their own country. The targets were set to represent the minima rather than maxima, but several NOCs appeared to regard them as a ceiling to be attained rather than a base from which to build. Others were justly proud that they had exceeded the targets by a considerable amount. There is scope for further emphasis on the desirability for NOCs to strive to achieve higher levels of equality in their governance structures from whatever base they start.

The recruitment process

The interviews with women in particular highlighted the importance of both encouragement and sponsorship of candidates by senior figures within the NOC, who showed belief in their ability to do the job, and also the importance of female role models. Secretary Generals were largely unaware of the critical importance of encouragement by experienced NOC members. It is ironic that, given the very well qualified nature of the female members, they should be less confident than some of their male counterparts; but being the first, or among the first, women to submit to election from a predominantly male electorate can be daunting. Acknowledging the difference that such encouragement has made may be helpful in promoting the active sponsorship of candidates by experienced members of the NOCs.

Two-thirds of NOCs reported taking special measures to recruit women and one-third reported not having attempted any measures. One indicated a backlash when attempts to vote through measures had been rejected by the NOC. There is no doubt that special measures have been effective for those NOCs that have adopted them. NOCs that have not yet met the 10 per cent target could learn from the experiences of NOCs that have taken special measures, both formal and informal, to successfully recruit women Executive Committee members.

Training, support and networking

Major sources of policy ideas on the development of women and sport were seen to grow directly out of the IOC organized regional seminars and other international forums on "Women in Sport". These meetings provided two critical ingredients for the development of policy – a source of policy ideas, which may be adapted and reshaped for local application elsewhere, but also as a source for promoting confidence and creating networks among women who may often be working alone or in small numbers on the Executive Committees. The importance of providing moral support for women seeking to make a contribution as a minority in the context of their own organization should not be taken lightly. Time and again the women interviewed referred to the importance of confidence in relation to their willingness to submit themselves for election, and their willingness to speak out in promoting policies for women and for the general population. It was equally clear from the feedback of Secretary Generals that while they understood the significance of the "Women in Sport" conferences and seminars for promoting policy ideas, the issues of confidence building and networking were not always fully appreciated.

The nature of the training needs cited by women was not unexpected. Management, sports administration, technical skills (sports law, sports medicine, coaching) were mentioned, together with the need to learn about successful initiatives elsewhere. However, a key element of the training and support requested was the exchange of ideas in seminars and workshops (rather than the passive receipt of ideas) such that networks might be established and maintained. Internet communication could be built into these initiatives to allow networking and mutual support groups to flourish outside the context of face-to-face meetings. Such networks might require some (light touch) management but would have the potential to capitalize on the investment made in training.

While the IOC Women in Sport seminars have been a very important means of support in facilitating confidence building, networking among women and providing project management tools, it may be appropriate to consider organizing seminars that include more men in the future. Several respondents pointed out that if gender issues are to become mainstream concerns and real progress made, men and women must work together to take responsibility for promoting gender equality in sport. So far women's awareness and understanding of gender issues has been raised through training, but there has been limited engagement on the part of men.

Next steps

The research has provided evidence of the way in which the policy targets have been successful, and sought the views of those most involved in its implementation – women Executive Committee members and NOC Secretary Generals. Many examples of good practice have been identified. Dissemination of the findings of the research should assist the Olympic Movement in the continued implementation and development of the policy. The areas in which further work would seem appropriate include work with Continental Olympic Associations of NOCs, Women's Committees of NOCs, and other members of the Olympic family, in particular International and National Federations. It is hoped that the experiences of those who have contributed to the research as respondents will assist in taking this work forward to be used to help NOCs achieve and exceed the 20 per cent target in the months leading up to December 2005.

Note

[1] The response rates of 49.7 per cent and 48.2 per cent provide very respectable return rates, and are well above industry norms (Market Research Society – see http://www.mrs.org.uk/).

YOUTH INSERTION AND VULNERABILITY REDUCTION THROUGH SPORT IN MOZAMBIQUE

IV

From 23 to 24 November 2005, a national workshop was held in Maputo, Mozambique, on the theme "Youth integration and vulnerability reduction through sports". With the intention of having sports recognized as a contributing factor to the national programme for decent work and national strategy for youth, the workshop identified key areas and possible activities for youth, especially skills development in the sports sector as tools of education, including HIV/AIDS prevention. The workshop also assessed the training needs of the Boane Sports Centre, as well as other similar projects in the country.

The first lady of the Republic of Mozambique, Mrs Maria da Luz Guebuza, opened the workshop as Sports and Development Ambassador. She recognized the potential of sports to contribute to reducing poverty through opportunities for the social and economic insertion of youth. Her Excellency Minister of Labour, Helena Taipo, also stressed the fact that sports are a catalyst for the development of societies in economic sectors such as tourism, health, and production of sports material and equipment, services and skills development.

In compliance with the ILO tripartite constituents' rule, the Ministry of Labour, the Ministry of Social Affairs, the employers' organizations and the trade unions took part in the consultation, while the officials of the Ministerio da Juventude e Desportes (Ministry of Youth and Sport) are the key focal point for the module "Sports and Social Integration". The Minister of Labour, the Minister of Youth and Sports, and representatives of the Ministry of Tourism have all pledged their support for the programme. This network, together with the UN country team, can facilitate the implementation of a national plan for sport and development of youth programmes and encourage youth insertion and the reduction of vulnerability through sport.

In this context, it was recommended that the Government assume responsibility for sport as one of the noted development strategies. Youth should be encouraged to develop a spirit of entrepreneurship in the sports sector and beyond. Therefore it was recommended that existing opportunities and trends should be identified to use sports for entrepreneurship development. Lastly, sports for people with a disability have received very little support from the Government; therefore, it was recommended that special attention should be paid to this group.

A new approach to socio-economic partnerships was carried out as a pilot project at the local level through cooperative development with women in Boane, Mozambique. The local development agency of Matola, in collaboration with the ILO, the NOC and the IOC, contributed by providing training to establish the cooperative. Additional training is required in management and marketing at this stage.

The pilot activity created a cooperative of women manufacturers and provided schoolchildren with a feeding programme and sport education by teachers and trainers. The goal of the cooperatives is that families and youth will be able to use and manage the sport facilities of the Boane Sports Centre according to local needs. As income is generated through the cooperatives, local production will be stimulated, local capacity will be strengthened, and women will be empowered. The ILO, among others, was called upon to provide expertise in capacity building and cooperative development. Clearly the pilot activity produced a breakthrough.

MDG implementation: Youth insertion and vulnerability reduction through sport in Mozambique

The Millennium Development Goals (MDGs) commit the international community to an expanded vision of development, one that vigorously promotes human development as the key to sustaining social and economic progress in all countries, and recognizes the importance of creating a global partnership for development. The goals have been commonly accepted as a framework for measuring development progress.

Through the implementation and success of the Five-Year Plan, the Poverty Reduction Strategy (PARPA) II (2006-09), Agenda 2025[1] and the MDGs themselves, an accelerated response to the adoption of a vulnerability reduction strategy and progress toward the achievement of MDGs in Mozambique is attainable.

Vulnerability reduction strategy

Integrated, multi-sectoral and accelerated responses are needed in order to create communities' competencies for poverty reduction through:

* local ownership of initiatives;
* strong local stakeholders involvement in decision-making;
* respect and attention to local culture and development approaches;
* vulnerable target groups with special focus on youth and women.

Youth insertion and reduction of vulnerability through sport in Mozambique

Sport is to be used as the vehicle for reducing the vulnerability of youth, through applying the model "Sport for All":

- holistic development approach for young people, fostering their physical and emotional health and building valuable social connections;
- opportunity for self-expression and personal identity through the individual and society;
- mitigation of the spread and impact of HIV/AIDS;
- healthy alternatives to harmful actions, such as drug and sex abuse, and involvement in crime;
- within schools, sport as an opportunity to practise tolerance, cooperation, respect, social inclusion, de-stigmatization and human rights (equity).

Reduced vulnerability and community competencies through sport

- build bridges short with longer-term initiatives;
- link "upstream" (political decisions) to "downstream" (community-based)
- interventions;
- build knowledge networks: schools, youth groups, etc.;
- create synergies between different levels;
- strengthen multisectoral integrated actions;
- build partnerships between all stakeholders.

Recommendations

Sports programmes should be based on the "sport for all" model: ensuring that all groups are given the opportunity to participate, particularly those who gain additional benefits such as women, persons with disabilities and young people.

- *Sport should be included in the development agenda:* calls for the incorporation of sport and physical activity into the development policies of countries, as well as the development agendas of national and international development agencies, with particular emphasis on young people.

- *Sport should be used as a programme tool:* urges governments and UN agencies to include the opportunity to participate in sport as an objective, as well as a tool to achieve the MDGs and the goals of other international conferences, and the broader aims of development and peace.

- *Sport should form part of development programmes:* recommends the inclusion of sport-related initiatives into the programmes of UN agencies and bilateral and multilateral partners, where appropriate and according to locally assessed needs.

- *Partnerships should be formed:* a global network on sport for development to facilitate partnerships between development partners and sport-related organizations, including sports federations and associations and the IOC, sport-related humanitarian NGOs, the private sector, athletes and teams, and volunteers.

- *Resources should be mobilized:* from national and international sources.

Note

[1] The objectives of Agenda 2025 are to: create a national consensus on a vision and a strategy for the development of Mozambique; increase the capacity of the country as a whole, and of key decision-makers to take on the leadership role in national development; and strengthen the involvement and participation of citizens in development.

INDEX

Note: Page numbers in *italic* indicate boxes, figures and tables. Subscript numbers appended to page numbers indicate endnotes. The term "athletics" refers exclusively to track and field, while "athletes" refers to sportspeople in general.

217